IFIP Advances in Information and Communication Technology

641

Editor-in-Chief

Kai Rannenberg, Goethe University Frankfurt, Germany

IFIP – The International Federation for Information Processing

IFIP was founded in 1960 under the auspices of UNESCO, following the first World Computer Congress held in Paris the previous year. A federation for societies working in information processing, IFIP's aim is two-fold: to support information processing in the countries of its members and to encourage technology transfer to developing nations. As its mission statement clearly states:

IFIP is the global non-profit federation of societies of ICT professionals that aims at achieving a worldwide professional and socially responsible development and application of information and communication technologies.

IFIP is a non-profit-making organization, run almost solely by 2500 volunteers. It operates through a number of technical committees and working groups, which organize events and publications. IFIP's events range from large international open conferences to working conferences and local seminars.

The flagship event is the IFIP World Computer Congress, at which both invited and contributed papers are presented. Contributed papers are rigorously refereed and the rejection rate is high.

As with the Congress, participation in the open conferences is open to all and papers may be invited or submitted. Again, submitted papers are stringently refereed.

The working conferences are structured differently. They are usually run by a working group and attendance is generally smaller and occasionally by invitation only. Their purpose is to create an atmosphere conducive to innovation and development. Refereeing is also rigorous and papers are subjected to extensive group discussion.

Publications arising from IFIP events vary. The papers presented at the IFIP World Computer Congress and at open conferences are published as conference proceedings, while the results of the working conferences are often published as collections of selected and edited papers.

IFIP distinguishes three types of institutional membership: Country Representative Members, Members at Large, and Associate Members. The type of organization that can apply for membership is a wide variety and includes national or international societies of individual computer scientists/ICT professionals, associations or federations of such societies, government institutions/government related organizations, national or international research institutes or consortia, universities, academies of sciences, companies, national or international associations or federations of companies.

More information about this series at https://link.springer.com/bookseries/6102

Luis M. Camarinha-Matos ·
Geert Heijenk · Srinivas Katkoori ·
Leon Strous (Eds.)

Internet of Things

Technology and Applications

4th IFIP International Cross-Domain Conference, IFIPIoT 2021
Virtual Event, November 4–5, 2021
Revised Selected Papers

 Springer

Editors
Luis M. Camarinha-Matos (iD)
Universidade Nova de Lisboa
Monte Caparica, Portugal

Srinivas Katkoori (iD)
University of South Florida
Tampa, FL, USA

Geert Heijenk (iD)
University of Twente
Enschede, The Netherlands

Leon Strous
De Nederlandsche Bank
Amsterdam, The Netherlands

ISSN 1868-4238   ISSN 1868-422X   (electronic)
IFIP Advances in Information and Communication Technology
ISBN 978-3-030-96468-9   ISBN 978-3-030-96466-5   (eBook)
https://doi.org/10.1007/978-3-030-96466-5

This Springer imprint is published by the registered company Springer Nature Switzerland AG
The registered company address is: Gewerbestrasse 11, 6330 Cham, Switzerland

Preface

The fourth IFIP International Internet of Things (IoT) Conference, that took place in a virtual mode during November 4–5, 2021, addressed both technology and applications. The topics presented reflected the variety of aspects with respect to IoT, aspects covered by IFIP's Domain Committee on IoT which organizes this annual event.

The IoT Technical Program Committee for this edition consisted of 53 members from 18 countries who considered 36 submitted abstracts with 33 full papers. The selection was based on the full papers. Each paper was on average refereed by four reviewers, using the single-blind review principle. In total, 15 papers were selected for presentation resulting in an acceptance rate of 45%.

This book contains the revised versions of the refereed papers presented at the conference. The papers were selected on the basis of originality, quality, and relevance to the topic. As expected, the peer-reviewed papers covered a wide array of topics that were clustered in five thematic sessions:

- Modernizing agricultural practice using IoT
- Cyber-physical IoT systems in wildfire context
- IoT for smart health
- Security
- Methods

The conference featured two keynote speakers. The first keynote was given by Schahram Dustdar from TU Wien, Austria. In his talk "Edge Intelligence - Engineering the Fabric of IoT, Systems, and People" he analyzed the role of IoT, edge, cloud, and human-based computing as well as AI in the co-evolution of distributed systems for the new decade. He identified challenges and discussed a roadmap that these new distributed systems have to address, and he took a closer look at how a cyber-physical fabric will be complemented by AI operationalization to enable seamless end-to-end distributed systems.

The second keynote on "Secure IoT by Design" was given by Saraju P. Mohanty from the University of North Texas, USA. A broad perspective of the vast multifaceted forms of cybersecurity attacks secure/security by design (SbD) solutions in IoT was presented. SbD advocates making security as a requirement right in the design phase so that retrofitting would not be needed. He presented SbD driven cybersecurity solutions for IoT using the hardware security primitive Physical Unclonable Function (PUF). This included the first-ever hardware-integrated blockchain (called PUFchain) whose architecture he has overhauled using SbD principles to be secure, energy efficient, and scalable, while running 1000X faster than original blockchain with Proof-of-Work (PoW).

In two panel sessions, one on IoT applications and one on IoT research, panel members presented their views and discussed questions about the main engineering challenges in IoT development and current IoT research challenges, about promising approaches to face such challenges, and a forecast on futuristic application scenarios and on emerging technologies that are likely to have an impact in the next 5–10 years. A summary of the panel sessions is included in this book as the first chapter.

We thank the authors and presenters, the panel members, the session chairs, the organizers of special sessions, the Program Committee, and the external reviewers for their hard work and contributions, and we look forward to their continued involvement.

We feel that all the contributions make the book a rich volume in the IFIP AICT series and we trust that the reader will be inspired by it.

December 2021

Luis M. Camarinha-Matos
Geert Heijenk
Srinivas Katkoori
Leon Strous

Organization

General Co-chairs

Geert Heijenk   University of Twente, The Netherlands
Leon Strous   De Nederlandsche Bank, The Netherlands

Program Co-chairs

Luis M. Camarinha-Matos   NOVA University of Lisbon, Portugal
Srinivas Katkoori   University of South Florida, USA

Publicity Chair

Suzan Bayhan   University of Twente, The Netherlands

Web Chair

Omkar Dokur   University of South Florida, USA

Technical Program Committee

Carmelo Ardito*   Politecnico di Bari, Italy
Nils Aschenbruck   University of Osnabrück, Germany
Suzan Bayhan   University of Twente, The Netherlands
Elisa Bertino   Purdue University, USA
Luis M. Camarinha-Matos*   NOVA University of Lisbon, Portugal
Nuno Carvalho   Universidade de Aveiro, Portugal
Augusto Casaca*   INESC-ID/IST, Portugal
Tibor Cinkler*   Budapest University of Technology and Economics, Hungary
Jose Neuman De Souza*   Federal University of Ceará, Brasil
Florin Filip   Romanian Academy of Sciences, Romania
Gordon Fletcher*   Salford University, UK
Rosanna Fornasiero   CNR, Italy
Rekha Govindaraj   IIT Kharagpur, India
Miria Grisot   University of Oslo, Norway
Geert Heijenk   University of Twente, The Netherlands
Jun Hu   Eindhoven University of Technology, The Netherlands
Chenglu Jin   CWI Amsterdam, The Netherlands
Yier Jin   University of Florida, USA
Robert Karam   University of South Florida, USA
Stamatis Karnouskos   SAP, Germany

Srinivas Katkoori*	University of South Florida, USA
Mehran Mozaffari Kermani	University of South Florida, USA
Arianit Kurti	Linnaeus University, Sweden
Maryline Laurent	Institut Mines-Telecom, France
Paulo Leitão	Instituto Politécnico de Bragança, Portugal
Tiziana Margaria	Lero, Ireland
Peter Marwedel	TU Dortmund, Germany
Vincent Naessens	KU Leuven, Belgium
Mário Nunes	INOV, Portugal
A. Luís Osório	Instituto Superior de Engenharia de Lisboa, Portugal
Fabio Paterno*	ISTI-CNR, Italy
Shilpa Pendyala	Intel, USA
Joachim Posegga	University of Passau, Germany
Franz Rammig	University of Paderborn, Germany
Sandip Ray	University of Florida, USA
Ricardo Reis*	Universidade Federal do Rio Grande do Sul, Brazil
Kay Roemer	TU Graz, Austria
Rajsaktish Sankaranarayanan	Intel, USA
Carmen Santoro	ISTI-CNR, Italy
Susana Sargento	University of Aveiro, Portugal
Damien Sauveron*	XLIM (CNRS/University of Limoges), France
Jürgen Schönwälder	Jacobs University Bremen, Germany
Abbas Shahim	Vrije Universiteit Amsterdam, Netherlands
Krassen Stefanov*	University of Sofia, Bulgaria
Leon Strous*	IFIP/De Nederlandsche Bank, The Netherlands
Himanshu Thapliyal	University of Kentucky, USA
Jean-Yves Tigli	Université Côte d'Azur/CNRS, France
A Min Tjoa*	Vienna University of Technology, Austria
Sebastiaan von Solms*	University of Johannesburg, South Africa
Ulrika H. Westergren*	Umeå University, Sweden
Marco Winckler*	Université Côte d'Azur, France
Li Da Xu*	Old Dominion University, USA
Hao Zheng	University of South Florida, USA

Additional Reviewers

Ilse Bohé	KU Leuven, Belgium
Rustem Dautov	SINTEF, Norway
Florian Frank	University of Passau, Germany
Victor Grimblatt	Synopsys, Chile
Thomas Hänel	University of Osnabrück, Germany
Phu H. Nguyen	SINTEF, Norway

Henrich C. Pöhls	University of Passau, Germany
Gérald Rocher	Université Côte d'Azur/CNRS, France
Alexander Tessmer	University of Osnabrück, Germany

*IFIP Domain Committee on IoT members

Contents

Summary of Challenges

Challenges in IoT Applications and Research

Luis M. Camarinha-Matos[1(✉)] and Srinivas Katkoori[2]

[1] School of Science and Technology and UNINOVA-CTS, NOVA University of Lisbon,
2829-516 Monte Caparica, Portugal
`cam@uninova.pt`
[2] CSE Department, University of South Florida, Tampa, FL 33620, USA
`katkoori@usf.edu`

Abstract. Internet-of-things (IoT) has great promise and immense potential in positively transforming the society for a better tomorrow. We can broadly approach the IoT system design from two perspectives, one from the basic research perspective and another from the applications perspective. Two panels have been organized on these topics to explore the relevant issues and challenges. The first panel entitled "IoT applications," with three panelists and the second panel entitled "IoT research," were organized as part of the IFIP IoT 2021 conference. Leading researchers participated in these panels sharing their research results, their views on the state-of-the-art, and promising future directions. In this article, we summarize the proceedings of the two panel discussions.

Keywords: Internet of Things · IoT engineering challenges · IoT research challenges · IoT trends

1 Introduction

The area of Internet of Things has gone a long way since the term was first coined by Kevin Ashton in 1999. Along the last decades various efforts have been made to extend the concept, not only in terms of its supporting infrastructure and technology, but also in terms of its social, legal, and ethical implications [1, 2]. As the number of "things" connected to Internet has rapidly grown, organizational issues and the inter-relation with other systems, under a cyber-physical systems perspective, became part of the agenda.

As reflected in the contents of IoT 2021 and its previous editions [3, 4], the Internet of Things is characterized by a multidisciplinary nature, where various engineering and technology-oriented fields need to be combined with socio-organizational, legal, economic, and business-oriented contributions. In fact, it is rather impressive the number of technical contributions featuring fundamental research, technological developments, and advanced applications, that have been published in the last years. Yet, many of these publications tend to emphasize the perspective of a single discipline. The IFIP IoT series of conferences aim at creating an environment where an integrated multi-disciplinary and even interdisciplinary perspective can be nurtured.

L. M. Camarinha-Matos et al. (Eds.): IFIPIoT 2021, IFIP AICT 641, pp. 3–10, 2022.
https://doi.org/10.1007/978-3-030-96466-5_1

It is important to reflect on recent achievements and identify current challenges and emerging trends in both research and advanced applications towards solving complex societal problems. For this purpose, two panels were organized at IoT 2021 aimed at bringing together different perspectives and contributing to identify future directions:

- Panel 1, devoted to IoT Applications, involving contributions from Paulo Leitão, Adrian Florea, and Gerd Kortuem, and moderated by Luis Camarinha-Matos.
- Panel 2, devoted to IoT Research, including contributions from Elisa Bertino, Marilia Curado, Carlo Fischione, and Paul Havinga, and moderated by Srinivas Katkoori.

This article briefly summarizes the main issues discussed in these panels, highlighting the main conclusions.

2 Challenges in IoT Applications

2.1 Scope

The scope of IoT applications has been progressively expanding to address more complex systems. More and more researchers are asked by funding agencies to position their work in the context of the United Nations goals for sustainable development (Agenda 2030) [5]. As society and its supporting systems are becoming hyper-connected, IoT needs to be considered in a more integrated and holistic perspective, which also demands adequate engineering methodologies. In order to guide the discussion of these challenges, the invited panelists were asked to organize their contributions according to three guiding questions:

- *What are the main engineering challenges in IoT development?*
- *What are the critical success factors in advanced IoT applications?*
- *Which futuristic application scenarios do you envision for the next 5–10 years?*

The following sections highlight the main ideas resulting from the panelists' statements and also from the discussion with the conference attendants.

2.2 Main Engineering Challenges in IoT Development

Despite the technological advances of last decades, there are still critical technological challenges requiring further developments. This includes:

- Security, privacy, and data protection mechanisms.
- Further developments in power supply for IoT devices (batteries and energy harvesting), low energy protocols and computing.
- More focus on "actuation" and not only on "sensing".
- Integration of AI and machine learning.
- Development and integration of bio devices.
- Development of very low cost IoT devices (for mass applications).
- Increased maturity of standards. Current multiplicity of standards is often an obstacle.

Complementarily, it is necessary to invest more on methodological approaches to deal with:

– Complex IoT-based systems design.
– Integration of heterogeneous and evolving systems.
– Interoperability, legacy systems, and ubiquitous connectivity.

On the modeling side, further efforts are needed on:

– Organizational models for complex IoT/CPS systems including a large number of devices and subsystems.
– Collaboration models for autonomous, semi-autonomous, and evolving systems of smart systems.
– Distributed cognition models.

Besides the applications in traditional domains, e.g., manufacturing/industry, healthcare, smart cities, it is necessary to facilitate the penetration of IoT in other domains not so widely addressed yet, e.g., agriculture, and wildfires management, which requires an understanding of the specific "culture" of those domains and the involved value creation processes.

IoT development also poses questions of a socio-technical nature, including:

– Education and upskilling of engineers with a multi-disciplinary culture.
– Coping with different cultures and terminology in different application domains.
– Understand and comply with ethical principles and data protection regulations.

As an overarching context, there is a need for a strong emphasis on sustainability:

– Towards sustainable IoT, including reducing electronic waste.
– Maximizing trust, through transparent and scrutable algorithms, including explainable AI.
– Maximizing protection towards verifiable secure IoT.

2.3 Critical Success Factors in Advanced IoT Applications

A crucial success factor is to develop an "IoT that we can control", an "IoT that we can context", and "IoT that we can rely on". Certainly, we cannot ignore IoT, which has become a kind of "societal infrastructure", but not always beneficial. As such, a democratic society should be able to decide on which levels of transparency and which kind of values it prioritizes.

This factor relates again to the issue of trust and scrutable systems and raised the question of "ethics embedded in systems". On this issue there was no consensus among participants, with opinions going from "yes, we should implement ethics in systems" to "no, we should not". Main arguments from the "no side" question the origin of the ethics principles, which are never perfect, not fixed, and evolving. As an alternative, it was pointed out that we need to be able to audit systems. Thus, we need to design systems to be auditable. Another opinion pointed out that more than auditable, we need verifiable systems.

Further discussed factors include:

- Properly engaging people in digital transformation.
- Improvement of connectivity, namely in remote and low population density areas.
- Coping with business goals (alignment between technological part and the business part), value creation, and solution impacts.
- Sustainable business models for new application domains such as agriculture.

2.4 Futuristic Application Scenarios for the Next 5–10 Years

A vast array of application scenarios was discussed, including improvements of current types of applications and disruptive directions. Examples:

- Combination of augmented reality and IoT for improved services and entertainment.
- Advanced smart city infrastructures, including smart mobility.
- Fully automated homes and their integration with smart grids, smart waste management, and other city infrastructures.
- Improved customer services and customer experience.
- Improved health monitoring and diagnosis with edible nano devices and wearable IoT.
- Intelligent industrial environments facilitating sustainability, resilience, and human-centric perspectives (towards Industry 5.0).
- Support of digital transformation.
- Use of nano devices in agri-food monitoring, traceability, and quality control.
- Precision farming and smart agriculture, resorting to IoT sensors and actuators. Examples: environment and crops monitoring, smart irrigation and fertilization, predictive analytics, plant disease detection and pest control, livestock tracking and geofencing, smart greenhouses, etc.
- Expanded IoT usage in climate monitoring and climate change prediction.
- Real-time monitoring of constructions (buildings, roads, infrastructures).

All these developments shall be driven by general sustainability concerns, and designed for transparency, accountability, and verifiability.

2.5 Concluding Remarks

As a final outcome of this panel, there is a general message of optimism regarding the high potential of IoT in helping to address major societal challenges and plenty of directions for a future applied research agenda. Nevertheless, all developments need to be human-centric, verifiable/scrutable, and responsible.

3   Challenges in IoT Research

3.1   Scope

IoT represents an ongoing technology transition bringing together many component technologies pertaining to diverse research domains such as internet, wireless communication, cloud computing, big data, data analytics, cybersecurity, etc. It is critical to identify immediate research challenges that needs to be met. While individually, impressive strides are being made in each of the constituent component technologies, what is critical and needed is a systems level thinking cross-cutting diverse research topics. Fortunately, this is happening in the form of many international research conferences focused on IoT (such as this conference) as well as dedicated tracks in established research conferences on the component technologies.

To guide the discussion of these challenges, the invited panelists in the second panel were asked to organize their contributions according to three guiding questions:

- *What are the current IoT research challenges?*
- *What are the promising approaches to face such challenges?*
- *What emerging technologies are likely to have an impact in next 5–10 years?*

The following sections highlight the main ideas resulting from the panelists' statements and from the discussion with the conference attendants.

3.2   Main Current IoT Research Challenges

Any practical IoT system is very complex due the scale (scalability) and diverse (heterogeneous) interacting component technologies (interoperability) [6]. The sheer complexity is overwhelming and gives rise to many research challenges. The IoT design problem is complicated as many of the challenges must be addressed simultaneously. The panel thinks that many research challenges are domain dependent (e.g., smart farming, healthcare IoT, industrial IoT, etc.). Further, the research complexity is captured well in the statement, *"IoT research is a system of systems research."*

The following are the main research challenges that the panel has identified as quintessential to be addressed with high-quality research:

- *Security and Trust* – The success of an IoT system depends on how secure it is. Naturally its wide-scale adaptability requires that it is trustable. Unfortunately, security and trust cannot be easily guaranteed. The definitions of security and trust itself changes depending on the IoT system at hand. Thus, domain dependent security challenges need to be understood well.
- *ML and IoT* – Many aspects of IoT are increasingly dependent on AI/ML which requires a lot of careful and high-quality research. IoT system automation can be accomplished with artificial intelligence. The system complexity necessitates that it learns by itself over time which perhaps is initially trained through supervised learning approach. ML model development from collection of training data to chosen model (network characteristics) to validation involves humans. It is critical that unintentional

biases should not seep into the model. Good processes must be developed that will help in collected "good" training data.

- *Data privacy* – IoT systems generate lots of data which can be sensitive (e.g., healthcare monitoring data) and must be protected. Ensuring data sovereignty must be researched wherein data ownership must be identified with data sharing rights assigned to the rightful owner. Privacy can have different definitions depending on the contexts. Privacy-by-design research is required wherein end users can easily opt-out and want to remain anonymous by choice. Currently, no such option exists. One possibility is to keep the data where it is generated and only share the insights from the data. If the data have to be transported, then automated network anonymizers need to be researched.
- *Energy efficiency* – One of the main bottlenecks is energy efficiency. The edge devices need to be constantly powered and their power must be managed to optimize the power consumption. While devices are cheap, powering them efficiently is a critical problem.
- *Connectivity and communication* – For IoT reliable and secure connectivity is very important. Cellular technologies such as 5G and upcoming 6G are critical to the success of IoT. Ubiquitous energy efficient connectivity must be researched. Bandwidth limitations is a well-known bottleneck to the success of IoT, research is needed to increase bandwidth. One challenge in wireless IoT is the difficulty in incorporating ML training and inference in real-time. Security in existing and evolving communication technologies needs further research attention.
- *Legacy systems* – It is important that legacy systems with old protocols must be brought in that requires convergence of old operational technology with information technology. Research is needed into how this transition can happen in a reliable and efficient manner.
- *Regulation and Certification* – While the regulation is not a complete answer to guarantee a safe and secure system, it has an important role to play in IoT system certification. Regulation may be difficult to enforce, however, there is a need for regulation that can bring awareness in the end users as well as the administrators of an IoT system. To the extent possible, component technologies should be certified.

3.3 Promising Approaches to Face the Challenges

The panel has suggested many promising directions to face the research challenges identified above. They are:

- *Safety and security research* - A systematic approach to security need to be adopted that in general will have four progressive stages: (1) prepare and prevent; (2) monitor and detect; (3) diagnose and understand; and (4) react, recover, and fix. Safety issues can be addressed by an approach for constrained reinforcement learning (well established technology). Systematic identification of vulnerabilities in existing technologies (such as 4G and 5G).
- *IoT standardization* – Standardization will result in methodical design (vs. adhoc design) that will help handle the IoT design complexity better. Legacy systems can interface better with standard modern technologies.
- *Design approaches* – As IoT system has foundation in diverse component technologies, a multi-disciplinary approach is needed. Such an approach will break silos and

will lead to more robust systems. Open system design approach is highly promising as this will lead to contributions from research community with crowdsourcing similar to what the software design world has seen. When an IoT system fails, there is a need for forensic analysis as to what happened and the order of events. Thus, forensic analysis tools for IoT need to be researched.

– *ML and IoT* - ML for wireless IoT can be achieved by: (a) data-driven optimization of network operations; (b) data-driven redesign of PHY or Link Level protocols; (3) redesign or adaptation of wireless access protocols to support ML services. Distributed ML over wireless IoT (Edge AI) is a promising direction due to resource constraints (processing, storage, and power). One aspect of IoT system is that humans interact in many ways (sometimes erroneously!) which necessitates smarter and adaptive algorithms.

– *Edge and Cloud Computing* - Ongoing research in edge computing is in the right direction particularly with embedded AI that can lead to smarter IoT systems with optimized resource orchestration. Battery free operation of edge devices is critical as current battery technology cannot meet the long-term needs of IoT without replacement/maintenance. Cloud computing research into big data, distributed computing, platform-as-service, etc., are important ongoing research that will greatly contribute to IoT success. Secure data spaces will enable secure multi-party computation and federated learning. The panel believed that federated learning is an important emerging technology with significant impact on IoT.

3.4 Emerging Technologies that are Likely to Have an Impact in the Next 5–10 Years

The panel identified many promising technologies many of which are already in advanced implementation stages, while some are very futuristic in nature:

– 5G, 6G, Mesh technologies.
– Standardization, Open system design approach, Event-driven IoT, Digital twins, Human IoT interfaces.
– IoT cyber threat intelligence, Root-of-trust HW approaches, Embedded AI enabling real-time interaction, privacy, and efficiency.
– Tiny ML, Federated AI.
– Data driven applications and society.
– Augmented and extended reality (metaverse), The Internet of senses (>5 years), Real-time music interaction over internet.
– Autonomous driving, Personal health monitoring, Smart Cities, Drones, Bio-nano things (IoBNT).
– Combined sensing and communication (optical and satellite communication).
– Quantum technologies (sensing, communication, computing).

3.5 Concluding Remarks

In conclusion, the panel agreed that IoT research is an exciting topic with interesting challenges. They encouraged young or starting researchers to consider IoT as their research field. The panel felt that there are many opportunities in the IoT field. If the research challenges are addressed successfully then it will solve many societal problems and positively contribute to the progress of humankind. IoT can make the world better and healthy (e.g., can we predict a pandemic?). For this we require a very careful approach to research both basic as well as applied research.

4 Conclusions

Both panels agree that IoT will be a major contributor to addressing big societal challenges such as global healthcare, global food system, wildfire management, sustainability, etc. There is a need for a multi-disciplinary perspective; technology-only approaches will fall short, they need to be judiciously combined with socio-technical research, ethics research, regulation and certification standards, appropriate education, and global awareness. IoT research and development shall be driven by general sustainability concerns, and designed for transparency, accountability, and verifiability. Future IoT applications include, for instance, Internet-of-senses, Internet-of-BioNanoThings, augmented and extended reality, improved health monitoring and diagnosis with edible nano devices.

Acknowledgments. We would like to thank the seven panelists and the conference audience for two thought-provoking and exciting panel discussions.

References

1. Sundmaeker, H., Guillemin, P., Friess, P., Woelfflé, S. (eds.): Vision and Challenges for Realising the Internet of Things. CERP-IoT, European Commission (2010)
2. Camarinha-Matos, L.M., Goes, J., Gomes, L., Martins, J.: Contributing to the Internet of Things. In: Camarinha-Matos, L.M., Tomic, S., Graça, P. (eds.) DoCEIS 2013. IAICT, vol. 394, pp. 3–12. Springer, Heidelberg (2013). https://doi.org/10.1007/978-3-642-37291-9_1
3. Strous, L., Cerf, V.G. (eds.): IFIPIoT 2018. IAICT, vol. 548. Springer, Cham (2019). https://doi.org/10.1007/978-3-030-15651-0
4. Casaca, A., Katkoori, S., Ray, S., Strous, L. (eds.): IFIPIoT 2019. IAICT, vol. 574. Springer, Cham (2020). https://doi.org/10.1007/978-3-030-43605-6
5. United Nations: Transforming our world: the 2030 Agenda for Sustainable Development (2015). https://sdgs.un.org/2030agenda. Accessed 30 Nov 2021
6. Hanes, D., Salgueiro, G., Grossetete, P., Barton, R., Henry, J.: IoT Fundamentals: Networking Technologies, Protocols, and Use Cases for the Internet-of-Things. Cisco Press, Indianapolis (2017)

Modernizing Agricultural Practice Using IoT

sFarm: A Distributed Ledger Based Remote Crop Monitoring System for Smart Farming

Anand K. Bapatla[1] , Saraju P. Mohanty[1(✉)] , and Elias Kougianos[2]

[1] Department of Computer Science and Engineering, University of North Texas, Denton, USA
anandkumarbapatla@my.unt.edu, saraju.mohanty@unt.edu
[2] Department of Electrical Engineering, University of North Texas, Denton, USA
elias.kougianos@unt.edu

Abstract. Crop monitoring systems are one of the important aspects of Smart Agriculture. Due to explosive growth of population there is an increase in demand for food products while urbanization is causing shortage in manual labor. As the yield of a crop is greatly affected by many climatic and environmental parameters, there is an urgent need for efficient crop monitoring. Rapidly advancing IoT (Internet of Things) technologies have shown very promising results and have automated most of the traditional processes in farming. An efficient Crop Monitoring System (CMS) is proposed which automates the monitoring by using the IoT and real-time data is shared securely using private IOTA Tangle Distributed Ledger Technology. The proposed application equips farmers with required information which will help them make decisions promptly based on the real-time environmental parameters of the crop and reduces human labor. Data privacy and security are other important aspects addressed in the proposed system by setting up a private IOTA Tangle. Unlike public distributed ledgers, private distributed ledgers provide data privacy and security by allowing only known participants to join the network, thereby limiting the adversaries trying to tamper with the data. Practical implementation of the proposed system is done and analyzed for scalability and reliability.

Keywords: Internet-of-Agro-Things (IoAT) · Smart agriculture · Crop monitoring systems · Farm monitoring systems · Distributed ledger · Blockchain · IOTA · Tangle distributed ledger · Real-time data sharing

1 Introduction

Agriculture is one of the sectors which has been highly influenced and benefited from the advancements in technology. From using human labor and indigenous tools which is referred as Agriculture 1.0, processes used in farming have been modified significantly by introducing the latest technological aspects for achieving better yield and making them climate-smart [17]. Different milestones in the history which have paved new ways for farming are shown in Fig. 1. Main driving forces for these revolutions are population, urbanization and demand for food products. According to Our World in Data [20], the global population is currently at 7.7 billion and is estimated 9 billion by

© IFIP International Federation for Information Processing 2022
Published by Springer Nature Switzerland AG 2022
L. M. Camarinha-Matos et al. (Eds.): IFIPIoT 2021, IFIP AICT 641, pp. 13–31, 2022.
https://doi.org/10.1007/978-3-030-96466-5_2

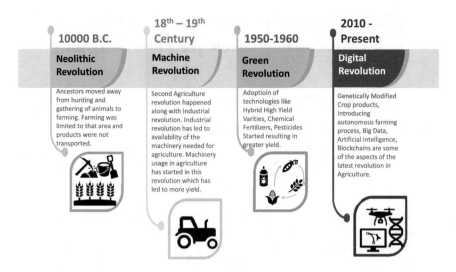

Fig. 1. Agricultural revolutions.

the end of 2050 which clearly shows rapid increase in demand for food products. Urbanization has led to reduction in availability of manual labor for farming tasks which has also been a limiting factor for reaching the demand. Another important factor affecting the food product yield is the availability of arable land and natural resources.

The Internet of Agro-Things (IoAT), Big Data (BD), Artificial Intelligence (AI), Machine Learning (ML), and Distributed Ledgers are some of the latest technologies which are driving the agricultural revolution 4.0 [24, 32]. The IoAT is agricultural things with capability of connecting and sharing data with each other using different Information and Communication Technologies (ICT's). Smart agriculture is a new agricultural trend which integrates different latest technologies to assist farming by providing real-time decision making capability along with intelligent control and minimal usage of resources, while making the yield high and predictable. One of the most important aspects of smart agriculture is real-time crop monitoring systems as yield is impacted by many external interactions like weather patterns, water scarcity, energy costs, etc. [10]. Such systems can help reduce the amount of human labor needed to monitor the farms throughout the time of crop and enable farmers to take prompt decisions. Multiple farm monitoring systems are already in place, both at the regional and national level, such as the Global Information and Early Warning System (GIEWS), Famine Early Warning System Network (FEWS NET), and Monitoring Agriculture with Remote sensing (MARS) [9]. These systems have shown how important is to have an efficient crop monitoring system in place but there is need for making these systems more robust and secure. A cyber-attack on such systems which are targeted at farms, food supply-chain and automated control mechanisms can cause catastrophic loss and also pose threat to the lives of consumers [11]. Along with this, integrating and maintaining such Collaborative Control Systems (CCS) is difficult and needs some conflict resolution among the components to improve the performance and prevent errors. The importance of such

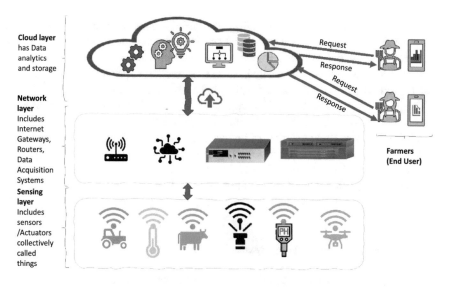

Fig. 2. Smart agriculture layered architecture.

conflict resolution systems and two novel Collaboration Detection and Prevention of Errors and Conflicts (CDPEC) algorithms are developed and analyzed in [2] which has significantly reduced the potential faults in such collaborative environments. A typical IoT architecture is shown in Fig. 2.

IoT devices are resource constrained and introducing complex encryption and decryption mechanisms cannot be a feasible solution. The cloud layer in a typical IoT architecture is capable of processing and storing large amounts of data and are generally a third party service which is a central entity. Access times from the cloud mainly depends on the network traffic and quality of network connection, which can be a problem in real-time systems like crop monitoring systems. Without proper security mechanisms in place, an adversary can perform a Distributed Denial of Service Attack (DDOS) and false data injection attacks. Apart from these there is always a chance of Single Point Of Failure (SPOF) as the whole system data are stored and processed at a central cloud server.

Distributed ledger Technology (DLT) is a novel approach of recording, sharing and synchronizing data across multiple data stores participating in the network which is analogous to network formed by the edge devices in IoT. Main components of DLT include nodes, transaction, consensus mechanism, shared ledger and cryptography. A participant in this peer-to-peer network who is responsible for generating the transaction and perform network operations is called a node. Each node in the network will have its own copy of the distributed ledger in order to make it tamper proof and has all the historical transaction data which can be traversed through to verify. Consensus mechanism is a set of rules which are accepted over the network and followed by all nodes to process an incoming transaction. DLT can help to solve these problems and eliminate the central authority. It also provides security and prevents tampering of the data, False data injections and spamming. The proposed sFarm system makes use of such a private DLT based on the Tangle Data structure for eliminating the need for central authority which will remove the latency and provide a real-time data sharing platform. Along with these attacks it also acts as a solution to provide data privacy and security while providing a resource friendly and cost-efficient architecture.

The paper is organized in the following sections: Sect. 2 gives an overview of prior related research work. Section 3 talks about the novel features of the proposed system. Section 4 will discuss how Distributed Ledger Technology is a viable solution for Crop Monitoring Systems and the type of distributed ledger to be used in Smart Agriculture. Section 5 provides the overview and working of the proposed system. Section 6 discusses the algorithm behind the proposed sFarm. Section 7 provides the implementation and analysis details and Sect. 8 provides the conclusion along with future research aspects.

2   Related Research Overview

The Blockchain and Distributed Ledger Technologies have been showing very promising applications in a variety of fields like Smart Healthcare [27, 29], Smart Transportation [5, 21] along with Smart Agriculture since the time financial solution Bitcoin [22]. Bitcoin was solely designed for keeping track of digital assets and it is very difficult to adapt it in other fields, hence different platforms like Ethereum, EOS, NEO, and IOTA have been designed. Different studies have been conducted to check the feasibility of the blockchain in Smart Agriculture applications.

A use case of precision agriculture was proposed in [16], an extensive analysis of combining DLT technologies with IOT devices as a data marketplace. DLT was also analyzed as a solution for cattle farms in [8] where poultry farm data has been stored on a public DLT and accessed using the Masked Authentication Messaging (MAM) data communication protocol. The current paper uses private DLT, and performance analysis of the proposed architecture is done to determine the throughput and reliability of the system. Recently, a secure data sharing platform was developed for Smart Agriculture in [30]. Smart contracts were used by different entities to determine the access policy. Smart Contracts on EOS platform are used in this to define the access policies. Managing IoT devices using the blockchain is presented in [13], one of the initial papers which has shown the potential usage of smart contracts in managing different IoT devices. An Ethereum smart contract based control was used. This work helped in understanding the potential usage of smart contracts in IoT device control but there will be large number of IoT devices while monitoring a farm and the Ethereum blockchain is not scalable and is not a feasible solution in crop monitoring systems. The main bottleneck in using blockchain technology is resource intensive consensus mechanisms like PoW which cannot be adapted into resource constrained environments like IoT. Research has been conducted in proposing new IoT friendly consensus mechanisms [25, 33] which helps in successfully adapting blockchain technology into applications like Smart Agriculture. Apart from crop monitoring systems, the blockchain shows potential applications in other important aspects of Smart Agriculture like efficient supply chain tracking. Supply chain is too complex and involves many parties in the process. Even with Enterprise Resource Planning (ERP) applications in place, there is still many transactions happening with blinded parties resulting in significant loss of crop and money. Many such farm-to-fork applications are also analyzed and implemented in [18, 19, 23].

As promising as DLT technology is for providing efficient solutions to scalability and providing a secured environment for IOT Applications, it is still being improved and is constantly evolving. Constant work is being done to remove the need for coordinator nodes and making it fully decentralized. Other works for curbing address reuse [31] and increasing scalability [3] for such tangle data structure based DLT's is also being analyzed to make it a feasible solution for IoT environments. A summary of related research is shown in Table 1.

Table 1. Related research and their importance

Related research	Contributions
Lamtzidis et al. [16]	Data Marketplace application using DLT and IoT technologies was designed and analyzed
Elham et al. [8]	Proposed a poultry farm monitoring system using public DLT and accessed using MAM data protocol
Rahman et al. [30]	Proposed a secure data sharing model for smart agriculture. Proposed model was implemented in EOS environment and analyzed
Huh et al. [13]	One of the initial papers which has shown the potential use of smart contracts in IoT environment. Different smart contracts were defined to control actuators like AC, Lights and Electric meters
Puthal et al. [25]	A light weight IoT-friendly consensus mechanism called Proof-of-Authentication (PoAh) is proposed replacing the resource consuming PoW and improved the transaction confirmation times
Malik et al. [19]	These authors have proposed a blockchain based solution for supply chain in smart agriculture. They made use of Access Control Lists (ACL) and Smart contracts to build a three-layered architecture
Madumidha et al. [18]	Authors had discussed about different entities participating in the supply chain of agricultural products and use-case analysis was done for using RFID and IoT systems

3 Novel Contributions

Below are the problems addressed and novel solutions proposed in current proposed sFarm application.

3.1 Problems Addressed in the Current Paper

The problems of current Crop Monitoring Systems addressed in the current paper are:

– Single point of failure by having a centralized data sharing platform.

- Centralized authorities controlling the shared data and monetizing without realizing benefits to farmers.
- Data security and privacy issues as IoT is a resource constrained environment.
- False data injection by adversary nodes present in the network.
- Network congestion bottleneck and delay in processing requests hindering real-time application performance.
- Delay in data sharing as the central server can be flooded.
- Denial-of-Service attacks can be performed by sending spam messages to central server.
- Cost of infrastructure usage and maintenance is usually high.

3.2   Novel Solutions Proposed

The novel contributions of the proposed sFarm are:

- Decentralized data sharing platform with real time data sharing.
- Providing a secure crop monitoring system to eliminate different security threats.
- Avoiding data tampering by providing a single source of truth using a distributed ledger.
- Continuous monitoring of different farm parameters and reporting to the farmer.
- Provide data privacy and security by implementing a private DL.
- Cost-efficient infrastructure for building and maintaining Real-Time Crop Monitoring Systems.

4   Is the Distributed Ledger a Feasible Solution?

Each application should be analyzed to determine if DL is an apt solution. A path to analyzing the feasibility of blockchain technology has been given in [26]. A similar analysis is performed for proposed sFarm to check the feasibility of DLT technology in Smart Agriculture.

Multiple untrusted participants in data sharing and the need to dissolve a central entity is one of the important characteristics for adapting a DLT solution [7]. Since there are multiple sensor nodes and many actuator nodes along with the farmers to monitor and take decisions in this smart agriculture architecture, DLT is a good choice. The data being monitored is used for real-time monitoring and analysis of the climatic and environmental cycles, there is no need for modifying the past stored data. As the transactions in DLT cannot be modified once approved, it is apt solution in the proposed sFarm.

DLT is a solution when the main concern in the data sharing is with data privacy and security [12]. IoT networks are prone for data leakage and data security issues because of lack of security measures in such constrained environments Private DL implemented in sFarm will limit and control the entities participating in the network operations thereby providing data privacy and security. Private DL will also prevent spamming of the network by filtering transactions coming from outside of network. The main characteristic of DL is providing a tamper-proof single source of truth which makes it a very good technology to be used in such crop monitoring systems like sFarm.

Table 2. Comparison of blockchain and IOTA tangle data structures

Feature	Blockchain	IOTA tangle
Structure	Special type of DAG where each block is connected to previous block using hash pointer	Data blocks flow in one direction and each block is connected to two other blocks using hash pointers
Security	Provides high security by using complex consensus	Provides less security compared to blockchain and is apt solution for not much critical applications needing scalability
Decentralization	Decentralized and no need for coordinator node	Less decentralization as there is a coordinator node
Cost of transaction	Certain transaction fee will be levied for each transaction and it may increase based on the traffic congestion	There are no miners in Tangle making it fee-less for sending transactions
Transaction time	Increases with increase in network traffic	Decreases with increase in network traffic
Scalability	Predetermined block sizes and block generation times will make the transactions to stall and limit the scalability	Each transaction node performs PoW for two tip nodes in tangle for it's transaction to be attached, hence making tangle highly scalable with large number of participants
Applications	Designed specifically for digital asset control and ownership	Designed for IoT Applications to reach the scalability and provide security

Most of the above discussed aspects are satisfied by the blockchain but the IOTA Tangle data structure is chosen because of its scalability and cost of infrastructure. Choosing IOTA Tangle enables the transactions to be processed in real-time and data is available readily to the farmers for making decisions. Each node in the network is responsible for performing required Proof-of-Work (PoW). The PoW used in IOTA is not complex as it is used only for preventing spamming whereas in blockchain PoW is used to provide immutability. Differences between the blockchain and IOTA Tangle are given in Table 2.

By taking all these factors into account, sFarm makes use of private IOTA Tangle for implementing the crop monitoring system.

5   Architectural Overview of sFarm

An architectural overview of the system is shown in Fig. 3. The main components of the proposed architecture are sensing nodes, edge nodes, private DLT network based on Tangle data structure, and users.

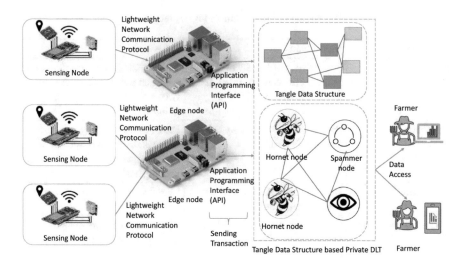

Fig. 3. Architectural overview of sFarm,

5.1   Sensing Nodes

Sensing nodes are placed at different locations of the field. The main responsibility of the sensing node is sensing the environmental parameters and sending the data to the edge devices. Sensing nodes are not capable of storing large data or perform high level computations. They should also be power efficient as the replacing and maintenance costs should be low as there will be potentially thousands of such devices in a large farm. The proposed monitoring makes use an MCU for connecting all sensors and to send the information to the edge devices for further processing. A simple sensing node is proposed in sFarm with a sensor to monitor air temperature, humidity and GPS sensor to track its location to map the spatial data. A block diagram of sFarm is shown in Fig. 4.

5.2   Edge Node

The edge node is responsible for collecting data from the sensing nodes. A single board computer is used as the edge device in the proposed sFarm application. Data from the MCU is sent to the edge device using a lightweight publish-subscribe network protocol. Unlike sensing nodes, edge nodes have both computational and data storage capabilities to manage large amounts of data. The data being sent from different sensing nodes will be collected and processed by using DLT client libraries and made into a transaction which is sent to the private DLTs using API calls.

The temperature and humidity sensor used can monitor the temperature ranges from 0–50 °C with an accuracy of ± 2 °C and humidity in the range of 20–90% RH with an accuracy of $\pm 5\%$ RH. The GPS module used is able to track 22 satellites on 66 channels to provide a location accuracy of 1.8 m. It has inbuilt internal patch antenna and also a U.FL connector is available to connect an external antenna. Power usage is very low and draws only 25 mA during tracking and 20 mA during navigation.

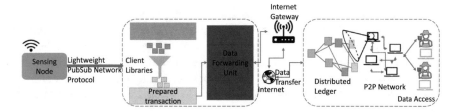

Fig. 4. Block diagram of sFarm.

6 Proposed Algorithm for sFarm

Environmental data from the field is collected by sensing nodes and is transferred to the edge node by using a lightweight pubsub network protocol. A sensing node publishes the data to a topic and each edge node is subscribed to multiple topics to receive data from multiple sensing nodes. The received data is pre-processed using client libraries and a transaction is formatted and generated. The edge node is also responsible for executing Proof-of-Work (PoW) for the tips selected in the tangle data structure. Once a valid nonce is computed, the transaction is sent to one of the nodes in the private DLT implemented. Transaction generation is shown in Algorithm 1. Once the transactions

---

Algorithm 1. Proposed Data Upload Algorithm for sFarm

Input: Temperature, Humidity and GPS Position data from sensing node
Output: Transaction Hash from Private Distributed Ledger
 1: A topic τ_S is created for each sensing node S
 2: Each edge node E can subscribe to topics from multiple sensing nodes
 3: E.subscribe(τ_S)
 4: **for** Every time interval t_i **do**
 5:     Prepare a message μ with Temperature (temp), Humidity(hum) and GPS data
 6:     S.Publish(τ,μ(temp,Hum,GPS))
 7: **end for**
 8: **while** Message $\in$ topic τ **do**
 9:     E $\leftarrow$ Receive(τ,μ)
10:     E runs Tip selection algorithm and get two tips $T1, T2$ from DLT
11:     Proof-of-Work(PoW) executed by edge node and Nonce η is computed
12:     Payload $\rho \leftarrow$ Client.preparePayload(μ(temp,Hum,GPS),η)
13:     Prepare Transaction $\Gamma \leftarrow$ Client.prepareTransaction(ρ,η)
14:     **if** Client Connected **then**
15:         result $\rho \leftarrow$ Connection.sendTransaction(Γ)
16:     **else**
17:         Connection $\leftarrow$ Client.connect(Provider URL, Port)
18:         result $\rho \leftarrow$ Connection.sendTransaction(Γ)
19:     **end if**
20:     return ρ.hash
21: **end while**

---

are added to the DL, a streams framework based data protocol is used for structuring and navigating through the data in the ledger securely. Within a private network the data being sent to the ledger may not be required to be encrypted as all the participants in network are trusted parties. If an access policy needs to be enforced on the data, public key encryption can be used to encrypt the data before sending it to the ledger and only authorized parties with private keys will be able to access the data. The data access algorithm is shown in Algorithm 2.

Algorithm 2. Proposed Data Access Algorithm for sFarm

Input: Root Node, Client Node, Port and Minimum Weight Magnitude (MWM)
Output: Organized data from tangle

1: A channel τ is created using streams framework
2: Publisher Υ has public key information K_{pub} of the intended recipient ρ and can encrypt data before sending to ledger
3: Recipient ρ subscribes to the channel of interest to receive messaged from Publisher Υ in real-time
4: ρ.subscribe(τ)
5: **while** Message $\in$ stream τ **do**
6:     Recipient ρ receives encrypted message ψ
7:     $\rho \leftarrow$ Receive(τ)
8:     Received encrypted data ψ is decrypted using private key $K_p rv$ of recipient ρ
9:     Decrypted message $\mu \leftarrow$ decrypt(ψ,$K_p rv$)
10:    Decrypted messages can be displayed on web pages using Application Programming Interfaces (API)
11:    **if** Node Not Connected **then**
12:        Connection $\leftarrow$ Client.connect(Client Node URL, Port)
13:    **end if**
14: **end while**

---

7   Implementation and Validation

7.1   Implementation

The sensing node which is placed at different locations of the field for sensing is shown in Fig. 5. In the implemented design both location and environmental parameter data is combined together and sent to the edge device which is responsible for preparing the IOTA transaction and send it to the IOTA Tangle DLT. Communication between the edge node and edge device is achieved in the implementation by using a message broker. A topic is defined, and the edge node makes use of this topic to publish the data updates from time to time. The edge device receives all these updates by subscribing to that topic. Once data is received by the edge device it acts as a client and uses client libraries for modifying the received data into a transaction and send it to the IOTA private tangle network. Data being sent from the sensing node is shown in Fig. 6.

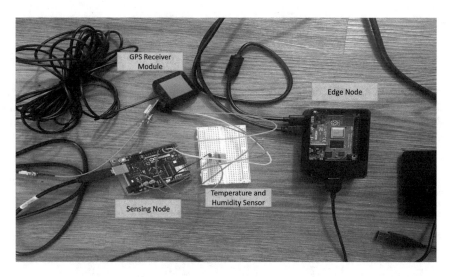

Fig. 5. Implemented sensing node along with edge device.

```
© COM12

 Humidity: 49.00%  Temperature: 21.70°C 71.06Location: 3312.7810N, 9709.4609W
 Location (in degrees, works with Google Maps): 33.2130, -97.1577
 Speed (knots): 0.02
 Angle: 23.56
 Altitude: 211.80
 Satellites: 9

 Humidity: 49.00%  Temperature: 21.70°C 71.06Location: 3312.7812N, 97095.4609W
 Location (in degrees, works with Google Maps): 33.2130, -112.5976
 Speed (knots): 0.03
 Angle: 20.55
 Altitude: 211.80
 Satellites: 9

 Humidity: 49.00%  Temperature: 21.70°C 71.06Location: 3312.7812N, 9709.4609W
 Location (in degrees, works with Google Maps): 33.2130, -97.1577
 Speed (knots): 0.03
 Angle: 50.07
 Altitude: 211.80
 Satellites: 9
```

Fig. 6. Continued readings from the sensing node.

7.2 Agriculture Datasets and Community Data Sharing Using the Proposed sFarm

The proposed sFarm architecture can also be used for community data sharing applications. Community data sharing platforms can help in educating farmers about the type of crop to be grown based on weather conditions, prevailing crop infections and many other important information that can be part of decision support tools. Three different datasets for crop recommendation, production, and yield are taken with different sizes of data and analyzed for the transaction times taken for each data to be uploaded to the distributed ledger. A Crop Recommendation Dataset [14] helps farmers in formulating a strategy based on different field parameters like Nitrogen, Phosphorous, Potassium, Temperature, Humidity, pH of soil and rainfall to determine the type of crop to be grown. Another dataset [15] with medium size focuses on the prediction of crop price yield by using different regional attributes. Along with these, a large dataset [1] provide information about the cop production in India over several years, is also used in this application. Average data upload times are computed in the implemented sFarm application for these three different datasets and the results are presented in Table 3.

Table 3. Average transaction times and estimated upload times for community data sharing using sFarm

Dataset	Size of dataset (in KB)	Number of records	Average transaction time (in sec)	Estimated upload times (in hr)
Crop recommendation dataset [14]	146.52	2200	1.01	0.31
Corn yield [15]	2781	23475	2.29	14.96
Crop production dataset [1]	14958	246091	1.24	85.04

The estimated time for uploading larger datasets increases rapidly when the size of data increases. This is due to the Proof-of-Work needed to be performed by the uploading client. PoW difficulty increases as the number of transactions sent by the same node increases within a short span of time to reduce spamming of the network. To avoid this, off-chain storage can be a solution or the data can be segmented and uploaded using different clients to reduce the upload times. In addition, remote PoW can also be implemented using more powerful hardware other than clients dedicated specifically for performing PoW required for transactions of client. If the data consists of images, uploading image data directly as the JSON input is not a feasible solution. A possible alternative approach is to upload these files on off-chain storage like AWS S3 bucket and store the Uniform Resource Locator (URL) information to DLT. This is analyzed in the proposed sFarm by storing the images from datasets [4,6,28]. Sample images of apple, grape and tomato leafs from the dataset are shown in Fig. 7. Different grades of pomegranate are shown in Fig. 8, and cabbage disease classification data are shown in Fig. 9.

7.3   sFarm Validation

Near real-time data availability is one of the main aspects of crop monitoring systems like the proposed sFarm for prompt actions to be taken by the farmer. For evaluating real-time operations, transaction confirmation times are evaluated. An edge node with a quad-core ARM A72 CPU with 4 GB RAM is considered and 50 test runs are

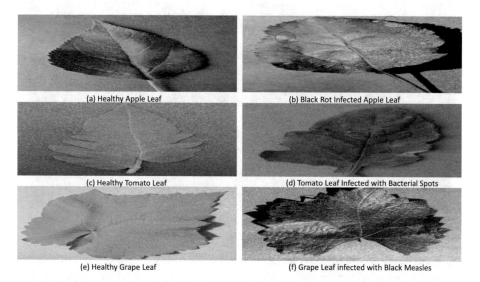

(a) Healthy Apple Leaf

(b) Black Rot Infected Apple Leaf

(c) Healthy Tomato Leaf

(d) Tomato Leaf Infected with Bacterial Spots

(e) Healthy Grape Leaf

(f) Grape Leaf infected with Black Measles

Fig. 7. Plant disease dataset [6] (a),(b) Shows healthy and black rot infected Apple leaves respectively (c),(d) Shows healthy and bacterial infected Tomato leaves respectively (e),(f) Shows images of healthy and black measles infected Grape leaves respectively

(a) Pomegranate with Superior G1 Q1 Quality

(b) Pomegranate with G2 Q1 Quality

(c) Pomegranate with G3 Q1 Quality

(d) Pomegranate with G3 Q4 Quality

Fig. 8. Pomegranate fruit quality dataset [28] Pomegranate classified into 3 Grades - G1,G2,G3 and each grade subdivided into 4 Quality labels Q1, Q2, Q3, Q4. (a) Shows the image of highest grade highest quality Pomegranate (b) Shows the highest quality of grade 2 Pomegranate with slight defects (c) Shows not ripe Pomegranate and comes under Grade 3 (d) Shows pomegranate With least quality and grade

Fig. 9. Cabbage disease dataset [4] (a) Image shows fresh un-infected cabbage Leafs (b) Shows image of Cabbage infected by back Moth (c) Shows image of infected Cabbage plant by leaf miner (d) Shows a Cabbage plant infected by Meldew

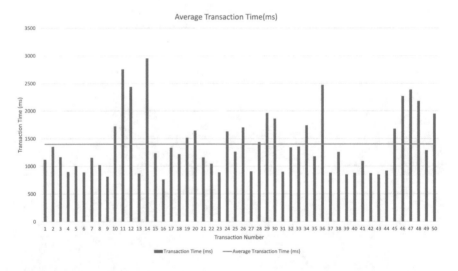

Fig. 10. Average transaction time for Private IOTA tangle node implemented in sFarm.

performed. Transaction confirmation times are noted for each test run and an average transaction time is computed. Figure 10 shows the transaction times and the average time. The average transaction times for the implemented sFarm application is 1401 ms. A 1.4 s delay is acceptable as the climatic and environmental changes are gradual and do not change within seconds significantly. As the farm size increases, the number of sensing nodes to cover the entire field increases in proportion to the farm area. Hence, the power consumption of each node should be minimal. Maximum current use for the

Table 4. Statistics of load testing performed on private tangle implemented for sFarm

Parameter	Value
Number of samples data transactions sent	1000
Load duration	1 min
Failed transactions	10
Percentage of error	1%
Average response time (ms)	7566.76
Minimum response time (ms)	1883
Maximum response time (ms)	25760
Median response time (ms)	7314.00
Throughput (transactions/second)	38.03

implemented end node including both temperature sensor and GPS module is 33.95 mA. Assuming all electronic devices in the sensing node are consuming maximum current, the amount of power consumed is estimated to be 0.169 W. Assuming 1000 such sensing nodes are running in the field continuously for 24 h, they will consume only 4.056 units of electricity which is very small. Considering the fact that usage of solar energy in fields is common, the cost of operating the proposed sensing nodes in large numbers is efficient and affordable.

The IOTA private tangle implemented for the proposed sFarm consists of two peer nodes along with a coordinator node. Transactions from the edge nodes will be sent to the peer nodes. As the number of edge nodes increases, the number of transactions reaching each peer node in the IOTA Tangle network increases. The throughput of the IOTA Tangle node helps in determining the scalability of the proposed model. Each peer node in the private Tangle of sFarm is designed with a Quad-core CPU with 4 GB of RAM. To determine the throughput of the node, 1000 sample messages are sent within a span of one minute to the same Hornet node. Response times and the error rates are measured to determine the scalability. Statistics of the test are given in Table 4.

Response time distribution for all 1000 sample data transactions sent is shown in Fig. 11. Average response time for these 1000 samples is 7566.6 ms. Even with such a large number of nodes sending transactions at the same time to a single node has resulted in only 1% failure and average response time of approximately 7.5 s. Hence, the throughput of each peer node is high enough to handle a large number of edge nodes at the same time. Latency from the peer node is another factor which needs analyzing to determine if it can support near real-time applications like sFarm. The request load is increased gradually over the time span of 1 min, and the number of success and failure responses are measured along with the median latency in receiving responses from the peer node and results are shown in Fig. 12. A comparative analysis with respect to transaction times and throughput is performed between [16] and the current paper implementation to analyze the benefits of using Private Tangle Data Structure based DLT over Public Tangle based DLT and is presented in Table 5.

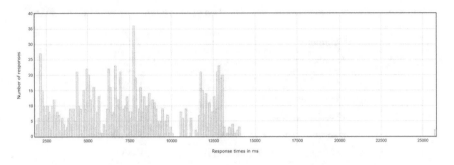

Fig. 11. Response time distribution for private IOTA tangle Node implemented in sFarm.

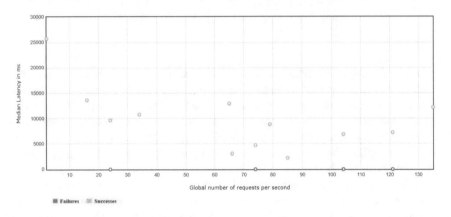

Fig. 12. Latency of peer node with increasing number of requests per second,

Table 5. Comparative analysis of results

Feature	Lamtzidis et al. [16]	Current paper
DLT platform	IOTA	IOTA
Type of DLT	Public	Private
PoW	Local	Local
Transaction time (in Sec)	60	1.8
Throughput (Tx/Sec)	5	38.03

8   Conclusions and Future Research

In this work we have proposed a novel idea of distributed ledger based Remote Crop Monitoring System which solves the problem of data privacy and security and provides an efficient and affordable Remote Crop Monitoring solution. It makes use of DLT along with the IoT to leverage a system which can solve the discussed problems with centralized data sharing platforms. Proof of concept is implemented for the proposed sFarm and is analyzed for scalability and reliability. Results from the analysis have shown that the proposed system can handle a large number (1000) of sensing nodes with an average latency of 7566.6 ms and 1% error rate making it an acceptable solution for small to large farms.

In future work, we will develop a full level prototype and deploy it in a real-time environment. Along with that, different techniques to reduce the latency further and provide a user-friendly GUI option for better accessibility to farmers will be analyzed. Our focus is on providing an efficient, affordable and robust solution for a Crop Monitoring System while maintaining data security and privacy. In addition, future work will be able to use AI/ML techniques to monitor the anomalies in environmental parameters and alert the user to take prompt decision.

Acknowledgment. This material is based upon work supported by the National Science Foundation under Grant number OAC-1924112. Any opinions, findings, and conclusions or recommendations expressed in this material are those of the authors and do not necessarily reflect the views of the National Science Foundation.

References

1. Abhinand: Crop production in india (2019). https://www.kaggle.com/abhinand05/crop-production-in-india. Accessed 10 July 2021
2. Ajidarma, P., Nof, S.Y.: Collaborative detection and prevention of errors and conflicts in an agricultural robotic system. Stud. Inf. Control **30**(1), 19–28 (2021). https://doi.org/10.24846/v30i1y202102
3. Alkhodair, A., Mohanty, S., Kougianos, E., Puthal, D.: McPoRA: a multi-chain proof of rapid authentication for post-blockchain based security in large scale complex cyber-physical systems. In: Proceedings IEEE Computer Society Annual Symposium on VLSI (ISVLSI) (2020). https://doi.org/10.1109/isvlsi49217.2020.00-16
4. Apuada, G.: Chinese cabbage disease dataset (2020). https://www.kaggle.com/giane901/chinese-cabbage-disease-detection. Accessed 10 July 2021
5. Bao, S., et al.: Pseudonym management through blockchain: cost-efficient privacy preservation on intelligent transportation systems. IEEE Access **7**, 80390–80403 (2019). https://doi.org/10.1109/access.2019.2921605
6. Bhattarai, S.: New plant diseases dataset (2019). https://www.kaggle.com/vipoooool/new-plant-diseases-dataset. Accessed 10 July 2021
7. Doku, R., Rawat, D.: Pledge: a private ledger based decentralized data sharing framework. In: Proceedings Spring Simulation Conference (SpringSim) (2019). https://doi.org/10.23919/springsim.2019.8732913
8. Elham, M.N., et al.: A preliminary study on poultry farm environmental monitoring using internet of things and blockchain technology. In: Proceedings 10th Symposium on Computer Applications and Industrial Electronics (ISCAIE) (2020). https://doi.org/10.1109/iscaie47305.2020.9108820
9. Fritz, S., et al.: A comparison of global agricultural monitoring systems and current gaps. Agric. Syst. **168**, 258–272 (2019). https://doi.org/10.1016/j.agsy.2018.05.010
10. Godfray, H.C.J., et al.: Food security: the challenge of feeding 9 billion people. Science **327**(5967), 812–818 (2010). https://doi.org/10.1126/science.1185383
11. Gupta, M., Abdelsalam, M., Khorsandroo, S., Mittal, S.: Security and privacy in smart farming: challenges and opportunities. IEEE Access **8**, 34564–34584 (2020). https://doi.org/10.1109/access.2020.2975142

12. Henry, R., Herzberg, A., Kate, A.: Blockchain access privacy: challenges and directions. IEEE Secur. Privacy **16**(4), 38–45 (2018). https://doi.org/10.1109/msp.2018.3111245
13. Huh, S., Cho, S., Kim, S.: Managing IoT devices using blockchain platform. In: Proceedings 19th International Conference on Advanced Communication Technology (ICACT) (2017). https://doi.org/10.23919/icact.2017.7890132
14. Ingle, A.: Crop recommendation dataset (2020). https://www.kaggle.com/atharvaingle/crop-recommendation-dataset Accessed 10 July 2021
15. kumar, S.: Crop price prediction (2019). https://www.kaggle.com/abhinand05/crop-production-in-india. Accessed 10 July 2021
16. Lamtzidis, O., Pettas, D., Gialelis, J.: A novel combination of distributed ledger technologies on internet of things: use case on precision agriculture. Appl. Syst. Innov. **2**(3), 30 (2019). https://doi.org/10.3390/asi2030030
17. Liu, Y., Ma, X., Shu, L., Hancke, G.P., Abu-Mahfouz, A.M.: From industry 4.0 to agriculture 4.0: Current status, enabling technologies, and research challenges. IEEE Trans. Ind. Inf. **17**(6), 4322–4334 (2021). https://doi.org/10.1109/tii.2020.3003910
18. Madumidha, S., Ranjani, P.S., Varsinee, S.S., Sundari, P.: Transparency and traceability: in food supply chain system using blockchain technology with internet of things. In: Proceedings 3rd International Conference on Trends in Electronics and Informatics (ICOEI) (2019). https://doi.org/10.1109/icoei.2019.8862726
19. Malik, S., Dedeoglu, V., Kanhere, S.S., Jurdak, R.: TrustChain: Trust management in blockchain and IoT supported supply chains. In: Proceedings IEEE International Conference on Blockchain (Blockchain) (2019). https://doi.org/10.1109/blockchain.2019.00032
20. Max Roser, H.R., Ortiz-Ospina, E.: World population growth. Our World in Data (2013). https://ourworldindata.org/world-population-growth
21. Mollah, M.B., et al.: Blockchain for the internet of vehicles towards intelligent transportation systems: a survey. IEEE IoT J. **8**(6), 4157–4185 (2021). https://doi.org/10.1109/jiot.2020.3028368
22. Nakamoto, S.: Bitcoin: A peer-to-peer electronic cash system. Cryptography Mailing list at (2009). https://metzdowd.com
23. Niya, S.R., Dordevic, D., Nabi, A.G., Mann, T., Stiller, B.: A platform-independent, generic-purpose, and blockchain-based supply chain tracking. In: Proceedings IEEE International Conference on Blockchain and Cryptocurrency (ICBC) (2019). https://doi.org/10.1109/bloc.2019.8751415
24. Pallagani, V., Khandelwal, V., Chandra, B., Udutalapally, V., Das, D., Mohanty, S.P.: dCrop: a deep-learning based framework for accurate prediction of diseases of crops in smart agriculture. In: Proceedings IEEE International Symposium on Smart Electronic Systems (iSES) (Formerly iNiS) (2019). https://doi.org/10.1109/ises47678.2019.00020
25. Puthal, D., Mohanty, S.P.: Proof of authentication: IoT-friendly blockchains. IEEE Potentials **38**(1), 26–29 (2019). https://doi.org/10.1109/mpot.2018.2850541
26. Puthal, D., Mohanty, S.P., Kougianos, E., Das, G.: When do we need the blockchain? IEEE Consumer Electron. Mag. **10**(2), 53–56 (2021). https://doi.org/10.1109/mce.2020.3015606
27. Qiu, J., Liang, X., Shetty, S., Bowden, D.: Towards secure and smart healthcare in smart cities using blockchain. In: Proceedings IEEE International Smart Cities Conference (ISC2) (2018). https://doi.org/10.1109/isc2.2018.8656914
28. Kumaran, A.: Pomegranate fruit dataset (2020). https://www.kaggle.com/kumararun37/pomegranate-fruit-dataset. Accessed 10 July 2021
29. Rachakonda, L., Bapatla, A.K., Mohanty, S.P., Kougianos, E.: SaYoPillow: blockchain-integrated privacy-assured IoMT framework for stress management considering sleeping habits. IEEE Trans. Consumer Electron. **67**(1), 20–29 (2021). https://doi.org/10.1109/tce.2020.3043683

30. Rahman, M.U., Baiardi, F., Ricci, L.: Blockchain smart contract for scalable data sharing in IoT: a case study of smart agriculture. In: Proceedings of IEEE Global Conference on Artificial Intelligence and Internet of Things (GCAIoT) (2020). https://doi.org/10.1109/gcaiot51063.2020.9345874
31. Shafeeq, S., Zeadally, S., Alam, M., Khan, A.: Curbing address reuse in the IOTA distributed ledger: a cuckoo-filter-based approach. IEEE Trans. Eng. Manag. **67**(4), 1244–1255 (2020). https://doi.org/10.1109/tem.2019.2922710
32. Udutalapally, V., Mohanty, S.P., Pallagani, V., Khandelwal, V.: sCrop: a novel device for sustainable automatic disease prediction, crop selection, and irrigation in internet-of-agro-things for smart agriculture. IEEE Sens. J. **21**(16), 17525–17538 (2020). https://doi.org/10.1109/jsen.2020.3032438
33. Yazdinejad, A., Srivastava, G., Parizi, R.M., Dehghantanha, A., Karimipour, H., Karizno, S.R.: SLPoW: secure and low latency proof of work protocol for blockchain in green IoT networks. In: Proceedings IEEE 91st Vehicular Technology Conference (VTC2020-Spring) (2020). https://doi.org/10.1109/vtc2020-spring48590.2020.9129462

Smart Agriculture Using Flapping-Wing Micro Aerial Vehicles (FWMAVs)

Shaik Abdullah[1](✉), Priyasha Appari[1], Srihari Rao Patri[1],
and Srinivas Katkoori[2]

[1] EEE Department, National Institute of Technology Warangal,
Warangal 506004, Telangana, India
{shaik_841972,appari_951939}@student.nitw.ac.in,
patri@nitw.ac.in
[2] CSE Department, University of South Florida, Tampa, FL 33620, USA
katkoori@usf.edu

Abstract. One of the main problems in smart agriculture is smart artificial pollination with Micro Aerial Vehicles (MAVs). With their small body size and dimensions, they hold the promise of substituting insect pollinators. We propose an improvised version of the previously designed insect-scale flapping-wing micro air vehicles (FWMAVs), namely Harvard RoboBee-like two-winged robot and the four-winged USC Bee+. This version attempts to solve the critical issue of low controllability observed in the previous prototypes which render them inefficient for practical applications such as artificial pollination. We reduce the number of actuators to just one and eliminate the dependency of pitch, roll, and yaw on the wing-movement by controlling the system with weight shifting mechanism controlled by electromagnets. We successfully validate the proposed design in Gazebo simulations. The proposed design requires less material and low manufacturing cost due to simpler design and low number of required parts. To the best of our knowledge, this design is the first of its kind which is a fully functional FWMAV suitable for artificial pollination.

Keywords: Aerial robotics · Microbotics · Actuators · Internet-of-Things (IoT) · Smart farming · Smart agriculture

1 Introduction

Bees and humming birds have always been the center of attention when it comes to fine controllability and precision. To replicate an automated model of them would be to construct a perfection incarnate aerial vehicle. The miniature size of the robot would enable applications such as artificial pollination, disaster management, search and rescue operations, etc.

Harvard RoboBee [2] and USC Bee+ [3] are the most mature designs in the literature, however, there are still challenges in terms of their stability and

© IFIP International Federation for Information Processing 2022
Published by Springer Nature Switzerland AG 2022
L. M. Camarinha-Matos et al. (Eds.): IFIPIoT 2021, IFIP AICT 641, pp. 32–47, 2022.
https://doi.org/10.1007/978-3-030-96466-5_3

controllability as they depend heavily on an actuator for each wing. Each wing is flapped at different frequency in order to cause an imbalance in equilibrium thus making the robot move in desired direction. Since these frequencies have to be changed at millisecond time scale, having high precision control is a big challenge.

We aim to solve this problem by using a single actuator and eliminating the dependence on wings alone for maneuvering. Instead we propose a model which changes direction by a weight shifting mechanism. The model would have both wings beating at same frequency and would determine the thrust of the body. The roll and pitch would be determined by a tiny weight attached to the robot at the bottom which would be fixed with a planar joint. This is similar in structure to the first of this type which was designed and termed the HMF [1]. We developed the model in ROS using python and then validated with simulations in Gazebo software.

The proposed solution will be easy to implement in a smart agriculture system for not only artificial pollination, but also various other applications such as plant health monitoring, etc. This model is simpler in structure, more robust and less power hungry compared to its counterparts in [2,3].

The rest of the paper is organized as follows. Section 2 motivates using IoT for smart agriculture. Section 3 presents the proposed vision of using beebots for smart pollination. Section 4 proposes the beebot design. Section 5 provides the design details. Section 6 reports the experimental results. Finally, Sect. 7 draws conclusions and outlines future work.

2   Smart Agriculture Using IoT-Related Work

Smart agriculture is an emerging concept that helps in managing farms using modern technologies to increase the quantity and quality of products while optimizing the human labor required. It is a big leap from traditional farming as it brings certainty and predictability to the table. The application of Internet-of-Things (IoT) to agriculture could be a life-changer for humanity and the whole planet.

On farms, IoT devices can measure all kinds of data remotely and provide this information to the farmer in real time. It is capable of providing information about agriculture fields which can be acted upon by the farmer. This paper aims at making use of the evolving IoT technology for enabling smart agriculture with automation. Together, they will be paving the way for what can be called a Third Green Revolution. The most common IoT applications in smart agriculture are sensor-based systems for monitoring crops, soil, fields, livestock, storage facilities, etc.

Currently, we witness how extreme weather, deteriorating soil, drying lands, and collapsing ecosystems make food production more and more complicated and expensive. It is projected that there will be more than 9 billion people inhabiting earth by 2050 which necessitates large scale food production.

Smart agriculture based on IoT is focused on helping farmers close the supply demand gap, by ensuring high yields, profitability, and protection of the environment. Monitoring environmental conditions is the major factor to improve yield of the efficient crops. Therefore, smart farming has a real potential to address all the needs in a safe, environmentally friendly, and resource-efficient approach. Moreover, it is a true way to scale down on the use of pesticides and fertilizers. This allows producing a cleaner and more organic final product compared to that from traditional agricultural methods. The ultimate result from this automated smart farming process would be high precision and control, eventually leading to considerable savings in all key resources.

Sushanth and Sujatha [6] propose a system that responds to the user input with the help of wireless communication (3G/4G). The system has a duplex communication link based on a cellular-Internet interface programmed through an android application that can be used to communicate with the beebot.

Multiple projects in the area of smart agriculture using IoT have been reported in the literature. In [7] algorithms were developed for predicting and monitoring plant health. [8] proposes a network of sensors for smart irrigation. [9] proposes better image acquisition algorithms based on cloud computing developed to solve problem of blurred images taken by mobile robots involved in smart farming. All of these works assert to the bright future of smart agriculture and IoT being the solution to many agricultural problems.

3   Smart Agriculture Using Beebots-Proposed Vision

Agriculture is the one of the largest sources of livelihood in India. It plays a crucial role in the economy. But there are some challenges being faced by the farmers. There is increasing pressure from climate change, soil erosion, biodiversity loss, fulfilling the demand and dealing with farming—plants, pests and diseases. Smart farming can solve some of these problems and allows farmers to grow crops in a more controlled and productive manner.

Research has shown that the presence of wild bees increases yields across many types of crops. The vast majority of plant species—almost 90%, in fact—rely on pollinators to reproduce. This means bees are responsible for one out of every three bites of food we eat. As pollinators, bees play a part in every aspect of the ecosystem. But there is a decline in bee population. There are many factors that contribute to pollinator decline—most of which are related to the climate crisis. Pesticides, fertilizers, parasites, biodiversity loss, deforestation, changes in land use, and habitat destruction are just a few of the reasons.

According to [10,11], pollination by honeybees and wild bees significantly increased yield quantity and quality on average up to 62%, while exclusion of pollinators caused an average yield gap of 37% in cotton and 59% in sesame. When we combine that with artificial pollination methods, efficiency in crop yield is bound to increase significantly.

This paper discusses the framework for next generation farming based on a combination of precision agriculture and robotic systems. The work focuses on using robotic bees in agriculture. To the best of our knowledge, this work is first of its kind on the application of Flapping-Wing Micro Aerial Vehicles (FWMAVs) in artificial pollination. The beebot can be equipped with a structure enabling artificial pollination, equipped along with the database of the farm, helping far more efficient form of pollination than hand pollination or actual bees. Futuristically, as suggested in [6] the beebot can be further equipped with visual sensors and converted into an IoT, which accesses the online database, helping to generate an outcome value/expected yield, health parameters of each plant in the farm, etc., as illustrated in Fig. 1. Beebots can be released in a desired area which are constantly connected as IoT devices to a common server for instructions and access to cloud computing, database, etc.

This work identifies problems of system adaption, usability, and feasibility, health of plants and users and energy consumption. The precise implementation and use of the model will make agriculture more profitable, efficient, environmental friendly and help make the most appropriate decisions.

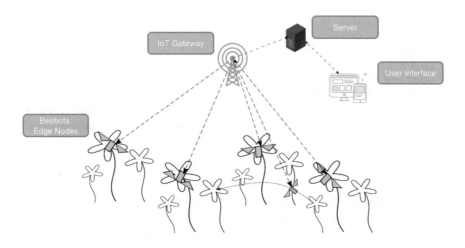

Fig. 1. A beebot based IoT system for artificial pollination

In [4], a clear picture and mechanism is proposed which shows how MAVs would perfectly fit under the umbrella of smart agriculture, how MAVs would be extremely efficient in collecting data, pollinating and monitoring, functioning as vital IoT devices. Robotics, automation, and cloud software systems are efficient tools for smart farming.

4 Proposed Beebot

Most of the mechanical design is extremely simple to manufacture. The body primarily consists of five components in total. Four of these are similar to the base model as proposed in [1]: the exoskeleton, transmission, wings, and actuators. In addition to that we add a small cap like structure to the bottom of the exoskeleton for carrying out the weight shifting mechanism.

4.1   The Exoskeleton

The exoskeleton or the air frame is primarily made of carbon fibre, which is light weighted and strong, ideal in case of an FWMAV. The structure is a hollowed out cuboid with some faces cut out. It would contain the actuators, weight shifting mechanism, and transmission.

4.2   The Wings

The wings are made of flexible material so as to be able to bend to provide the thrust. The wings are composed of a structural frame and spars (veins) made from carbon fiber and the membrane made from polyester film. The materials are chosen such that they remain rigid under various flight conditions. Each wing is 1.5 cm long, and along with the exoskeleton, the wingspan amounts to just 3.5 cm.

4.3   Actuation

The actuator chosen for this application is a bio-morph piezoelectric actuator. These actuators are chosen because of the fact that in their normal mode of operation they have too short a stroke to be useful for micro-robots. They can respond at high frequencies, many small displacements can be added together to give large net motion.

4.4   Transmission

The wing stroke is directly controlled by the actuator and transmission. Wing rotation takes place with a flexure joint in between the output of the transmission and the wings. This flexure is parallel to the wingspan direction and the joint takes care of over rotation of the wing. This system is actuated in only one degree-of-freedom.

4.5   Weight Shifting Mechanism

A tiny weight put in a cap is attached to the bottom of the body of the robot. The cap has four electromagnets which control the x- and y-coordinates of the weight within the cap. This enables weight shifting and hence resulting in the tilting of the body of the robot.

5   Proposed Design

We adopt the basic model described in [1]. It was capable of only a single vertical degree of freedom. The novelty of work is to implement the weight shifting mechanism that overcomes the drawbacks of existing designs. We add a small weight at the bottom of the body and shift it to shift the centre of mass of the whole robot resulting in a tilt thus developing a horizontal component to the thrust generated by the wings.

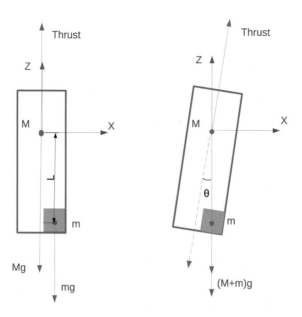

Fig. 2. Illustration of weight shifting mechanism

5.1 System Dynamics

The net force exerted by the wings on the body is balanced by sum of the weight of the body and the resultant thrust as

$$m\ddot{r} = -mgn_3 + fb_3 \tag{1}$$

where b_3 is vector along the axis of the body and n_3 vector along universal z-axis and r is the resultant force vector.

The change in orientation is given by:

$$\dot{q} = \frac{1}{2}q * p \tag{2}$$

The rotational force is given by:

$$J\dot{\omega} = -\omega \times J\omega + \tau \tag{3}$$

5.2 Actuator Command Generation

Let m be mass of the smaller shifting weight and M rest of the mass of the body, which results in the tilting of the body by an angle θ (Fig. 2). In equilibrium conditions, for F representing the thrust generated by the flapping of wings on the body,

$$F \cos \theta = (M + m)g \tag{4}$$

where body tilt angle, θ is

$$\theta = \arctan \frac{x_{COM}}{L} \tag{5}$$

Where L represents vertical distance between centre of mass and the smaller mass m and x_{COM} represents shift in centre of mass due to shifting of weight by distance x from (0,0). x_{COM} is calculated as

$$x_{COM} = x \frac{m}{M + m} \tag{6}$$

We compute similarly along the y-axis.

While the horizontal component provides for motion:

$$F \sin \theta = (m + M)a \tag{7}$$

Hence we can control two parameters, F and x.

F is directly proportional to the speed of flapping of wings and can be input as a product of height required and a constant K.

x will be run through a PID controller to determine how fast and in which direction the body will move.

5.3   Weight Shifting Mechanism

To be able to displace the weight m through an amount x, we use electromagnetic force. The electromagnetic force generated is

$$F = \frac{\mu_o}{4\pi} \frac{m_1 m_2}{r^2} \tag{8}$$

Considering two electromagnets opposite to each other with magnetic poles m_1 and m_2 at a distance of r units from each other attached to the edge of the cap.

So, force by first electromagnet is given by

$$F_1 = \frac{\mu_o}{4\pi} \frac{m_1 m_i}{x^2} \tag{9}$$

and force by second electromagnet by

$$F_2 = \frac{\mu_o}{4\pi} \frac{m_2 m_i}{(r - x)^2} \tag{10}$$

where r is the diameter of the cap, x distance required to move, m_i the induced magnetic moment in the weight, and m_1 and m_2 are the magnetic moments of the two electromagnets. Net force would be a difference of these two forces resulting in acceleration of the small weight

$$F_{resultant} = F_1 - F_2 = ma \tag{11}$$

where a is the acceleration and m mass of the weight.

Now to move the weight through a distance l,

$$l = \frac{at^2}{4} \tag{12}$$

for a zero initial velocity, considering an immediate deceleration of the same amount after $t/2$ time has passed.

5.4   Attitude Controller

Based on the information regarding orientation of the body received from the IMU, we run the following control loop.

$$Roll = e_r K_p + K_i \int e_r dt + K_d \frac{de_r}{dt} \tag{13}$$

where e_r represents the error in roll, i.e., the difference between the desired orientation and current orientation, K_p, K_i, and K_d represent PID gains.

$$Pitch = e_p K_p + K_i \int e_p dt + K_d \frac{de_p}{dt} \tag{14}$$

where e_p represents error in pitch.

Now, we define the amount of change in position of the weight along x-axis and y-axis as

$$x = Roll - Throttle \tag{15}$$

$$y = Pitch - Throttle \tag{16}$$

which is then used to calculate the required force and electromagnetic field induction by Eqs. (11) and (12).

5.5   Position Controller

Position controller is comprised of two sub-algorithms. The first sub-scheme generates the magnitude of the thrust force, f; the second sub-scheme generates the desired attitude. In specific, f is computed as

$$f = f_a^T b_3 \tag{17}$$

$$f_a = -K_p(r - r_d) - K_d(\dot{r} - \dot{r}_d) - K_i \int (r - r_d)dt + mgn_3 + m\dot{r}d \tag{18}$$

where K_p, K_d, and K_i are positive definite diagonal gain matrices; and r_d is the desired position of the robot's center of mass.

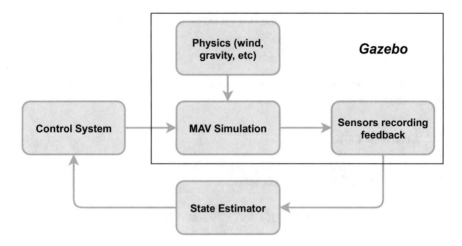

Fig. 3. Proposed beebot ROS architecture

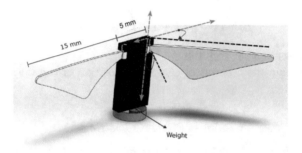

Fig. 4. Structure of the beebot

5.6   ROS and Simulation

We validated the model using Gazebo simulation. It is a robot simulation software which contains a physics engine that primarily helps with rapidly testing algorithms, designing robots in a realistic scenario.

The system includes the CAD design translated into URDF which represents the physical and collisional properties of the model. A feedback controlled control system is designed taking input from the body of the robot and giving output as torque required to apply on the joints.

The basic architecture, as shown in Fig. 3, of the MAV includes a control system node which publishes input values to the simulated Beebot body in Gazebo. It also accepts input from the simulation's physics node providing for external influences such as wind, gravity, collision, etc. The simulated sensors record data which is processed by a state estimator and the processed feedback is given back as input to the control system node.

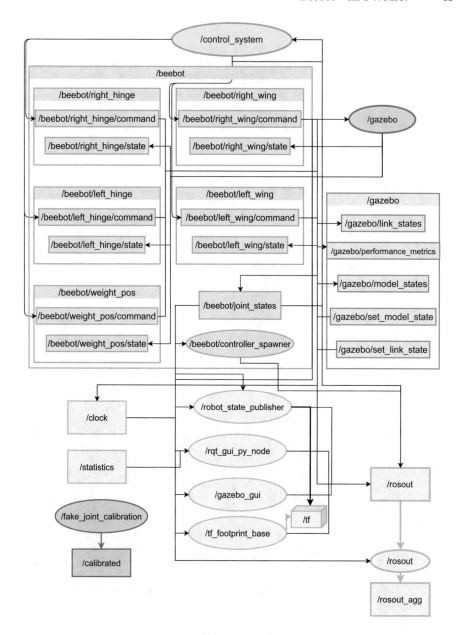

Fig. 5. Flow chart of the ROS architecture

The architecture of ROS nodes and ROS topics has been quite simple and intuitive. The robot was designed as a simple cuboid with two wings attached by hinges. The wings themselves can rotate in order to properly provide for thrust as shown in Fig. 4.

Each hinge and wing has a joint each, making it total four joints. Every joint has its own topic declared on which command is published. A single node containing the control system algorithm, takes in the position and state of the wings as inputs and gives command to the joints in a feedback controlled loop structure as shown in Fig. 5.

As shown in the Fig. 4, a forward flap would not only mean yaw movement of the wings but also a negative pitch. Similarly for a backward flap, a negative yaw along with a positive pitch.

6   Experimental Results

We prototyped and tested the control system algorithms using ROS and Gazebo. The prototype has a wingspan of 3.5 cm and weight of 145 mg. Each wing is 15 mg, the additional weight structure 30 mg, and the body itself 85 mg. We tested a wide range of values for taking off and landing, and successfully managed to fly vertically, hover the robot and tilt it in the desired direction.

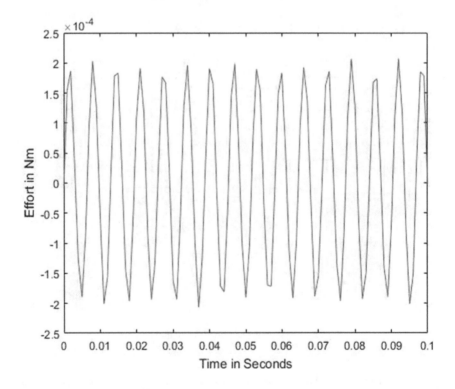

Fig. 6. Input values for the wings

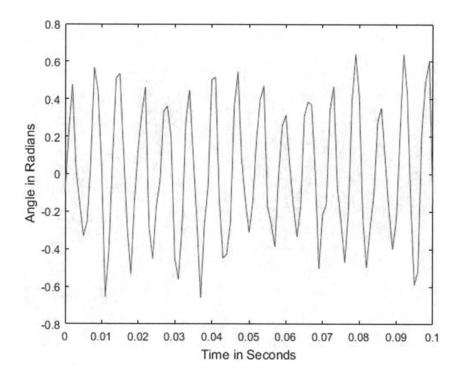

Fig. 7. Flapping pattern

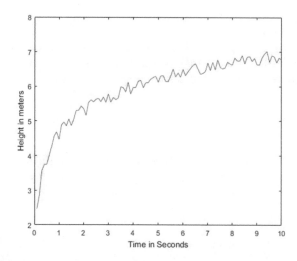

Fig. 8. Altitude gained as a function of time. The beebot flies vertically and stops at a height of 7 m.

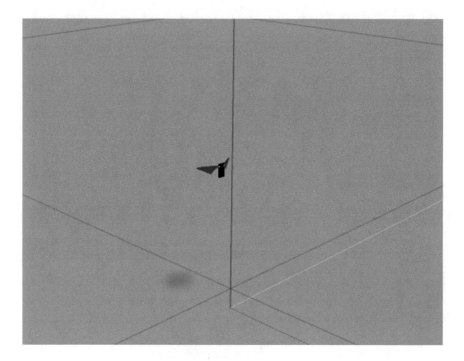

Fig. 9. Gazebo image of beebot

6.1   Flight

The flapping frequency observed 150 Hz at which the robot took off at a reasonable speed. Figure 6 shows the take-off mode with the command given in terms of Newton-meters and the wing responding accordingly measured in radians (Fig. 7).

6.2   Hover

Figure 8 shows the position of the beebot as it tries to stabilise itself at a point in the simulation at a height of 7 m with a flapping frequency 120 Hz (Fig. 9).

6.3   Tilt

After adding the extra weight, we set to trying to get the robot body to tilt. We had the body tilting at roughly 30° as shown in Figs. 10 and 11. This is accomplished by keeping the additional weight in a cap attached to the bottom of the body, with its weight being roughly 30 mg. The weight moved at a distance of 2.5 mm within the cap to achieve this value of tilt.

This shows how we can easily acquire the tilt required to move in the xy plane by just attaching a small structure at the bottom containing a weight.

Fig. 10. Gazebo image of the beebot tilting forward

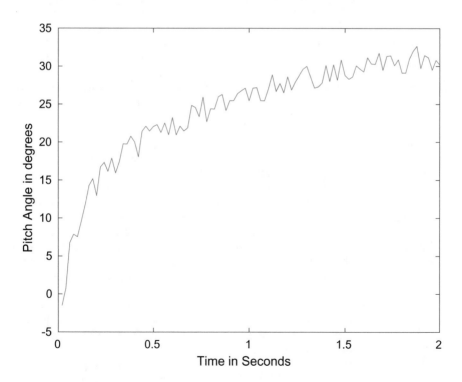

Fig. 11. Graph representing change in pitch of the beebot as weight gets shifted

It is moved around to apply torque and tilt the body by whichever amount and direction we need seamlessly and instantaneously, resulting in a compact mechanical structure, and a simple control system design.

7   Conclusions and Future Work

We have proposed a light FWMAV for artificial pollination and validated it in simulation. We proposed a simpler design with a weight shifting mechanism that can be used to control the robot to move in desired direction. The future work includes prototyping and testing for artificial pollination in real farms. Some of the challenges would be controlling the yaw of the robot and making it resistant and stable to wind.

References

1. Wood, R.J.: The first takeoff of a biologically inspired at-scale robotic insect. IEEE Trans. Robot. **24**(2), 341–347 (2008). https://doi.org/10.1109/TRO.2008.916997
2. Ma, K.Y., Felton, S.M., Wood, R.J.: Design, fabrication, and modeling of the split actuator microrobotic bee. In: IEEE/RSJ International Conference on Intelligent Robots and Systems, pp. 1133–1140 (2012). https://doi.org/10.1109/IROS.2012. 6386192
3. Yang, X., Chen, Y., Chang, L., Calderón, A.A., Pérez-Arancibia, N.O.: Bee+: a 95-mg four-winged insect-scale flying robot driven by twinned unimorph actuators. IEEE Robot. Autom. Lett. **4**(4), 4270–4277 (2019). https://doi.org/10.1109/LRA. 2019.2931177
4. Chen, Y., Li, Y.: Intelligent autonomous pollination for future farming - a micro air vehicle conceptual framework with artificial intelligence and human-in-the-loop. IEEE Access **7**, 119706–119717 (2019). https://doi.org/10.1109/ACCESS. 2019.2937171
5. Zhang, J., Fei, F., Tu, Z., Deng, X.: Design optimization and system integration of robotic hummingbird. IEEE Int. Conf. Robot. Autom. (ICRA) **2017**, 5422–5428 (2017). https://doi.org/10.1109/ICRA.2017.7989639
6. Sushanth, G., Sujatha, S.: IOT based smart agriculture system. 2018 International Conference on Wireless Communications, Signal Processing and Networking (WiSPNET), pp. 1–4 (2018). https://doi.org/10.1109/WiSPNET.2018.8538702
7. Kumar, S., Chowdhary, G., Udutalapally, V., Das, D., Mohanty, S.P.: gCrop: Internet-of-Leaf-Things (IoLT) for monitoring of the growth of crops in smart agriculture. In: 2019 IEEE International Symposium on Smart Electronic Systems (iSES) (Formerly iNiS), pp. 53–56 (2019). https://doi.org/10.1109/iSES47678. 2019.00024
8. de Oliveira, K.V., Esgalha Castelli, H.M., José Montebeller, S., Prado Avancini, T.G.: Wireless sensor network for smart agriculture using ZigBee protocol. In: 2017 IEEE First Summer School on Smart Cities (S3C), pp. 61–66 (2017), https://doi. org/10.1109/S3C.2017.8501379
9. Xu, X., Li, X., Zhang, R.: Remote configurable image acquisition lifting robot for smart agriculture. In: IEEE 4th Advanced Information Technology Electronic and Automation Control Conference (IAEAC), pp. 1545–1548 (2019). https://doi.org/ 10.1109/IAEAC47372.2019.8997721

10. Chautá, A., Mellizo, S.A., Campbell, M.A.B., Thaler, J.S., Poveda, K.: Effects of natural and artificial pollination on fruit and offspring quality. Basic Appl. Ecol. **13**(6), 524–532 (2012), ISSN:1439-1791. https://doi.org/10.1016/j.baae.2012. 08.013

11. Stein, K., et al.: Bee pollination increases yield quantity and quality of cash crops in Burkina Faso, West Africa. Sci. Rep. **7**. https://doi.org/10.1038/s41598-017- 17970-2

Smart Lysimeter with Crop
and Environment Monitoring
Enhanced with Pest and Crop Control

Carlos Almeida[✉], João C. Martins[✉], João Miguel Santos[✉],
and José Jasnau Caeiro[✉]

Instituto Politécnico de Beja, Beja, Portugal
{carlos.almeida,joao.martins,joao.santos,j.caeiro}@ipbeja.pt

Abstract. A model of a smart lysimeter, adopting an IoT approach, enhanced with pest and crop state analysis is presented. Besides the measurement of the traditional evaporation-transpiration balance, the lysimeter senses additional parameters like the soil temperature and humidity at different depths; air temperature and humidity; sunlight exposition (visible and infrared). Additionally, the system can capture high-resolution images of the target culture. These images are locally processed for data reduction and the main features are stored in a remote platform afterwards. The main goal is the monitoring and enhancement of the global crop yield. This lysimeter also provides data for a global water resources system that integrates information from several sources: lysimeters, weather stations, water quality monitoring systems, *etc*.

1 Introduction

Modern agriculture is supported by sensor networks and the Internet of Things (IoT) is part of this trend, bringing new types of sensors, reducing its cost and providing large amounts of relevant data. This opens the possibility for novel types of data analysis related with crop and pest control, with the application of new types of pattern recognition techniques and the use of approaches based on artificial intelligence, namely machine learning techniques.

The use of the IoT paradigm allows the monitoring of crops in real-time, making possible to generate early alerts from the analysis of the collected data to support timely decisions by the farmer related with crop and pest control and harvesting [12].

Water is fundamental for socio-economic development, paramount for the production of food, for energy generation, for the maintenance of healthy ecosystems, and, as a result, essential for the humankind survival.

Given its scarcity, careful management of the water resources, particularly in its use in agriculture, which is responsible on average for 70% of all freshwater consumption [6], has become more and more important.

© IFIP International Federation for Information Processing 2022
Published by Springer Nature Switzerland AG 2022
L. M. Camarinha-Matos et al. (Eds.): IFIPIoT 2021, IFIP AICT 641, pp. 48–63, 2022.
https://doi.org/10.1007/978-3-030-96466-5_4

The lysimeter is an important instrument to measure the watering needs for a particular type of culture, climate and soil. Lysimeters measure the evapotranspiration (ET) of plants and have been used in agriculture for more than a century. Their primary purpose is to quantify the water requirements of plants in order to provide only the amount of water needed for their healthy growth.

Evapotranspiration is the quantity of water loss by the plants through evaporation and through transpiration. In a culture, there is a water balance due to the water inflow and outflow. In the input water there is water from rain, irrigation and condensation. In the output water there is the drained water, that infiltrates into the soil, the evaporation and transpiration. Figure 1 illustrates the water cycle system in plant culture.

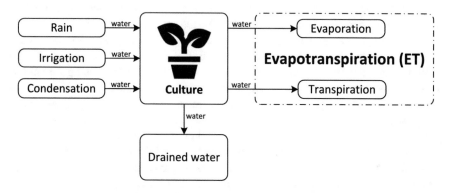

Fig. 1. Evapotranspiration diagram.

Until about a decade ago, lysimeters were mostly used by educational and research institutions due to their relatively high cost, but the emergence of new technologies, materials and sensors, allowed the construction of high-tech and low-cost weighing lysimeters. The use of an smart lysimeter which, in addition to the traditional measuring of ET, senses other parameters related to the soil, atmosphere and the culture, which were not previously available, with a low production and installation cost, enhances its widespread use with the potential increase in crop yield in terms of quality and quantity with the optimization of resources, namely water.

In [14], the ET of desert plants is quantified using simple moisture sensors at various depths and pressure sensors associated to a microcontroller to visualize data and keep the soil moisture at a certain level. The presented lysimeter do not use water weighing.

To quantify the ET of large fields, [13] combines data from remote sensing, meteorological data, and a traditional lysimeter with weight sensors, making it possible to estimate the ET of large crops. In [8], a smart ET estimation is presented. The authors employ a fuzzy neural network to estimate the ET of a greenhouse plantation from the temperature, humidity and atmospheric pressure data features. After training the neural network and calibration of the system with a local weighing lysimeter, the ET is predicted.

When a high precision estimate of the ET is required, a weighing lysimeter is preferred. It is usually composed of two vessels, one with the soil with the plants and a second vessel that collects the drainage water. By measuring and comparing the weight of the soil vessel with the weight of the drainage vessel, it can estimate the ET with high precision. Different soils exhibit different water infiltration rates. At start, the infiltration rate is fast but, as the water moisturizes the soil, it becomes stable, and the use of a weighing lysimeter allows to assess both situations with increased accuracy. The use of several soil moisture sensors at different depths allows the characterization of the water percolation along the soil depth. In [7], an accurate water infiltration balance is presented recurring to a precision weighing lysimeter demonstrating that the weighing lysimeters present the best estimation for the ET in terms of precision.

From the image processing and analysis of the growing plants it is possible to infer its health and to identify and control pests. In [9], a study of application of image analysis techniques is described, where the most promising techniques to detect diseases on the plants' leaves and fruits, and to classify the disease, are presented. The paper [10], makes an extensive review about the application and importance of machine vision in precision agriculture. In [11] an image processing system is described to identify the type of plant from the leaves' veins.

This paper describes a smart lysimeter that, additionally to the ET, measures additional ambient and soil parameters, namely: the air temperature and humidity; the visible luminosity; the infra-red luminosity; the soil temperature and the humidity at different depths. Additionally acquires images of the target culture for posterior analysis for crop and pest control.

The remaining of this paper describes the architecture and the instrumentation, in terms of hardware and software, of a smart lysimeter. Section 2 presents the general architecture of the smart lysimeter; Sect. 3 describes the implementation of the experimental prototype in terms of its structure, hardware and software; Sect. 4 presents the obtained experimental results and the paper ends with the conclusions in Sect. 5.

2   Smart Lysimeter Architecture

A drawing of the physical structure of the smart lysimeter is presented in Fig. 2. It is structurally composed by three different vessels complemented with a set of sensors. The top vessel contains the soil with the plants. The middle vessel collects the wastewater drained from the soil of the top vessel whose weighing allows the calculation of the ET. This wastewater is transposed afterwards to the bottom vessel so that it can be later used for further chemical and physical analysis. As an example, it can be used for a percolation study.

The lysimeter architecture is designed with currently available IoT technologies, namely: low cost sensors, low power microcontrollers (MCU) and long range communications. The design has the purpose of achieving a low cost and high

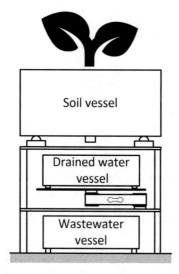

Fig. 2. Lysimeter physical structure.

performance system by following the IoT paradigm. A layered view of the system architecture is displayed in Fig. 3. It can be decomposed into three main parts: the *i)* physical layer, where the sensors acquire data and where some early processing is done, which forwards the information to the cloud layer; *ii)* the cloud layer that is responsible for: the communications, the storage and data analysis, thus generating alarms related to the crop and pest control; and finally, at the top, *iii)* the application layer provides services to the different types of users according to their specific role.

Since there is the need to have different polling times to collect the data and to execute different functions, the physical layer is decomposed into two modules: the lysimeter module and the camera module.

The lysimeter module contains the sensors to measure the soil and environmental parameters, namely the soil temperature and the humidity at different depths. It weighs the soil vessel and the drained water to calculate the evapotranspiration, and measures the ambient temperature, the humidity and the light intensity. The sensors are connected to a low-power MCU that manages the acquisition and transmission of data to the cloud through a radio-frequency telecommunication SoC module. The MCU also manages and supervises the power supply by powering on all circuits when acquiring, processing and transmitting the sensors' data to the cloud layer. Afterwards, it powers off the subcircuits (sensors and SoC) in order to save power when the module is in standby, and turns on power again after the preset time polling.

The camera module is responsible for the image acquisition from the camera sensor. The camera sensor is connected to a SBC that acquires, preprocess and sends images to the cloud layer using an Internet connection. The SBC power is controlled by a low-power MCU to save energy: the MCU starts up the SBC when it is programmed to take an image (1 or 2 times a day is enough); after this, the MCU powers off the SBC to save energy.

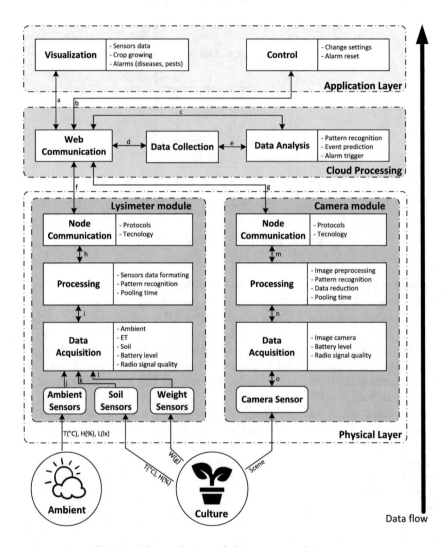

Fig. 3. A layered view of the system architecture.

The cloud layer manages the data reception from different lysimeters. It encompasses database storage and the different services related to data processing, like pattern recognition, namely machine learning for event prediction. It triggers alarms related to crop monitoring and/or pest control. At the top is the application layer. Its purpose is to provide different services to end users, like system configuration, data analysis and visualization, alarms setting and display, etc.

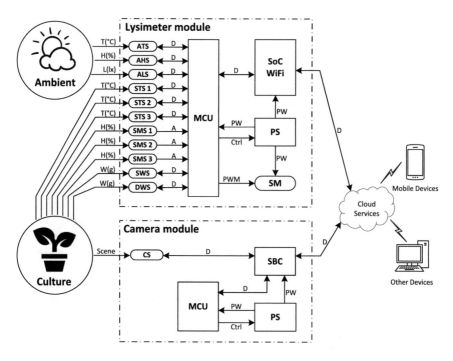

Fig. 4. Lysimeter system hardware architecture.

A lower level system hardware architecture is depicted in Fig. 4. The set of acronyms displayed in the figure and their related meanings are presented in Table 1.

Table 1. Lysimeter hardware acronyms.

	Description		Description
MCU	Microcontroller Unit	SoC	System on Chip (WiFi)
ATS	Ambient Temperature Sensor	AHS	Ambient Humidity Sensor
ALS	Ambient Light Sensor	STS	Soil Temperature Sensor
SMS	Soil Moisture Sensor	SWS	Soil Weight Sensor
DWS	Drained water Weight Sensor	SM	Waste Vessel Servo Motor
SBC	Single Board Computer	CS	Camera Sensor

3   Experimental Prototype

The described IoT based lysimeter architecture led to a prototype that is described in this section. Low-cost off-the-shelf components, without compromising the technical quality of the final result, were chosen for the implementation of the lysimeter prototype, bringing a clear cost benefit. Open source software tools were adopted whenever possible.

3.1   Lysimeter Module

The hardware structure of the lysimeter module is displayed in Fig. 5. A description and the listing of the components used to implement the lysimeter, along with its most important specifications, is presented in Table 2. An MCU from the MSP430 family, the MSP430G2553, is chosen, due to its very low power consumption and cost. It provides analog and digital ports to connect and control sensors. It has an I2C communications bus, used for sensors with I2C support, and an UART interface for connection to the SoC. The soil vessel is equipped with a set of corrosion resistant humidity and moisture capacitive sensors (CSMS), placed at different depths. The soil vessel is weighted using four load cells (4×50 kg load cells). These are part of the branches of a half Wheatstone electrical bridge, connected to one channel of a HX711 amplifier/ADC, that communicates with the MCU using a proprietary clocked digital output. The other channel of the HX711 module is connected to a load cell (1×10 kg) that weights the drained water vessel. The lysimeter has an ambient light sensor, the TSL2561, that integrates visible, and visible plus infrared sensing. The system also measures ambient temperature and humidity with a SHT30 sensor.

The module is powered from a 1 W solar panel and stored in a MR18650 Li-Ion battery cell. To control the battery charge it is used a TP4056 module. The power switch is done with a DMP2022LS P Channel MOSFET transistor, that can control up to 10 A. To control the drain water valve it is used a commercial HS422 servo-motor controlled by a PWM signal. For the communications with the cloud it is used a Wi-Fi SoC ESP8266-01 module. The set of components adopted for the prototype implementation is presented in Table 2.

The MSP430 MCU also manages the power provided to the different subsystems. It monitors the battery voltage and powers ON/OFF the sensors and the telecommunications SoC. The MCU also activates a servo motor which controls the valve that transfers the water from the drained water vessel to the wastewater vessel. The MSP430 MCU also sends the sensors' data to the ESP8266 module through the UART connection. The ESP8266 has a MQTT client application to transmit the data to the cloud. If pressed quickly, the multifunction button wakes up the module and a new sensor read loop is started. The MCU and telecommunications SoC software is developed with the GNU C programming language toolchain.

3.2   Camera Module

The hardware structure of the camera module is displayed in Fig. 6. A description and listing of the main components used to implement the module, along with its most important specifications, are presented on Table 3.

This module also uses the MSP430G2553 MCU, from the MSP430 family, to supervise the battery status and the power of the camera module, namely of its SBC.

The SBC is a Raspberry Pi 3B+ (RPi) which is a compact, yet powerful small computer on a single board, with extensive wireless communications (Wi-Fi and Bluetooth) and a MIPI interface that can be connected to a series of different image cameras, besides a set of GPIO pins. The RPi is responsible for the image acquisition and pre-processing. It is equipped with a with high resolution (8 Mpx) Raspberry Pi Camera Module 2, with a IMX219 Sony image sensor. It makes a local backup of the images and sensors' data and sends it periodically to the cloud. The module's power system is similar to the one of the lysimeter module, complemented with a DC/DC converter to supply the SBC with the proper voltage (+5 V). The module also possesses a multifunction button that when pressed wakes up the module and a new sensor read cycle is started automatically. The RPi has three software libraries installed: paho MQTT client, Pyserial, and Picamera. It runs a set of Python scripts to control the system: acquire images, communicate with MCU, and communicate with the cloud.

A pair of photos of the system is presented in Fig. 8. The lysimeter and the associated camera can be seen in these pictures. The camera setup is presented with greater detail in the picture on the right side of figure.

This experimental prototype uses Wi-Fi communications. However, for a system to be deployed in the open field, other communications solutions, like LoRa/LoRAWAN [5], NB IoT [2], or SIGFOX [3] can be easily adopted to transmit small packets of data. To transfer images, a higher band communications protocol must be used like an Internet LTE connection, for instance.

The camera module can be used as stand-alone system, to acquire and process images that can be provided to a previously trained machine learning model, running directly on the SBC, that can trigger alerts related to the crop state and culture health, and send them to the cloud and, ultimately, reach the user/farmer.

3.3   Lysimeter Software

The MCU software is developed with the Code Composer Studio suite [1], with the C/C++ programming language. The software is used for the control of data acquisition. The information is sent to the SBC using serial communications.

The SBC is running the Raspberry Pi OS, a Debian Linux operating system for ARM based architectures. The image acquisition and processing applications are developed using the Python programming language. They depend on the PiCamera package and also on the OpenCV Python bindings. A *crontab* script launches the applications at the predefined times. The images transfer is

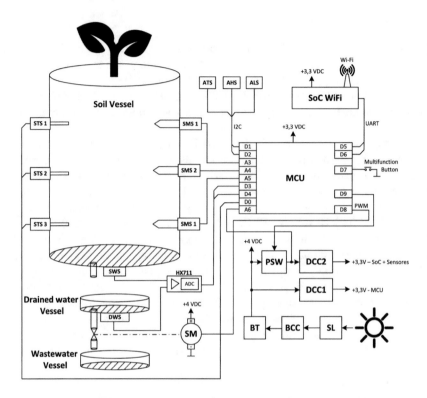

Fig. 5. Lysimeter module hardware diagram.

secured by the SSH protocol using public-key cryptography. Whenever the SBC is powered up it waits for the MCU data, converting it to a JSON (Javascript Object Notation) object that is sent to a MQTT server. Afterwards a picture is taken, locally processed and sent to the storage server. After this sequence of procedures the SBC is shut down. In case the data cannot be sent to the remote server, the software stores a backup locally.

For the prototype's cloud software proof of concept, a virtual machine was created. It runs the Ubuntu Server 20.04 LTS Linux distribution. All the software services are launched as Docker containers. This Docker software stack is composed by the *mosquitto* MQTT server; the Node-RED low code Node.js based server; the MongoDB non relational database server; the TensorFlow CNN (Convolutional Neural Network) machine learning based application and the ATMOZ/SFTP secure file storage server. This container technology based approach ensures an easy and reliable software services deployment stack, as seen in Fig. 7.

Table 2. Lysimeter module hardware components

	Description	Model	Specification
MCU	Microcontroller	MSP430G2553	16 MHz, 16 KB/512B
SoC	System on Chip	ESP8266-01	Wi-Fi 3.3 VDC
ATS	Ambient Temp. Sensor	SHT30	(I2C) −40 °C–80 °C, ±0.3 °C
AHS	Ambient Humid. Sensor	SHT30	(I2C) 0–100% RH, ±2.0%
ALS	Ambient Light Sensor	TSL2561	(I2C) Visible and IR sensor
STS	Soil Temperature Sensor	DS18B20	(1 Wire) −10 °C–85 °C, ±0.5 °C
SMS	Soil Moisture Sensor	CSMS	(An) Grove Capacitive Sensor
SWS	Soil Vessel Weight Sensor	HX711	4 cells with 1/2 bridge
DWS	Drained Water Weight Sensor	HX711	1 cell - Wheatstone Bridge
SM	Servo Motor	HS422	(PWM) 180°, torque 3.3 Kg/cm
SL	Photovoltaic Solar Panel	FAL09004	5 VDC 1 W 110 × 60 mm
BCC	Battery Controller Charge	TP4056	1 A 1xBAT Li-Ion
BT	Li-Ion Battery	INR18650-35E	3.6 V 3500 mAh Samsung
PSW	Power Switch	DMP2022LSS	−10 A P-MOSFET
DCC1	DC/DC Converter MCU	MCP1700-3302	3.3 V 250 mA LDO
DCC2	DC/DC Converter	MCP1700-3302	3.3 V 250 mA LDO

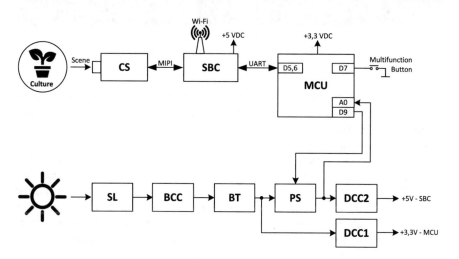

Fig. 6. Camera module hardware diagram.

4 Experimental Results

The prototype is assembled as described, including its programming and configuration. A photo of the prototype being used to monitor strawberry plants, with a detail of the camera set (right-top) and the water vessels (right-bottom) is shown in Fig. 8. The Node-RED flow for the data acquisition process is presented in Fig. 9.

Table 3. Camera module hardware components

	Description	Model	Specification
CS	Camera Sensor	RPi Cam. Mod. 2	IMX219 8 Mpx sensor
SBC	Single Board Computer	RPi 3B+	1.4 GHz BCM2837 4 GB
MCU	Microcontroller	MSP430G2553	16 MHz, 16 KB/512B
SL	Photovoltaic Solar Panel	FAL09004	5 VDC 1 W 110 × 60 mm
BCC	Battery Controller Charge	TP4056 Module	1 A 1xBAT Li-Ion
BT	Li-Ion Battery	INR18650-35E	3.6 V 3500 mAh Samsung
PSW	Power Switch	DMP2022LSS	−10 A P-MOSFET
DCC1	DC/DC Converter	MCP1700-3302E	3.3 V 250 mA LDO
DCC2	DC/DC Converter	VMA402 Module	5 V 2 A Step-Up LM2577

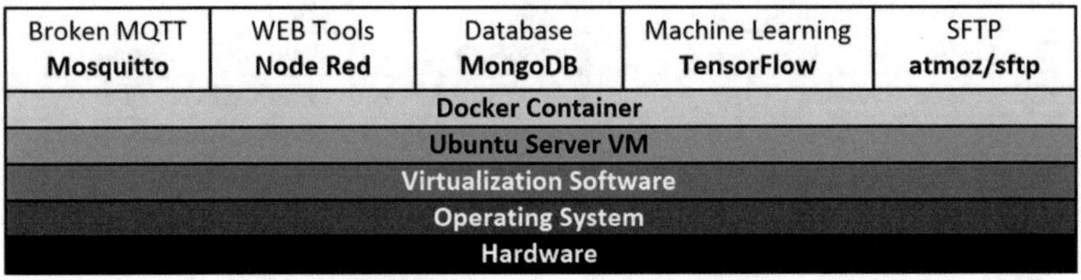

Broken MQTT **Mosquitto**	WEB Tools **Node Red**	Database **MongoDB**	Machine Learning **TensorFlow**	SFTP **atmoz/sftp**
Docker Container				
Ubuntu Server VM				
Virtualization Software				
Operating System				
Hardware				

Fig. 7. Cloud services virtualization

The current values of the gathered data are visualized in a dashboard using a computer based web browser client or from a smartphone, Fig. 10. The values that are collected during the previous 2 days period are made available with the Node-RED Dashboard web server, as can be seen in Fig. 11.

A high resolution image of the plants, acquired by the camera module, is shown in Fig. 12. On the right, a detailed image of the fruit is presented, from where it is possible to detect, by a trained eye, a significant set of plant diseases. However, the goal is to have a machine learning based system, running in the cloud servers, able to detect the state of the fruits, the possible plant diseases, and to automatically fire up an alarm and send the corresponding alert to the users by email or SMS.

The web service is compatible with modern PWA (Progressive Web Apps [4]). It is thus possible to access the lysimeter data from any mobile device through a smartphone app similar interface.

The images are stored using the SFTP (Secure File Transfer) protocol. An example of a captured image from strawberry plants can be seen in Fig. 12.

From experience, the sensors' data can be collected with a time interval between 10 min to 30 min, and since the plant evolution is very slow it is enough to capture one or two images per day, by choosing the time of day with the best light conditions.

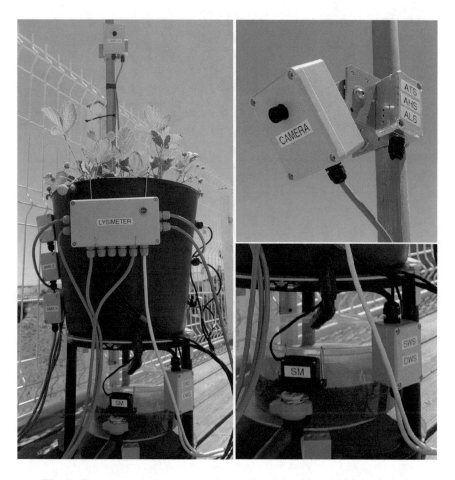

Fig. 8. Prototype appearance and some hardware details (right figure).

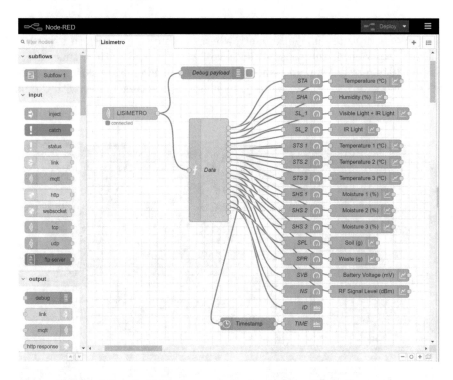

Fig. 9. NodeRed flow (graphical program), showing the data acquisition process.

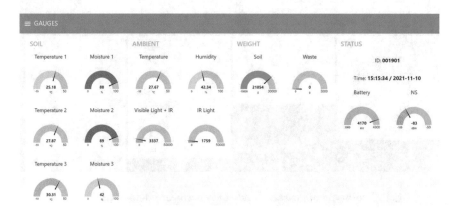

Fig. 10. NodeRed dashboard output (web browser/smartphone).

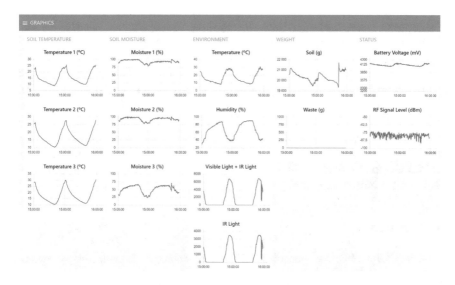

Fig. 11. NodeRed dashboard with graphs of the last 24 h data.

Fig. 12. Example of a captured raw image (left) with a zoomed detail (right).

5   Conclusions

The lysimeter prototype presented shows the application of the IoT paradigm to solve a common and fundamental problem in agriculture – the measurement of the evaporation-transpiration balance. Additionally, several other physical parameters of the soil and surrounding environment, and the collection of images for monitoring the plants' evolution are added. This data can be used to detect diseases and plagues using a machine learning based system. The proposed lysimeter system offers an integrated low-cost and energy efficient solution for the evaporation-transpiration balance measure that can be used in different locations and scenarios.

The next steps in the development of the smart lysimeter are the collection of a large dataset, imagery and sensor data, from crop and soil monitoring, to develop and train a machine learning model to detect if plants are growing as expected or if there are problems related to the crop development and potential diseases. The integration of the smart lysimeter into an overall water resources system that gathers information from various other sources, including weather stations, water quality monitoring systems, water evaporation monitoring systems, lake and river water level monitoring systems, *etc.* is also planned. A data model based on modern pattern recognition systems, machine learning, and artificial intelligence software will allow to relate all data collected in order to predict events and monitor long-term threats to water resources.

References

1. CCSTUDIO IDE, configuration, compiler or debugger. TI.com. https://www.ti.com/tool/CCSTUDIO
2. Narrowband - Internet of Things (NB-IoT). https://www.gsma.com/iot/narrowband-internet-of-things-nb-iot/
3. SIGFOX.COM. https://www.sigfox.com/en
4. What are Progressive Web Apps? https://web.dev/what-are-pwas/
5. What is LoRaWAN® Specification. https://lora-alliance.org/about-lorawan/
6. The World Bank: Water in agriculture (2020). https://www.worldbank.org/en/topic/water-in-agriculture
7. Ávila Dávila, L., et al.: A compact weighing lysimeter to estimate the water infiltration rate in agricultural soils. Agronomy **11**(1), 180 (2021). Number: 1 Publisher: Multidisciplinary Digital Publishing Institute. https://doi.org/10.3390/agronomy11010180. https://www.mdpi.com/2073-4395/11/1/180
8. Hernández-Salazar, J.A., Hernández-Rodríguez, D., Hernández-Cruz, R.A., Ramos-Fernández, J.C., Márquez-Vera, M.A., Trejo-Macotela, F.R.: Estimation of the evapotranspiration using ANFIS algorithm for agricultural production in greenhouse. In: 2019 IEEE International Conference on Applied Science and Advanced Technology (iCASAT), pp. 1–5 (2019). https://doi.org/10.1109/iCASAT48251.2019.9069533
9. Hungilo, G.G., Emmanuel, G., Emanuel, A.W.R.: Image processing techniques for detecting and classification of plant disease: a review. In: Proceedings of the 2019 International Conference on Intelligent Medicine and Image Processing, IMIP 2019, pp. 48–52. Association for Computing Machinery (2019). https://doi.org/10.1145/3332340.3332341
10. Mavridou, E., Vrochidou, E., Papakostas, G.A., Pachidis, T., Kaburlasos, V.G.: Machine vision systems in precision agriculture for crop farming. J. Imaging **5**(12), 89 (2019). Number: 12 Publisher: Multidisciplinary Digital Publishing Institute. https://doi.org/10.3390/jimaging5120089. https://www.mdpi.com/2313-433X/5/12/89
11. Selda, J.D.S., Ellera, R.M.R., Cajayon, L.C., Linsangan, N.B.: Plant identification by image processing of leaf veins. In: Proceedings of the International Conference on Imaging, Signal Processing and Communication, ICISPC 2017, pp. 40–44. Association for Computing Machinery (2017). https://doi.org/10.1145/3132300.3132315

12. Vitali, G., Francia, M., Golfarelli, M., Canavari, M.: Crop management with the IoT: an interdisciplinary survey. Agronomy **11**(1), 181 (2021). Number: 1 Publisher: Multidisciplinary Digital Publishing Institute. https://doi.org/10.3390/agronomy11010181. https://www.mdpi.com/2073-4395/11/1/181
13. Yang, G., Zhao, C., Xu, Q.: Spatial-temporal analysis of field evapotranspiration based on complementary relationship model and IKONOS data. In: 2013 IEEE International Geoscience and Remote Sensing Symposium - IGARSS, pp. 2836–2839 (2013). ISSN: 2153-7003. https://doi.org/10.1109/IGARSS.2013.6723415
14. Zhu, W., Tian, Y., Wang, S.: Design of non-weighing type desert plant lysimeter observation system based on PIC18. In: 2013 6th International Conference on Information Management, Innovation Management and Industrial Engineering, vol. 3, pp. 42–44 (2013). ISSN: 2155-1472. https://doi.org/10.1109/ICIII.2013.6703608

Cyber-Physical IoT Systems in Wildfire Context

Fuel Break Monitoring with Sentinel-2 Imagery and GEDI Validation

João E. Pereira-Pires[1]([✉]), Valentine Aubard[2], G. Baldassarre[2], José M. Fonseca[1], João M. N. Silva[2], and André Mora[1]

[1] Centre of Technology and Systems/UNINOVA, School of Science and Technology, NOVA University of Lisbon, 2829-516 Caparica, Portugal
`je.pires@campus.fct.unl.pt, {jmf,atm}@uninova.pt`
[2] Forest Research Centre, School of Agriculture, University of Lisbon, 1349-017 Lisbon, Portugal
`{vaubard,isa124928,joaosilva}@isa.ulisboa.pt`

Abstract. Mediterranean Europe is strongly affected by wildfires. In Portugal, the Portuguese Institute for Nature Conservation and Forests (ICNF) implemented the national fuel break (FB) network responsible for fire control and suppression. FBs are regions where vegetation is reduced to break up the fuel continuity and create pathways for the firefighting vehicles. The efficiency of this strategy relies on the correct implementation of FBs and on periodic fuel treatments. Multispectral imagery from Sentinel-2 (with high temporal and spatial resolution) facilitates the monitoring of FBs and the implementation of methodologies for their management. In this paper a two stages methodology is proposed for monitoring FBs. The first stage consists in detecting fuel treatments in FBs, to understand if those were correctly executed. This is done through a change detection methodology with resource to an Artificial Neural Network. The second stage monitors the vegetation recovery after a fuel treatment, to aid the scheduling of new treatments, ensuring the efficiency of FBs during the fire season. Both methodologies resort to reflectance bands and spectral indices from Sentinel-2; and timeseries and objects, exploiting the temporal and spatial information. The two stages were tested in different regions across the Portuguese territory, demonstrating their usability for all the national fuel break network. The detection of treatments achieved a relative error lower than 4%, and the vegetation recovery cycle estimated by the second stage match the expectations from ICNF.

Keywords: Sentinel-2 · Change detection · Fuel breaks · Remote sensing · Wildfires · Vegetation recovery · Fuel treatments · GEDI · Artificial neural network · Spectral indices

List of Abbreviations

ANN   Artificial Neural Network
EO   Earth Observation
ExG   Excess of Green

L. M. Camarinha-Matos et al. (Eds.): IFIPIoT 2021, IFIP AICT 641, pp. 67–85, 2022.
https://doi.org/10.1007/978-3-030-96466-5_5

ExR   Excess of Red
FB   Fuel Break
FBN   Fuel Break Network
FH   Forest Height
FL   Fuel Load
FT   Fuel Treatment
GEDI   Global Ecosystem Dynamics Investigation
LiDAR   Light Detection And Ranging
NDVI   Normalized Difference Vegetation Index

1 Introduction

Wildfires are destructive events that occur recurrently during summer seasons. These disasters are common in several regions of the world, of which can be highlighted: the western states of the United States [1]; south-western Canada [2]; Mediterranean Europe (Portugal, Spain, France, Italy, Greece) [3]; and south-eastern Australia [4, 5]. None of these countries had found yet a solution for preventing and efficient suppression of wildfires. Since the current strategies for the suppression and available resources are not sufficient, proactive measures had been applied during the preparation of summer seasons.

In Portugal, the Portuguese Institute for Nature Conservation and Forests (ICNF) defined the Fuel Break Network (FBN), as a firefighting strategy. A Fuel Break (FB) consists of a strip of land which was artificially modified to reduce its Fuel Load (FL) [6]. This is achieved by decreasing and/or removing the vegetation within the FB through Fuel Treatments (FT). An image of an implemented FB is shown in Fig. 1. The technical specifications of a FB defined by ICNF are the following [7]:

- Composed by three parts: Fuel Interruption, Fuel Reduction, and Road Network. The FB has a minimum width of 125 m;
- Fuel Interruption: all the vegetation is removed and have minimum width of 10 m;
- Fuel Reduction: reduction of the vegetation by imposing a minimum distance between trees tops and a pruning height, and a minimum width of 60 m;
- Road Network: a pathway for the firefighting vehicles, with a minimum width of 5 m. It is in the middle of the FB, having a Fuel Interruption and a Fuel Reduction area to each side.

A graphical scheme of a FB is presented on Fig. 2 for an easier understanding. The FBN is responsible for compartmentalize the forest, which allows a better control of wildfires and slows down its propagation. Adding to its proactive effects, the road network creates better conditions for the firefighters.

A key factor for the effectiveness of the FBN in preventing the occurrence of wildfires is the correct implementation and maintenance of its FBs. The management and monitoring of the FBN is responsibility of ICNF. To accomplish it they need to periodically schedule FTs for the FBs and the implementation of new FBs (from now on both will be

Fig. 1. Ground observation of a Fuel Break. (Source: http://www2.icnf.pt/).

referred as FT), which are executed by Local Authorities. Concretely the ICNF needs to guarantee that FTs are correctly performed and to periodically assess the FL of FBs scheduling the necessary FTs. Currently, both activities are done by inspection of earth observation satellite imagery and ground observation of the FBs. The first approach is a time-consuming process and prone to errors, the latter is also time-consuming (due the extension of the FBN) and it is an expensive process.

The increasing number of Earth Observation (EO) missions, the quality of the data acquired from remote sensing platforms, and sensors specifically developed for vegetation monitoring, allows the implementation of new methodologies for forest management. Within the EO platforms, Sentinel-2 (S2, from the Copernicus mission) presents a set of attracting features. Briefly, it carries a multispectral sensor acquiring the reflectance in 13 spectral bands (including 3 on the red edge spectrum, which is recommended for vegetation monitoring), a revisit period of 5 days (suitable for monitoring), and a spatial resolution of 10 m and 20 m for majority of the bands (which gives sufficient information for analyzing FBs). In addition to S2, Global Ecosystem Dynamics Investigation (GEDI) is a Spaceborne Light Detection and Ranging (LiDAR) sensor optimized to measure the vertical structure of vegetation [8, 9]. GEDI acquires several variables of the forest, including the Forest Height (FH), with a spatial resolution of 25 m. Despite its measurement's suitability for the problems that ICNF needs to address, it is a sampling mission which compromises its usage for monitoring.

In this paper is proposed a semi-automatic methodology to support the FBN management that fulfils the following requirements:

- Detect the month when a FT was executed on a FB from predefined shapefile;
- Avoid detecting incomplete FTs (that cover less than 75% of the FB);
- Estimate FL growth in a FB after a FT;
- Must be a generic methodology that works for regions with different conditions (land cover, weather, geographic location, etc.).

This methodology is divided in two stages: the detection of FTs and estimation of the FL growth since the last FT. The proposed methodology performs an object analysis, instead of pixel analysis, which enhance the spatial information, and generate timeseries from the S2 reflectances and the derived spectral indices, to enhance the temporal information. The detection is ensured by an Artificial Neural Network (ANN) that outputs and the FL estimation is based on the analysis of the Normalized Difference Vegetation Index (NDVI) timeseries.

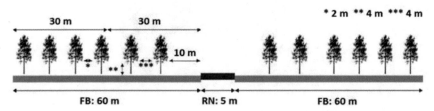

Fig. 2. Technical specifications of a fuel break in the Portuguese fuel break network [7].

ICNF provided the FBN's shapefile, the information of where and when FTs have been executed, which was used during the ANN training, validation, and error estimation. The select error metrics were relative error, recall (producer's accuracy), precision (consumer's accuracy), and F1-Score, as suggested in [10]. Next a dataset of incomplete FTs (with three different levels of coverage) was tested. Relatively to the FL estimation, the results were validated by ICNF and observation of S2 images. Finally, the pair NDVI/GEDI's FH was evaluated by the Pearson's Correlation, which provides a more precise validation of the usage of NDVI for assessing the FL increase in a FB.

There are no significant studies in the literature regarding change detection related to FTs or FBs. However, there are many published works about change detection methodologies. In [11] space-time features were exploited to detect forest disturbances using two consecutive observations and in [12] annual composites were used for detecting changes. In [13–15] methodologies to identify changes on the land and their type are proposed. In all these works Landsat imagery was used, which has a revisiting period of 16 days (three times the revisiting period of S2) and relied in more than one previous observation of the change event.

The studies of vegetation monitoring, FL accumulation, usually rely on the estimation of FH and aboveground biomass. Several methodologies are already implemented using different sensors' types (LiDAR [16, 17], Optical [18–20], SAR [21]), but the estimation models rely in in-situ measurements (which are spatially limited, time-consuming, and may be destructive), and are not generalizable for different regions.

This paper is written through five sections: this Sect. 1 concerning the introduction and state of art; the Sect. 2 dedicated to the material and methods, all the data used in this article is presented, the used methods are exposed, and the explanation of how the methodology was validated. Next in Sect. 3 the results and a brief description of them is provided; and the final two Sects. 4 and 5 are dedicated to the discussion and conclusions of the developed work.

2 Materials and Methods

2.1 Study Areas

The implementation and validation of the proposed methodology relied in 19 study areas across the national territory, described in Table 1. As is shown, they vary in terms of land cover (including 6 different types, and areas with multiple types) and geographic location, creating richer datasets.

For the FT detection training and validation four of the 19 study areas were used. In the selected areas FT had been executed between 2017 and 2018. The available samples from this period were divided into the training and validation dataset, and the defined error metrics computed. Next, the detection was tested in real-case scenarios: 14 regions treated in the first semester of 2020; and a FB outside the FBN that belongs to the National Power Network treated in 2018 (Marisol). Also, a specific test regarding the performance of the methodology for incomplete FTs was performed.

The FL growth estimation was tested in four areas treated during 2017 and 2018. ICNF validated the obtained results. Finally, the usage of the NDVI for the estimation was evaluated data other four study areas (due the fact the GEDI mission only provides data after April 2019).

2.2 Data and Tools

The main data sources used in development and validation of the proposed methodology were:

- FBN shapefile provided by ICNF;
- S2 imagery from mid-2015 to mid-2020;
- FH measurements from samples acquired in 2020 by GEDI.

The FBN shapefile is composed by the polygons corresponding to the FBs under authority of the ICNF (note that not all FBs are already implemented). Additionally, a polygon for Marisol was designed by the authors based on S2 imagery.

S2 is a constellation of two satellites platform (S2-A and S2-B) that carries a multispectral sensor measuring the reflectance in 13 spectral bands, covering the visible, vegetation red edge, near infrared, and shortwave infrared spectrum's regions. For this methodology Level-1C products (top-of-atmosphere radiance) due its availability since mid-2015. With a revisiting period of five days and spatial resolutions of 10 m and 20 m (bands with a spatial resolution of 60 m were not used due the minimum width of 125 m of FBs) it is a suitable platform for monitoring the FBN. From the authors' previous works, regarding the FT detection [22], bands 2, 3, and 4 were used to compute the spectral indices Excess of Green (ExG) and Excess of Red (ExR), and band 5 was used directly. Relatively to the FL growth bands 4 and 8 were used to compute the NDVI for the estimation. All used observations were downloaded from Copernicus Open Access Hub.

GEDI is a LiDAR sensor carried by the International Space Station, optimized for forest measurement. The mission started operating in April 2019, it acquires 25 m resolution samples, and has a coverage between the $51.6°$ N and 51.6 S, promising to sample 4% of the Earth's Surface [8, 9]. GEDI Level-2B products were used, concretely the RH100 parameter which corresponds to the sample FH [23]. Since it is a sampling mission, this information is not suitable for monitoring, so it was used to validate the usage of the NDVI in the FL growth estimation. To guarantee the quality of the GEDI data,

Table 1. Study areas description. Usage: 1 – Fuel Treatment training & validation; 2 – Fuel Treatment test; 3 – Fuel Load growth test; 4 – NDVI validation.

Study area	Relative location in country	Land cover	Usage
Amieria	Inland center	Eucalyptus and cork tree forest	2
Besteiros	Inland center	Eucalyptus, pine, and cork tree forests	2
Cabro-Baixo	Inland center	Agriculture, cork oak forests, shrubs	2
Canedo	Inland north	Pine forests	2, 4
Capinha	Inland north	Eucalyptus forests	2, 4
Casa Nova	South	Cork oak forests, shrubs	2
Famalicão	Inland north	Pine forests	2
Fundão	Inland north	Eucalyptus and pine forests, shrubs	1, 3
Marisol	Coast center	Eucalyptus forests	2, 3
Monte Zorra	Coast south	Cork oak forests, shrubs	2, 4
Monte Velho	South	Cork oak forests, shrubs	2
Paradelhas	Inland north	Shrubs	2, 4
Pincho	South	Agriculture, shrubs	2
Salir	South	Cork oak forests	2
Seia	Inland north	Artificial Territories, shrubs	1
Serra dos Candeeiros	Coast center	Agriculture, shrubs	1, 3, 4
Sertã	Inland center	Shrubs	1, 3
Terras Ordem	South	Pine forests	2
Vale Grou	South	Eucalyptus and cork oak forests, shrubs	2

only samples the meet the minimum quality requirements were used (samples with the quality flags l2a_quality_flag and l2b_quality_flag set).

Quantum GIS (QGIS) and several python modules were used for the methodology implementation. QGIS is an open-source geographic information system which includes several useful features for working with Remote Sensing data. Also, it allows the automation of tasks through its python console and by the development of plug-ins. The main python modules used in this methodology were: GDAL and Scikit-Learn.

2.3 Time Series Generation

The time series generation is ensured by the pre-processing stage. The analysis is performed at object level, i.e., within the FB area and is shared by the FT detection and FL growth estimation. In Fig. 4 it is presented an info graph describing the object time series generation. It consists in the following steps:

1. Correction of observations' geolocation errors;
2. Generation of the object values for all required reflectance bands;
3. Computation of the time series with a month timestep;
4. Computation of the spectral indices;
5. Estimation of the month values, when there no available observations.

ESA reported in [24] that S2 observations may suffer of an translational geolocation error up to 1.5 pixels, which corresponds to a maximum of 15 m error for the 10 m resolution bands and 30 m for the 20 m resolution bands. For most applications, this error may be neglected, however due the minimum width of 125 m of a FB, this error can negatively influence the results. The correction algorithm used in step 1 is presented in [25], and used in [22, 26], and it decreases the maximum error to 1.5 m and 3 m per resolution, which is negligible for the proposed methodologies.

In step 2 the object value is computed. An object is a group of adjacent pixels, being used in this methodology the group of pixels within a FB polygon. The objective of this work is to detect FTs on FBs, so the usage of an object approach is also consequence of the defined requirements. Also, change detection application benefits from the spatial information obtained using this approach [15] which agrees with the Tobler's first law of geography. The used metric for the object value were the mean value of the pixels within the FB.

Step 3 builds up the basis of the proposed methodology. Change detection applications try to find significant changes in data to understand if it was a real change and not a pseudo change (phenology, illumination, external effects) [12], and this is not an exception. FT detection relies on the comparison of consecutive values and FL growth estimation on the inter-annual comparison of values, being fully dependent of the generated time series from this step. Time series using all observation are very noisy, so this step also reduces the noise (as shown in Fig. 3), which improves the ability of the FT detection in avoiding pseudo changes and the quality of the FL growth estimations. In [22] a mean and a median noise filter were tested, exhibiting similar results, however the mean filter was chosen since it offers a more defensive approach, detecting less FTs but with more ability to discard false FT. This was decided by the authors because detecting a false FT is worse than not detecting a FT, in this specific case.

From the reflectance bands time series, in Step 4 are generated the time series for the spectral indices. Alternatively, the spectral indices time series may be computed on a pixel-based approach, where the index is calculated for each pixel and after the object value obtained in step 2. However, the authors demonstrated in [22] that the difference relatively to this approach is negligible, with the advantage that it is less time-consuming. The outputs of this step are the NDVI, ExG, and ExR time series.

Despite the revisiting period of 5 days, the cloud cover lead to the unusability of several S2 observations. On some winter months, there are no available observations, so it is needed a step 5 where a value per attribute is estimated for the months without usable observations. If there are two months without data, it is estimated a value just for the first month. In the evaluated study areas, there were no cases with two consecutive months without data, especially after the launching of S2-B. A very simple approach was used, the values of the previous month were used as values of the month without observations.

Each stage has a specific final pre-processing step. For the FT detection the final step consists in the data set generation for the ANN. For the FL growth estimation, a moving average (with a window size of three months) is applied as another noise reduction technique. Although it is suitable for this stage, for the FT detection it may smooths the data at the point of masking FTs.

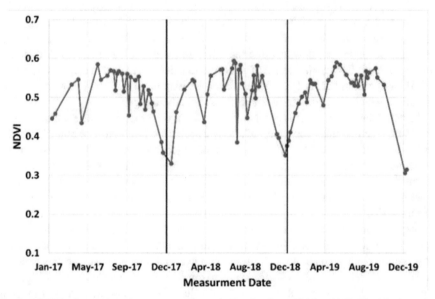

Fig. 3. NDVI's time series of a non-treated area in Fundão from 2017 to 2019. The black vertical lines highlight the one-year period.

2.4 Fuel Treatments Detection

The first stage of the proposed methodology is the FT detection. The methodology is prepared to identify three types of FTs:

1. On FBs that not periodically treated;
2. On FBs that periodically treated;
3. That occur in two consecutive months.

Type 1 are the easiest FTs to detect due being the ones where more FL is removed. Therefore, the effect on time series is more significant, also in the observations, as seen in Fig. 5 a), b), and Fig. 6 (blue curve). In Type 2 when the FTs are executed, the amount of FL is lower than in Type 1, because is not yet a dangerous situation, but it requires maintenance. FTs are not instantaneous events. Usually, they are observed in just one month. However sometimes observations of consecutive months show FL reduction. In those cases, it is just expected to detect a FT on the month with higher FL reduction. Type 2 and 3 have a less impact on the time series and in the observations (as seen in Fig. 5 c), d) and Fig. 6, orange curve), being harder to distinguish from phenology.

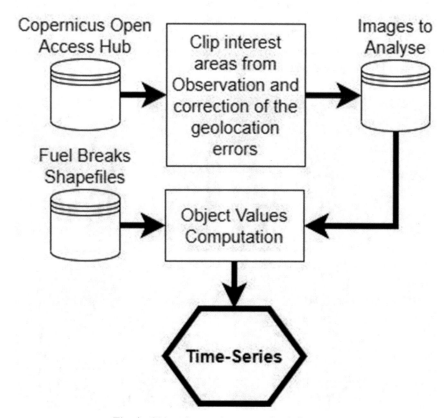

Fig. 4. Object time series generation info graph.

The FT detection is guaranteed by an ANN that use as features: reflectance B5, ExG, and ExR for the month being evaluated and the previous month (a total of 6 features). Several ANN structures were tested using one and two hidden layers, and its quality assessed by its accuracy and detection recall. From [22] was concluded that the best structure was an ANN using one hidden layer with 53 neurons. The input layer used a neuron per feature, and since it is a binary classification, the output layer constituted by one neuron. The main challenge of the proposed ANN is to identify Type 2 FTs, distinguishing them from phenology phenoms.

2.5 Fuel Load Growth Estimation

FL growth estimation, stage 2, completes the monitoring of the FBN. Vegetation is constantly growing in forests and after a FT is just a matter of time for vegetation to start regenerating, consequently increasing the available FL within the FBs. ICNF is responsible for scheduling regular FTs in the FBN, ensuring its efficiency and low fire risk. Due to the flora diversity in Portugal and that not all FBs are already being treated periodically, it is required a generic approach which allows the monitoring of the FBN. The drawback of using this approach is that there are not computed absolute metrics as the FH and Aboveground Biomass, as in [19, 20, 27], which usually are developed for specific areas and conditions. Instead, it yields an estimate of the percentage of the regenerated FL comparing with the state before the FT.

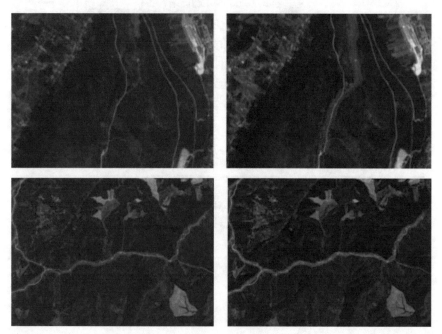

Fig. 5. TCI images previous and after fuel treatments: a), b) - Serra dos Candeeiros; c), d) - Fundão.

The first feature of this stage is the ability of self-learning, by analyzing data before the FT, of when is supposed to perform a FT in that FB, and of the NDVI's time series behavior relatively to the FB land cover and environmental conditions. Despite this sensibility of the NDVI (as seen in Fig. 3), the index reflects the FL growth, increasing its value until reaching the pre-FT values (as seen in Fig. 7). This is done through an adaptive reference system, where the maximum (*max*) NDVI of the 6 months before the FT is defined as the max FL NDVI measurement, and the NDVI's local minimum (*min*) after the FT defines the min of the FL's scale. Although only one measurement is needed before the FT to establish the FL's scale *max*, is expected a better behavior of the method if it has the six previous months' values. Usually, the NDVI's time series starts reflecting the vegetation regeneration in the 6 months after the FT. So, for NDVI's measurements acquired after the FT, but before the NDVI's local *min*, the method automatically estimates 0% of FL, since it is not verified in the time series any FL growth.

The second feature is the robustness against the vegetation phenology effects. As seen in Fig. 7, the presented NDVI's time series has a growing trend, but due its peaks and valleys behavior, it is not clear how the FL increases along time (especially when there is a decrease on the NDVI's values without any vegetation reduction). As it is observed in Fig. 3, phenology in time series behaves like a periodic signal with a one-year period, implying that measurements of the same month in different years are subjected to the same environmental conditions. To take advantage of this, the proposed method estimates the monthly FL growth from the NDVI's inter-annual difference, instead of using the difference of consecutive measurements. In the 12 months after the FL starts growing, it is used the difference of the month being analyzed and the local *min*, and afterward the inter-annual difference is used. This is required since the inter-annual difference before and after the FT, which leads to a wrong estimation of the FL growth. As the reader may observe, it is assumed that yearly FL growth is linear, however it does not mean that the estimation is linear (as it is seen in 0). It is explained due the fact that for each new estimation, new inter-annual measurements are used, leading to new linear regressions whose slopes are constantly changing and tend towards zero with time.

By combining the two identified features (self-learning and robustness to phenology) we modeled the FL growth using Eq. (1) and (2), where i is the month being estimated, j the month used for the difference (for the first year it ranges from 1 to 11, after that it is equal to 12), and k the number of months after the FT. The first term corresponds monthly FL growth and the second is the scaling term. Each monthly value should be added to the previous month estimation to get the current FL state. Despite being an incremental approach, the method is able to include treatments within the FB. If a vegetation reduction occurs within the FB, there will be a decrease in the FL estimations, which shows the reliability of the method.

2.6   Error Estimation

Different validation and error estimation were used in the two stages of the FBN monitoring. For the FT detection the available data for the ANN implementation was divided into training and validation set (with the proportion 67%–33%, respectively). For the training set a cross-validation was applied for the error estimation. After defining all the ANN parameters, the assessment using the validation set was performed. To test the method for incomplete FTs, nine FBs that were incompletely treated were evaluated. Finally, a real case scenario was tested, applying the detection stage for the first semester of 2020 and Marisol (treated in 2018). These results were validated by visualization of the S2 imagery, and by the pixel-based detection proposed by the authors in [26, 28]. The metrics presented are the Relative Error, and to evaluate the ability of the code in detecting FTs and avoiding false detections the Recall, Precision, and F1-Score, as proposed in [10].

The FL growth estimation was validated by visualization of S2 Imagery and by ICNF who corroborated the obtained results. To have a numerical assessment of the proposed

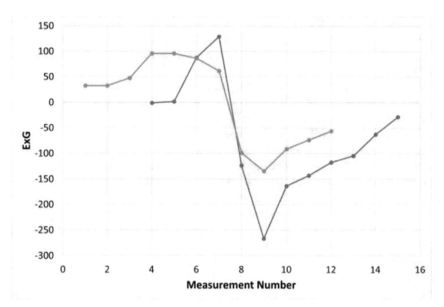

Fig. 6. ExG's time series: *blue* - Serra dos Candeeiros, type 1; *orange* – Fundão, type 2. The mean value of each time series was subtracted, and the time scale adjusted to enhance the comparison of the fuel treatments types. (Color figure online)

method, an indirect test was executed with resort to GEDI data. The FH is not the same as the FL but are correlated. The test consisted in obtaining 50 sample pairs of FH and NDVI and computing the Pearson's correlation to evaluate if NDVI is an indicator of the FH, and consequently of the FL. The samples were from treated FBs and surrounding areas where no FT was performed.

3   Results

3.1   Fuel Treatment Detection Results

The error estimation in the FTs detection was performed with the training and validation set, and with the test set where the method was applied to a real case scenario. The training, validation, and test set had 633, 311, and 641 samples respectively, being the results presented in Table 2.

From the presented results it can be concluded that the FTs detection method is accurate. From the relative error it is not expected to have misdetections above the 4%. Regarding the recall it was obtained 77% in the validation phase and 85% in the test phase, which shows the ability of the method in detecting FTs. However, the precision values are lower, 64% and 73%, which shows that some false detection will occur. Finally, the F1-Score, which reflect both previous metrics, shows that that the method is reasonably good in the FTs detection. Giving a more detailed description of the test set,

$$Growth_i = \frac{NDVI_i - NDVI_{i-j}}{j} \times \frac{1}{(Reference_{Max} - Reference_{Min})} \tag{1}$$

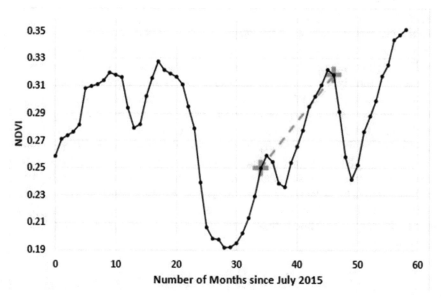

Fig. 7. NDVI time series of Fundão between July 2015 to May 2020. The crosses mark points 34 and 46, used to calculate the inter-annual difference.

$$FL\,Growth = \sum_k Growth_k \qquad (2)$$

was composed by 34 FBs where a FT as occurred. There were five non detected FTs, and 11 misdetections. These misdetections do not correspond to incomplete FTs. The confusion matrix is presented in Table 3.

To assess the method's robustness against incomplete FTs, nine incomplete FTs were tested. They were divided into three groups of completeness: 0–25%; 25–50%; and 50–75% (above 75% it is considered a complete FT). The results are shown in Table 4. There were no misdetections for FTs that covered less than 50% of the FB extension. Only on the two cases tested for the 50–75% completeness one was wrongly detected as FT.

Considering all the tests, the FT detection method has proved to be able to accurately detect FT and is guaranteed and its application to real cases scenarios.

3.2 Fuel Load Growth Estimation

In Fig. 8 the results of the FL growth estimation for four different study areas are presented. It should be noted that with this method, phenology effects were strongly reduced. Next, it is seen that the FL growth estimation curves begin with a nearly linear growth and start to decrease after 15 months. This was expected, and can be consequence of NDVI saturation, a characteristic of the spectral indices [29]. The comparison with the S2 imagery is consistent with estimations. In Fig. 9, images before and after the FT are presented. Figure 9 a) and Fig. 9 d) are visually similar and the last FL estimation was 100%, reinforcing the method's efficiency. FTs are usually schedule by ICNF to a specific FBs every 2 to 3 years. The FL growth estimations start stabilizing 24 months after the FL started growing, which agrees with the ICNF procedures and validates the presented results. The estimation for Serra dos Candeeiros showed that it can adjust to new FBs implementations. The decrease on FL after month 30 is not an error, it was due to a new FT. Finally, we can divide the results into two groups: Marisol and Serra dos Candeeiros that exceeded the 100%; and Fundão and Sertã that stabilize at the 100%. The FBs on the second group were already being periodically treated, opposing the others, what showed that study areas where the NDVI was not saturated lead to better estimations. The final validation step was the comparison between the FH measurements from GEDI and the NDVI measurements from S2, that are summarized in Fig. 10 and Table 5. It is immediately seen that there is a correlation between both variables, and that correlation is higher if the samples are grouped by study areas. The figures confirm it, being the full dataset Pearson's correlation equal to 0.69, and when grouping by study areas the average correlation increases to 0.84, with values ranging from 0.76 to 0.98, as shown in Table 5.

Table 2. Fuel treatments detection results. Recall, precision, and F1-score computed relative to the detection.

	Training set	Validation set	Test set
Recall	97%	77%	85%
Precision	89%	64%	73%
F1-score	93%	70%	78%
Relative error	3.3%	2.5%	2.5%

Table 3. Confusion matrix for the test set.

		Validation	
	Class	FT	No FT
Detection	FT	29	11
	No FT	5	598

Table 4. Results for incomplete FTs.

Completeness	Number of cases	Misdetections
0–25%	3	0
25–50%	4	0
50–75%	2	1

4   Discussion

The results presented in Sect. 3 showed that the proposed methodology is capable to monitor the FBN in two stages: detecting FTs and identifying when a FB needs a new FT. Starting with the FT detection a high accuracy on the results was achieved for a diverse dataset (in terms of geography, land cover, and seasonality). Also, the detection was performed comparing two consecutive observations opposing the need of more observations as in the previous works presented in Sect. 0. The method achieved similar results to the aforementioned works, with the advantage of being tested in a more heterogenous dataset. This lead us to expect that the methodology would work for unknown areas (as occurred with the test set). However, in [13–15] the proposed methodologies had the ability to identify the changes typology (land cover, land use).

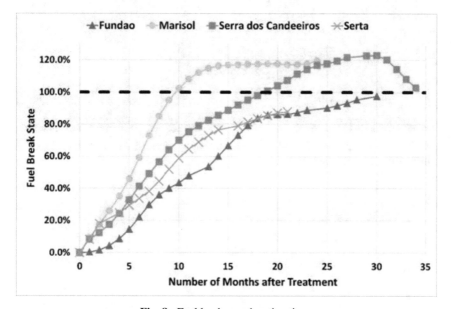

Fig. 8. Fuel load growth estimations.

For the second stage, FL growth estimation, a new robust method was successfully designed, where the phenology effect was strongly reduced, being capable to estimate the FL on a FB and identifying when a FB needs to be treated. The validation with GEDI data showed a high correlation between the FH and NDVI, and it is higher if data is grouped by study areas. These results showed ability to self-adapt to the region where the estimation is being performed. The tradeoff was not calculating absolute metrics as the FH or the aboveground biomass, as in the works presented during the introduction.

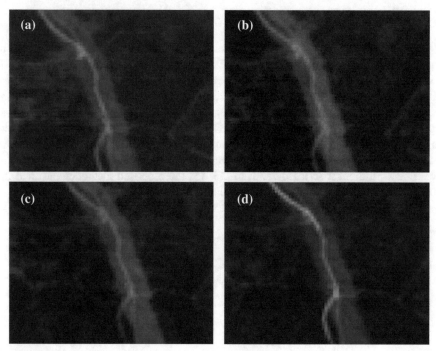

Fig. 9. TCI images from Fundão. a) Before treatment; b) Right after treatment; c) 2-year after treatment; d) 3-year after treatment.

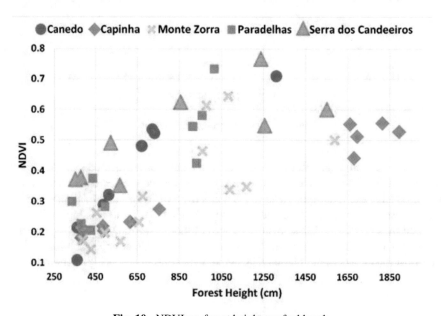

Fig. 10. NDVI vs. forest height per fuel break

Table 5. Pearson's correlations between forest height and NDVI.

Study area	Pearson's correlation
Canedo	0.92
Capinha	0.98
Monte Zorra	0.76
Paradelhas	0.89
Serra dos Candeeiros	0.77
Full Dataset	0.69

5   Conclusion and Future Work

In this paper it is proposed a semi-automatic methodology for monitoring FBs subject to different conditions (land cover, weather, geographic location, etc.). It is composed by two stages responsible for detecting FTs in the FBN and to estimate the FL growth in the treated FBs. Both stages resort to S2 periodic observations, being exploited the spatial and temporal features of the data by the generation of objects and the respective timeseries.

The detection stage achieved an error bellow of 4% for the training, validation, and test set; and a minimum F1-Score of 70% for the three sets. Also, it is demonstrated its ability to avoid the detection of incomplete FTs since it has not detected any FT where the treated area is 50% or less of the FB's area. However, in the interval [50%, 75%] it is not guaranteeing the ability to avoid the false detection.

The FL growth stage yields periodic estimation of the FB state in terms of FL accumulation. It relies on the NDVI's timeseries and it is a self-learning method that uses measurements before the FT to establish a FL's scale, so it can adapt to different FBs. Also, the estimation of the growth uses the inter-annual difference of two observations instead the difference of two consecutive observations, so it can reduce the phenology noise present on data. The method was validated by ICNF, the expected cycles between FTs were achieved (2.5 to 3 years), and the comparison between NDVI and GEDI's FH exhibit significant correlation values.

Finally, since the shapefiles relative to the FBs are designed by the user, so it is not yet a fully automatic methodology, and its performance decreases with incorrect designs of shapefiles.

Future work will includes the automatization of the generation of the shapefiles of the FBs, using the methodology proposed in [28]; recover observations not used due its atmospheric conditions; test new features (as textural features) to estimate the FL growth; use spectral indices not based on the normalized difference to decrease the saturation effect [29]; and start estimating biophysical parameters as the FH and aboveground biomass.

Acknowledgements. The authors would like to acknowledge Fundação de Ciências e Tecnologia (FCT) for funding the projects FUELMON (PTDC/CCI-COM/30344/2017) and foRESTER

(PCIF/SSI/0102/2017), and the Research Units, Centre of Technology and Systems – Uninova (UIDB/00066/2020) and Forest Research Centre (UIDB/00239/2020). Also, the ICNF deserves an acknowledgment for presenting us with the topic and supplying data regarding FB treatments. João E. Pereira-Pires thanks the Fundação para a Ciência e Tecnologia (FC&T), Portugal for the Ph.D. Grant 2020.05015.BD.

References

1. Barbero, R., Abatzoglou, J.T., Larkin, N.K., Kolden, C.A., Stocks, B.: Climate change presents increased potential for very large fires in the contiguous United States. Int. J. Wildl. Fire **24**(7), 892 (2015). https://doi.org/10.1071/WF15083
2. Tymstra, C., Stocks, B.J., Cai, X., Flannigan, M.D.: Wildfire management in Canada: review, challenges and opportunities. Prog. Disaster Sci. **5**, 100045 (2020). https://doi.org/10.1016/j.pdisas.2019.100045
3. San-Miguel-Ayanz, J., et al.: Forest Fires in Europe, Middle East and North Africa 2018. Publications Office of the European Union, Rome (2019)
4. Chuvieco, E., et al.: Historical background and current developments for mapping burned area from satellite earth observation. Remote Sens. Environ. **225**(March), 45–64 (2019). https://doi.org/10.1016/j.rse.2019.02.013
5. Bowman, D.M.J.S., Williamson, G.J., Abatzoglou, J.T., Kolden, C.A., Cochrane, M.A., Smith, A.M.S.: Human exposure and sensitivity to globally extreme wildfire events. Nat. Ecol. Evol. **1**(3), 1–6 (2017). https://doi.org/10.1038/s41559-016-0058
6. Ascoli, D., Russo, L., Giannino, F., Siettos, C., Moreira, F.: "Firebreak and Fuelbreak", in Encyclopedia of Wildfires and Wildland-Urban Interface (WUI) Fires, pp. 1–9. Springer International Publishing, Cham (2018)
7. DPFVAP – ICNF: Primary Fuelbreak Network Manual. Portugal (2014)
8. Potapov, P., et al.: Mapping global forest canopy height through integration of GEDI and Landsat data. Remote Sens. Environ. **253**, 112165 (2021). https://doi.org/10.1016/j.rse.2020.112165
9. Healey, S.P., Yang, Z., Gorelick, N., Ilyushchenko, S.: Highly local model calibration with a new GEDI LiDAR asset on google earth engine reduces Landsat forest height signal saturation. Remote Sens. **12**(17), 2840 (2020). https://doi.org/10.3390/rs12172840
10. Barsi, Á., Kugler, Z., László, I., Szabó, G., Abdulmutalib, H.M.: Accuracy dimensions in remote sensing. Int. Archiv. Photogram. Remote Sen. Spatial Inf. Sci. **XLII–3**, 61–67 (2018). https://doi.org/10.5194/isprs-archives-XLII-3-61-2018
11. Hamunyela, E., Reiche, J., Verbesselt, J., Herold, M.: Using space-time features to improve detection of forest disturbances from Landsat time series. Remote Sens. **9**(6), 1–17 (2017). https://doi.org/10.3390/rs9060515
12. Hermosilla, T., Wulder, M.A., White, J.C., Coops, N.C., Hobart, G.W.: An integrated Landsat time series protocol for change detection and generation of annual gap-free surface reflectance composites. Remote Sens. Environ. **158**, 220–234 (2015). https://doi.org/10.1016/j.rse.2014.11.005
13. Wang, W., Chen, Z., Li, X., Tang, H., Huang, Q., Qu, L.: Detecting spatio-temporal and typological changes in land use from Landsat image time series. J. Appl. Remote Sens. **11**(3), 035006 (2017). https://doi.org/10.1117/1.JRS.11.035006
14. Zhu, Z., Woodcock, C.E.: Continuous change detection and classification of land cover using all available Landsat data. Remote Sens. Environ. **144**, 152–171 (2014). https://doi.org/10.1016/j.rse.2014.01.011

15. Hao, Y., Chen, Z., Huang, Q., Li, F., Wang, B., Ma, L.: Bidirectional segmented detection of land use change based on object-level multivariate time series. Remote Sens. **12**, 478 (2020). https://doi.org/10.3390/rs12030478

16. Ku, N.W., Popescu, S.C.: A comparison of multiple methods for mapping local-scale mesquite tree aboveground biomass with remotely sensed data. Biomass Bioenerg. **122**(January), 270–279 (2019). https://doi.org/10.1016/j.biombioe.2019.01.045

17. Lee, J., Im, J., Kim, K., Quackenbush, L.: Machine learning approaches for estimating forest stand height using plot-based observations and airborne LiDAR data. Forests **9**(5), 268 (2018). https://doi.org/10.3390/f9050268

18. Lang, N., Schindler, K., Wegner, J.D.: Country-wide high-resolution vegetation height mapping with Sentinel-2. Remote Sens. Environ. **233**, 111347 (2019). https://doi.org/10.1016/j.rse.2019.111347

19. Puliti, S., et al.: Modelling above-ground biomass stock over Norway using national forest inventory data with ArcticDEM and Sentinel-2 data. Remote Sens. Environ. **236**, 111501 (2020). https://doi.org/10.1016/j.rse.2019.111501

20. Wittke, S., Xiaowei, Y., Karjalainen, M., Hyyppä, J., Puttonen, E.: Comparison of two-dimensional multitemporal sentinel-2 data with three-dimensional remote sensing data sources for forest inventory parameter estimation over a boreal forest. Int. J. Appl. Earth Observ. Geoinf. **76**, 167–178 (2019). https://doi.org/10.1016/j.jag.2018.11.009

21. Cougo, M.F., et al.: Radarsat-2 backscattering for the modeling of biophysical parameters of regenerating mangrove forests. Remote Sens. **7**(12), 17097–17112 (2015). https://doi.org/10.3390/rs71215873

22. Pereira-Pires, J.E., Aubard, V., Ribeiro, R.A., Fonseca, J.M., Silva, J.M.N., Mora, A.: Semi-automatic methodology for fire break maintenance operations detection with sentinel-2 imagery and artificial neural network. Remote Sens. **12**(6), 909 (2020). https://doi.org/10.3390/rs12060909

23. Dubayah, J.R., Tang, H., Armston, J., Luthcke, S., Hofton, M., Blair, J.B.: GEDI L2B canopy cover and vertical profile metrics data global footprint level V001. In: NASA EOSDIS Land Processes DAAC (2020). https://doi.org/10.5067/GEDI/GEDI02_B.001

24. Clerc, S.: MPC Team: S2 MPC - L1C Data Quality Report - ESA (2020)

25. Guizar-Sicairos, M., Thurman, S.T., Fienup, J.R.: Efficient subpixel image registration algorithms. Opt. Lett. **33**(2), 156 (2008). https://doi.org/10.1364/ol.33.000156

26. Pereira-Pires, J.E., et al.: Pixel-based and object-based change detection methods for assessing fuel break maintenance. In: 2020 International Young Engineers Forum (YEF-ECE), July 2020, pp. 49–54 (2020). https://doi.org/10.1109/YEF-ECE49388.2020.9171818

27. Lang, N., Schindler, K., Wegner, J.D.: Country-wide high-resolution vegetation height mapping with Sentinel-2. Remote Sens. Environ. **233**(April), 111347 (2019). https://doi.org/10.1016/j.rse.2019.111347

28. Aubard, V., Pereira-Pires, J.E., Campagnolo, M.L., Pereira, J.M.C., Mora, A., Silva, J.M.N.: Fully automated countrywide monitoring of fuel break maintenance operations. Remote Sens. **12**(18), 2879 (2020). https://doi.org/10.3390/rs12182879

29. Mutanga, O., Skidmore, A.K.: Narrow band vegetation indices overcome the saturation problem in biomass estimation. Int. J. Remote Sens. **25**(19), 3999–4014 (2004). https://doi.org/10.1080/01431160310001654923

A Study on Small Sensor Node Antenna Performance Camouflaged Under Grassland Fire

Tiago E. S. Oliveira[1,2], Mário Vala[1,3], Stefânia Faria[1,2], João R. Reis[1,2], Nuno Leonor[1,2], and Rafael F. S. Caldeirinha[1,2(✉)]

[1] Instituto de Telecomunicações, Leiria, Portugal
[2] Politécnico de Leiria, Leiria, Portugal
rafael.caldeirinha@ipleiria.pt
[3] Instituto Superior Técnico, University of Lisbon, Lisbon, Portugal

Abstract. In this paper, the impact of vegetation and fire on the radiation pattern of a small antenna to be used in a WSN sensor node, is studied. The proposed antenna used in this study is based on a differential patch design, tuned to operate in the 2.4 GHz frequency band. The antenna presents a reduced size of $45 \times 45\,\mathrm{mm}^2$ ($0.36\lambda \times 0.36\lambda$). The simulations were carried using a full-wave EM solver (CST MWS) considering four different scenarios: the first scenario only containing the antenna placed on the ground to serve as reference; in the second scenario vegetation was introduced to serve as the "normal" state of the terrain surrounding the sensor node; the third scenario includes the impact of surrounding fire considering the permittivity expected during such an event; and the last simulation was performed to include all the previous components simultaneously.

Keywords: Sensor node · Patch antenna · Grassland · Wildfire

1 Introduction

Wildfires are the uncontrolled fires that spread in non-urban areas. Their destructive potential may result in fatalities and loss of properties and natural landscape [1]. The consequences are, often, irreversible damages to the atmosphere and environment. Some examples such as the Dwellingup (1961) and Lara (1969) wildfires in Australia [2], the 2017 tragic wildfire episode in Portugal [3] and also the seasonal wildfires in California have demonstrated the fragility of keeping large grassland and forest areas without remote monitoring.

According to government records, 84% of all wildfires from 1992 to 2012 were human-induced in the United States [4] and this statistic is even higher for fires in Europe, which reaches 95% [5]. The necessity of a comprehensive system providing real-time information from extensive vegetation areas has become crucial. Detecting a fire in its early stages contributes to a faster reaction from the fire

© IFIP International Federation for Information Processing 2022
Published by Springer Nature Switzerland AG 2022
L. M. Camarinha-Matos et al. (Eds.): IFIPIoT 2021, IFIP AICT 641, pp. 86–95, 2022.
https://doi.org/10.1007/978-3-030-96466-5_6

fighters and thus a better control over the wild fire, preventing a the spread of devastation.

Wireless Sensor Networks (WSNs) are commonly proposed in the literature as a solution for an early stage fire-detection system implementation [6–8]. A WSN is typically composed of one or more Base Stations (BS) and multiple Sensor Nodes (SN), being that the SNs have the task to retrieve data from the environment and send it to the BS, where it is stored to be processed and analysed [9,10]. Thus, SN which employ fire or smoke detection capabilities [11] can be used to create a fire-detection system that covers a wide vegetation area.

To build a robust detection network, particularly for early fire detection, WSN networks benefit from having several sensor nodes scattered in large natural areas, e.g. large portions of forest, with the purpose of environmental monitoring. Therefore, it is desirable that SN are as compact and concealed as possible, with small form factors, to reduce the visual impact when deployed in the field, in large scale. Thus, to maintain the small size of the SN, the antenna size is an important factor to have in consideration at the design stage, particularly if relatively high gain antennas (>3 dBi) are required. In [12], the authors have already presented a slotted differential patch antenna operating at 2.4 GHz ISM band for SN usage which utilises the ground plane as shielding for possible electromagnetic noise produced from the circuitry.

The existence of heavy fire plumes as a result from overall combustion of vegetation will change the dielectric properties of the media around the antenna, as studied in [13], leading to changes in the effective permittivity and possible degradation of the antenna performance, which may affect antenna impedance matching and the shape of the radiation pattern. To this extent, the work presented herein aims at the study of the effects of both the environment (soil and undergrowth) and the fire in the overall performance of an antenna specially designed to be used in a sensor node.

This paper is organised as follows: in Sect. 2 the antenna used in this study is presented, where its standalone performance is evaluated; in Sect. 3 the results of the simulations carried out are presented for four different scenarios, that allow to draw conclusions of the enveloping environment effects on the radiation pattern of the antenna. Lastly, in Sect. 5, the main conclusions of this work are presented, as well as some directives to future work.

2   Sensor Node Antenna

The SN antenna being used in this study was firstly presented by the authors in [14] and further optimised by the authors in [12]. This differential antenna was designed to meet specific project requirements, namely to be utilised in a differential RF system set by the sensor node radio front-end architecture. The system that employ an output differential RF signal on the radio frequency system-on-chip (RF SoC) benefit from the intrinsic suppression of the common mode current [15] eliminating the need of Integrated Circuitry (ICs) for filtering processes, leading to an overall reduction of the sensor nodes size.

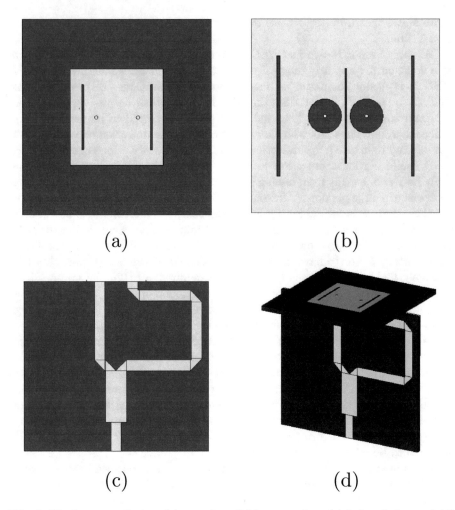

Fig. 1. Final antenna design: (a) top view, (b) bottom view, (c) balun design and (d) differential patch antenna coupled to balun.

The proposed antenna, depicted in Fig. 1, is based on a differential microstrip patch using etched resonating slots to reduce the overall size of the patch. Moreover, two circular slots were added around the feeding points that ensure an input impedance of 100 Ω [12]. A great advantage of this design relies in the ground plane which provide shielding from possible electromagnetic noise produced by the circuitry present in the SN.

The optimised antenna design [12] has dimensions of 45×45 mm^2, operating at 2.4 GHz, with 160 MHz of bandwidth, with 5.1 dBi of gain. The final layout (top and bottom) of the antenna can be observed in Figs. 1a, b, respectively.

For simulation purposes the antenna was coupled to a balun which is composed by a quarter-wave transformer and a 180° phase shifter, as shown in

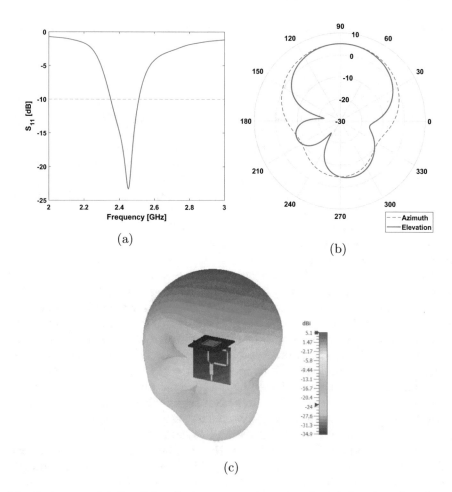

Fig. 2. Antenna (a) S_{11}, (b) radiation pattern (on azimuth and elevation planes) and (c) 3D representation of the radiation pattern.

Fig. 1c. The balun was incorporated in these simulations in order to have a differential signal as the input of the antenna when considering only one input port. This configuration (presented in Fig. 1d) allows the analysis of some antenna parameters that could not be obtained while using only the antenna (*e.g.* S_{11}). However, as mentioned before, the antenna is thought to be coupled to a differential RF SoC when implemented in a real scenario. Both the antenna and balun were design using a double sided FR-4 substrate, with $\varepsilon_r = 4.4$ and $tan(\delta) = 0.014$.

According to the simulations depicted in Fig. 2a, it is possible to observe a $S_{11} <$-10 dB, between 2.36 and 2.51 GHz, i.e. 160 MHz of bandwidth (6.7% of centre frequency). At the centre frequency, the antenna presents a realised gain of 5.1 dBi, with a broadside radiation pattern, characterised by having 79° and

100° of Half-Power Beamwidth (HPBW), in the main antenna planes, as shown in Fig. 2b.

3   Scenario Definition and Case Studies

Following the full characterisation of the antenna, the next step was to start building the simulation environment to be as close to reality as possible in the event of the start of a wildfire in the vicinity of the antenna.

The first simulation performed was when the forest soil was considered below the antenna. For this simulation a $50 \times 50\,cm^2$ ($4\lambda \times 4\lambda$) square with a depth of $20\,cm$, being the antenna placed $5\,mm$ above the centre, as shown in Fig. 3a. The material used for the soil already existed in CST Material Library as *Loamy Soil (wet)*, presenting an $\varepsilon_r = 13.8$ and $tan(\delta) = 0.18$. These dimensions are thought to be enough since only the elements near the antenna will have a significant impact on its radiation pattern.

Following this simulation, a layer of vegetation was added above the soil and surrounding the antenna. A 3D model of tall grass was used as depicted in Fig. 3b. The dielectric properties were taken from [16] for a moisture content of 45%, where $\varepsilon_r = 10$ and $tan(\delta) = 0.4$ were considered for simulation purposes.

Lastly, fire was introduced in the simulation to ascertain how it would impact the antenna performance. In order to obtain the dielectric characteristics of fire, another simulation tool, Fire Dynamic Simulator (FDS), which is a computational fluid dynamics solver released by the National Institute of Standards and Technology (NIST) [17], was used. In FDS it is possible to realistically simulate a fire environment and obtain some parameters such as gas densities and temperature profiles. In post-processing, from this data, it is possible to obtain the electron density and collision frequency that can subsequently be used to calculate the permittivity, as described in [3]. The fuel and burner characteristics were introduced and temperature and density profiles of the environment were extracted in order to calculated the electrical permittivity in a fire region [18]. Even though the fire is a turbulent media, characterised by fast and random variations (fire plumes) overtime, for simulation purposes only a single frame (single time instant) has been considered. For such frame, several permittivities and conductivities ranging from air characteristics $\varepsilon_r = 1$ and $tan(\delta) = 0$ to $\varepsilon_r = 0.9535$ and $tan(\delta) = 0.1343$ were obtained in FDS software and imported to CST, resulting in the 3D scenario presented in Fig. 3c.

4   Simulation Results and Discussion

In each one of the scenarios described above, both the S_{11} and radiation pattern of the antenna were analysed to infer how these would be affected with the presence of the soil, vegetation and fire, individually.

The simulated S_{11} is depicted in Fig. 4. From the results, it can be seen that by adding the soil to the simulation, a degradation of 1.7 dB (from −23.3 dB to −21.6 dB) in antenna matching is observed. On the other hand, when vegetation

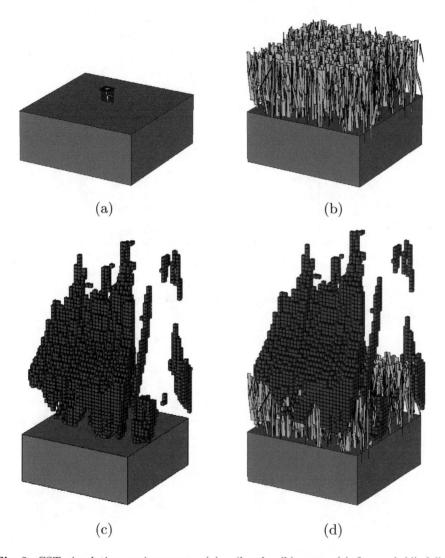

Fig. 3. CST simulation environments: (a) soil only, (b) grass, (c) fire and (d) full scenario.

is considered, the S_{11} almost remains unchanged. However, when the fire is taken into consideration, the S_{11} value decreases to -18 dB, presenting a difference of 5 dB from the case with only the antenna. This indicates that the fire has a significant impact in the antenna performance. Lastly, for the complete scenario, there is not a large difference in the S_{11} when compared to the previous set of simulations.

In terms of the radiation pattern of the antenna in its main planes, i.e. azimuth and elevation, there are also some differences for the various scenarios,

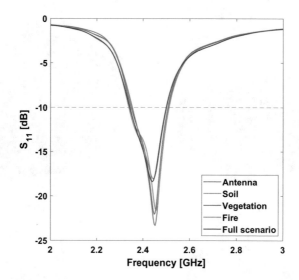

Fig. 4. Antenna S_{11} for all scenarios considered.

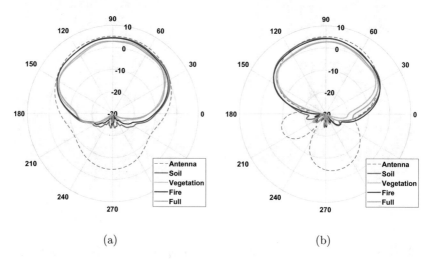

(a)   (b)

Fig. 5. Antenna radiation patterns for the different scenarios: (a) azimuth and (b) elevation.

as shown in Fig. 5. Note that to match the coordinate system of the simulation (CST MWS) the boresight direction is set to $+90°$ in azimuth and elevation. The first and most visible difference occurs when the soil is introduced in the model. Due to high ε_r and $\tan(\delta)$ of the material considered, the back lobe is severely attenuated (with consequent front to back lobe level enhancement), also verifying a small decrease in gain of 0.6 dB, i.e. from 5.1 to 4.49 dBi. Moreover, it can also be noticed a decrease in the realised gain of around 2 dB, when vegetation

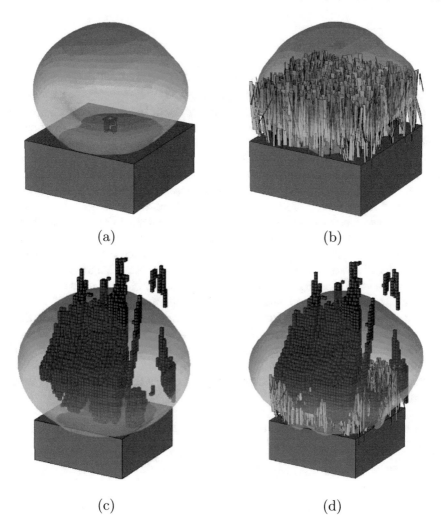

Fig. 6. 3D radiation patterns: (a) soil only, (b) grass, (c) fire and (d) full scenario.

is included in the simulation model. For this particular case, it can also be seen
a slight deformation in the shape of the radiation pattern, also visible in the 3D
radiation patterns of Fig. 6. The simulation with fire also resulted in a decrease
in the gain of around 0.8 dB, when comparing with the radiation pattern of
Fig. 2. Lastly, with the scenario containing both vegetation and fire, the antenna
gain decreases from 5.1 to 3.01 dBi (a difference of 2.1 dB). These results show
that the fire still has an impact on the gain of the antenna even when vegetation
is present. However, the decrease observed in the full scenario is smaller than
that of the superposition of the vegetation and fire scenarios (Figs. 6b and 6c),
due to the overlapping of the fire with the vegetation.

5   Conclusions

This paper presents the impact of grassland fire in the performance of a Sensor node antenna for wireless sensing networks. Firstly, a small antenna designed to be used in a sensor node operating in the 2.4 GHz frequency band, was presented. Based on previous work conducted by the authors, the antenna presents a realised gain of 5.1 dBi over a band of operation of 160 MHz (6.7% of central frequency).

This antenna was then involved by soil, vegetation and fire, approximating the model to a real case scenario of a wildfire. A study for each of the identified parameters was performed by simulation, to ascertain the impact of each model component in antenna performance. From the simulation results, it was observed that all these factors have impact in the performance of the antenna, deteriorating both the S_{11} and the radiation pattern. For a small area of simulation of $50 \times 50\,cm^2$ and considering only a single frame of a propagation fire, a decrease up to 2 dB of the maximum antenna gain was observed. This attenuation however is expected to be higher if considering larger combustion scenarios or taller grass which automatically generate higher fire plumes.

Future work will address further simulations with different vegetation densities and types, different time instants of fire, as well as an increase in the overall simulation environment size in order to ascertain at which distance the surroundings of the antenna will not have an important impact on its performance. The antenna prototyping and its testing in a real scenario is also thought to be done in the near future.

Acknowledgments. This research was partially supported by FCT under the projects WSN-EM (PTDC/EEI-EEE/30539/2017), RESCuE-TOOL (PCIF/SSI/0194/2017) and by FCT/MCTES through national funds and when applicable, co-funded EU funds under the project UID/EEA/50008/2021.

References

1. Minas, J.P., Hearne, J.W., Handmer, J.W.: A review of operations research methods applicable to wildfire management. Int. J. Wildland Fire **21**, 189–196 (2012)
2. Mphale, K.M.: Radiowave propagation measurements and prediction in bushfires. Ph.D. dissertation, School of Mathematical and Physical Sciences - James Cook University (2008)
3. Faria, S.S., Leonor, N., Fernandes, C.A., Felicio, J., Salema, C., Caldeirinha, R.F.: Radiowave propagation modelling in the presence of wildfires: initial results. In: 2020 14th European Conference on Antennas and Propagation (EuCAP), IEEE (2009)
4. Balch, J.K., Bradley, B.A., Abatzoglou, J.T., Nagy, R.C., Fusco, E.J., Mahood, A.L.: Human-started wildfires expand the fire niche across the united states. In: Proceedings of the National Academy of Sciences, vol. 114, p. 201617394 (2017)
5. San-Miguel-Ayanz, J., et al.: Comprehensive Monitoring of Wildfires in Europe: The European Forest Fire Information System (EFFIS) (2012)

6. Sittakul, V., Pasakawee, S. and Jan-im, C.: Wireless sensor network for wildfire detection and notification via walkie – talkie network. In: 2019 16th International Conference on Electrical Engineering/Electronics, Computer, Telecommunications and Information Technology (ECTI-CON), IEEE (2019)
7. Verma, S., Kaur, S., Rawat, D.B., Xi, C., Alex, L.T., Jhanjhi, N.Z.: Intelligent framework using IoT-based WSNs for wildfire detection. IEEE Access **9**, 48185–48196 (2021)
8. Ateeq, Z., Momani, M.: Wireless sensor networks using image processing for fire detection. In: 2020 5th International Conference on Innovative Technologies in Intelligent Systems and Industrial Applications (CITISIA), IEEE (2020)
9. Assim, M., Al-Omary, A.: Design and implementation of smart home using WSN and IoT technologies. In: 2020 International Conference on Innovation and Intelligence for Informatics, Computing and Technologies (3ICT), IEEE (2020)
10. Fahmi, N., Al Rasyid, M.U.H., Sudarsono, A.: Smart environment: accuracy of a server side model in design topology WSN and IoT. In: 2019 International Electronics Symposium (IES), IEEE (2019)
11. Gaur, A., et al.: Fire sensing technologies: a review. IEEE Sens. J. **19**(9), 3191–3202 (2019)
12. Oliveira, T.E.S., Reis, J.R., Vala, M., Caldeirinha, R.F.: High performance antennas for early fire detection wireless sensor networks at 2.4 GHz. In: 10th IEEE-APS Topical Conference on Antennas and Propagation in Wireless Communications APWC (2021)
13. Faria, S., et al.: Analytical studies of refractive index variation in pine needles media under wildfire conditions. In: 2021 15th European Conference on Antennas and Propagation (EuCAP), IEEE (2021)
14. Wang, S.-J., Li, L., Fang, M.: A novel compact differential microstrip antenna. Progress Electromag. Res. Lett. **57**, 97–101 (2015)
15. Bourtoutian, R., Delaveaud, C., Toutain, S.: Differential antenna design and characterization. In: 2009 3rd European Conference on Antennas and Propagation, pp. 2398–2402 (2009)
16. Shrestha, B.L., Wood, H.C., Sokhansanj, S.: Modeling of vegetation permittivity at microwave frequencies. IEEE Trans. Geosci. Remote Sens. **45**(2), 342–348 (2007)
17. McGrattan, K., McDermott, R., Hostikka, S., Floyd, J., Vanella, M.: Fire Dynamics Simulator. sixth edition ed. (2018)
18. Mphale, K.M., Heron, M.L.: Plant alkali content and radio wave communication efficiency in high intensity savanna wildfires. J. Atmospheric Solar-Terrestrial Phys. **69**, 471–484 (2007)

A Data Fusion of IoT Sensor Networks for Decision Support in Forest Fire Suppression

João P. Oliveira[1,2](✉), Miguel Lourenço[1,2], Luís Oliveira[1,2], André Mora[1,2], and Henrique Oliveira[3,4]

[1] Department of Electrical Engineering, NOVA School of Science and Technology, Caparica, Portugal
{jpao,l.oliveira}@fct.unl.pt, mag.lourenco@campus.fct.unl.pt
[2] Centre for Technologies and Systems (CTS) UNINOVA, Caparica, Portugal
atm@uninova.pt
[3] Instituto de Telecomunicações, Lisbon, Portugal
hjmo@lx.it.pt
[4] Instituto Politécnico de Beja, Beja, Portugal

Abstract. The extent and impact of wildfires are expected to increase as a consequence of climate changes, pushing forest and firefighting management decision-making process to be supported by Cyber-Physical-Systems (CPS) that are capable to promote collaborative decision processes. New IoT tools and frameworks fuse scientific knowledge and diversity of sensor data will contribute to improve strategic resources allocation, with the aim of protecting lives, assets, and the environment. The presented IoT CPS which is tunned as a decision support system (DSS) is adapted for the Portuguese wildfire context. It is composed by a geographic information system (GIS) online framework, a mobile client application and a set of portable multi-sensor devices.

Keywords: Multi-sensor technology · Internet of Things ·
Cyber-physical-system · Decision support system · Wildfires

1 Introduction

The concept of interconnection of physical objects based on the Internet of Things (IoT) is forcing significant changes in traditional sensor monitoring microsystems, namely in terms of cost, flexibility, security, resilient communications. Moreover, all processes involve the heterogeneous integration of diverse technologies including physical, communications and networking, and cloud computing. This cooperation between virtual cyber and real physical object entities represents the evolution of the IoT into a Cyber-Physical System (CPS) strategy, [1].

The dynamics of the physical processes integrated with those of the software and networking, facilitates the design and analysis of complex smart systems. For example, the optimization of modern systems applications, including decision support systems

L. M. Camarinha-Matos et al. (Eds.): IFIPIoT 2021, IFIP AICT 641, pp. 96–108, 2022.
https://doi.org/10.1007/978-3-030-96466-5_7

for firefighting as illustrated in Fig. 1. In this example, several multi-parameter sensors and actuators IoT nodes are positioned at several entry points inside this ecosystem. A decision support system with fusion of data originated from distinct sources, including sensors that interface with the physical domain, constitutes a CPS in which the software and hardware are closely interlaced. In these types of complex scenarios, usually, several persons are involved in the decision-making process, requiring an appropriate computer-based collaborative support system.

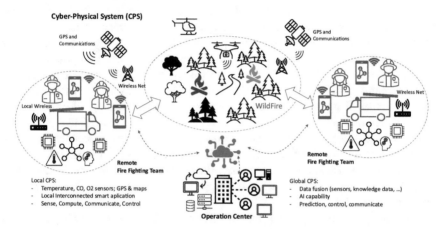

Fig. 1. A cyber-physical system concept for forest fire fighting.

In the last 20 years, Portugal has been severely affected by large wildfires, with almost three million hectares burnt, resulting in dramatic consequences in both social, economic, and environmental domains. The strong incidence of forest fires in the country is due to a joint effect of several reasons namely the significant changes in the climate during the year, ranging from rainy to extreme drought periods and hot temperatures (especially during the summer season), leading to a greater production of plant biomass, thus culminating in large wildfires [2]. To support the management of firefighting resources during these wildfire events, a strong effort in developing new approaches based on geographic information systems (GIS) has been conducted by the scientific community [3, 4].

The classical fire-fighting system centralizes much of the information at the command centers. In the field, commanders, with limited computing resources, mostly resort to military cartography for registering and planning of the operational response. Additionally, the access and registration of historical data from the wildfire scenario is still a bottleneck due to limited reliable resources being one of them the communication subsystem.

In past years, several methodologies were implemented, aiming the development of better DSSs for wildfire management based on GIS technology [5, 6]. In Greece, Virtual-Fire was proposed in 2013 [7] and later, the same research team proposed AEGIS [8] as a WebGIS Tool, to aid in prevention and combat of wildfires. It integrates spatial and map data, as well as vehicle's location, water, and fuel supplies, among other infrastructures, weather data, fire risk assessment maps and fire spread modelling. The Wideland Fire

Decision Support System (WFDSS) [9, 10] is the system used in the US, offering some similar features as the VirtualFire, and also includes a module for financial risk analysis. In Portugal, the MacFIRE Project is another WebGIS, launched by the Municipality of Mação, incorporating mapping data, vehicle's location, fire front severity classification and its location (manually done), ignition points of a fire, among other features [11].

The use of Wireless Sensor Networks (WSN) has been extensively studied in the literature mainly as fire detection systems to alert of potential wildfire spots in an early stage of propagation [12, 13]. These solutions can be extended to monitor the progression of wildfires and provide very useful data for more accurate fire spread simulations. However, they present downsides that reduce its applicability since when it comes to wildfire detection and monitoring, typically WSNs need to be designed for large areas involving a significant number of devices spread over the terrain. This poses multiple challenges such as when nodes fail or are destroyed by the fire, they need to be repaired or replaced, causing significant logistical challenges, considering such an extensive area. Also, technical challenges like the need for a network interface in each node or in a central gateway, which may be challenging since forests may not have a consistent internet or mobile coverage. Energy harvesting on the nodes is also a concern especially if they are installed in the tree trunks as they may not have much sun and wind exposure.

Hence, passive WSNs do not offer a significant value especially considering other existing fire detection solutions that cover extensive areas and do not require as much maintenance [14, 15].

This paper presents a Decision Support System (DSS) whose effectiveness relies on a reliable fusion of data coming from several and distinct sources. To support this integration, the DSS consists of an online GIS framework, a mobile client application, and a multi-sensor IoT node to support this integration. Section 2 presents a high-level architecture for the proposed DSS, whose major components blocks are described in Sects. 3 and 4.

2   A Data Fusion Based DSS High-Level Architecture

A Decision Support System (DSS) that leverages multi-sensor technologies and GIS functionalities is proposed to be a tool for decision-makers to analyze spatial and temporal data to take effective decisions during wildfires. Figure 2 shows the general architecture of the presented DSS.

This DSS is divided into three components: (1) a GIS service; (2) a mobile client application; and (3) a portable IoT Multi-Sensor Device:

1. The GIS online service was configured with a set of feature layers that host the relevant operational data which were published as an GIS feature service, allowing its use by several client applications through its Application Programming Interface (API). The available layers are used to store multiple types of data, such as: (i) the obstacles in the road that might affect the route taken by vehicles; (ii) the vehicles position and state, which is represented by different symbology to inform whether a certain vehicle is in a dangerous situation; (iii) the water supply locations; and (iv) fire-front severity and their location. The data is stored on a GIS database for

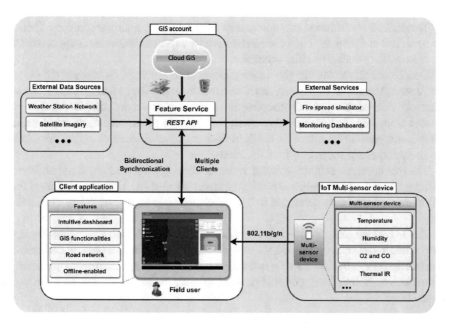

Fig. 2. The proposed DSS architecture.

later analysis and fire reproduction, allowing the decision makers to study the effect of their strategies. These layers can be easily and centrally configured and according to the user needs.

2. The mobile client application is the gateway to access all the operational data on the GIS online service, providing the user with GIS functionality to analyze and manage this type of data. This application contains visualization dashboards to facilitate the decision-making process, as well as alerts that warns the user about certain events. Finally, a road network dataset is configured in a local file geodatabase resident in the client application device's storage. The application generates routes between multiple places and find the shortest path to the nearest water supply location. All the work done on the client application is stored on a local sync-enabled file geodatabase that can be periodically synchronized with the GIS online webservice.

3. The IoT Multi-Sensor Device provides critical sensor data and gives insight about the current circumstances of the theatre of operations. Its main objective is to geolocate firefighting vehicles, whilst monitoring parameters such as temperature, humidity, oxygen and carbon monoxide concentrations inside the vehicle and the temperature surrounding it. It also collects remote sensed infrared data to create thermal images from scanning the region affected by a wildfire during the aftermath analysis. The client application generates alerts based on this sensor data that can be a lifesaving in situations, such as, a forest track machine operator working in a low oxygen environment.

The data fusion solution presented aims at aggregating multiple sources of heterogeneous data and display it in a comprehensive way to be an important support tool for decision-makers during wildfire scenarios.

Data fusion allows the merging of multiple and heterogeneous sources of data to produce a more consistent, organized, and accurate information by reducing redundancy and uncertainty on the data [16]. By coupling the derived information from the multiple data sources alongside the empirical knowledge of wildfire management, decision-makers can use this system as a tool to enhance their situational awareness and take faster, comprehensive, and more informed decisions.

The core component of this solution is the mobile application where users can interact with the system and visualize the relevant operational data. This application gathers multiple sources of data being the IoT Multi-Sensor Device one of the key sources of data.

The IoT Multi-Sensor node is integrated in the system in such a way that leverages both its multi-sensor technologies, with the available mobile device sensors and network interface to form a unified sensing node. By using the existing smartphone platform, it can act as a complementary portable gateway to relay the IoT Multi-Sensor node's data to the server.

3 Mobile Application

The Mobile Client Application is the core component of the proposed DSS that aggregates all the relevant data and functionality in a practical User Interface (UI). An initial assessment was made to gather the necessary requirements based on the end-user's feedback to which the system's architecture was designed around.

Figure 3 shows the key features implemented in the Mobile Client Application as well as the information sources that are jointly processed and correlated.

One of the most important features is the ability to operate offline, since internet connectivity may not always be available on the field, thus potentially undermining an effective and fast operational response. To achieve this goal, a workflow that includes a data synchronization step is designed to enable a seamless user experience in both online and offline environments.

As mentioned, a synchronization mobile geodatabase is created from a sync-enabled GIS online service that is stored locally on the mobile device, allowing the user to work offline by editing the geodatabase locally and later synchronizing its changes with the service. While offline, the mobile geodatabase keeps track of local edits that are later synchronized with the service, and changes made on the service by other users can also be received when the device is back online. The main advantages of this type of workflow are: not be dependent on a continuous internet connectivity, and not having to pre-plan map areas ahead of time to take them offline onto the mobile device, thus improving the system's flexibility.

By leveraging the GIS technology, we could also implement key functionalities that enable the user to create, manage and store spatial and non-spatial data. To achieve this, the ArcGIS Runtime SDK for Android is used [17], which provides a set of tools and documentation to implement the necessary features in a customized application.

Fig. 3. The mobile client application key features.

An GIS webservice is created through a data schema that was designed for the user requirements, to provide all the necessary operational data that is stored in the user account. This enables the establishment of a collaborative environment, where multiple users can be working on the same data, which is critical during wildfires,

A custom road Network Dataset was also created for the terrain knowledge (in this case from the Municipality of Mação in Portugal) that allows users to generate routes between multiple locations in this region, thus enabling to find the shortest path to the closest water supply locations. By incorporating a dynamic component, this feature allows generating routes according to the conditions of the road network. This is particularly important during wildfires since certain roads cannot be crossed due to the fire front being nearby or existing fallen trees or holes in the road. In this scenario, routes are calculated taking into consideration these dynamic factors that will avoid putting firefighters in dangerous situations and speed-up the operational response.

Finally, an intuitive and easy-to-use user interface (UI) is the key for allowing users to quickly navigate through the system and assess the situation on the field. This requires a comprehensive data visualization experience for the user, to provide location awareness and accelerate the planning of effective strategies to suppress wildfires. To meet this requirement, the UI is organized into three areas:

- Alerts area, allows the user to get access to alerts about vehicles in danger or abnormal sensor readings from the IoT Multi-Sensor Device that could indicate the presence of dangerous situations.

- Map area, displays a map and provides GIS functionalities that allow the user to manipulate geographical data associated with the map such as adding, editing or deleting features, adding or removing attachments, generating routes between locations.
- Data Visualization area, allows the visualization of data from features on the map such as sensor readings from the IoT Multi-Sensor Device and information about the vehicles on the field. It also provides relevant statistics such as the number of vehicles.

To address the limitation of the mobile platform screen dimensions, three tabs were implemented to display each of the three areas mentioned above on smartphone's UI. Figure 4 shows the Mobile Client Application UI with visualization tabs.

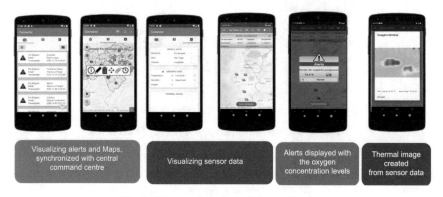

Fig. 4. The user interface of the application.

To provide the network dataset to the client application there were two options to be considered: the first option was to provide it through a web service that would require an internet connection upon its use; the second option was to be available through a geodatabase on the device. Considering that the internet connectivity may not always be available, the network dataset was provided through a geodatabase on the local device's storage.

The application lets the user find the closest water supply spot on the map relative to his location. These water supply spots are represented in a particular Feature Layer and classified by either fixed water supply, which includes lakes, damns or reservoirs, or mobile water supply such as pump trucks. To generate a route, it is important to consider the existence of obstacles such as fallen trees. A Feature Layer was created to contain them and is used to determine the closest water supply point.

In Fig. 5 it is evident the impact of existing obstacles on the road that will yield a different path generated. By introducing this dynamic component, users can have access to an updated road network according to real-time conditions that should prevent them from wasting time that is a critical resource during a wildfire and may be the difference between having a wildfire under control or not. Moreover, this feature could potentially avoid firefighters from getting into life-threatening scenarios such as what happened in

Pedrógão Grande, Portugal in 2017 [18]. Further work will be conducted to parameterize the Network Dataset according to the type of vehicle, considering a vehicle's dimension and weight when calculating paths to avoid going through impassable roads for certain vehicles.

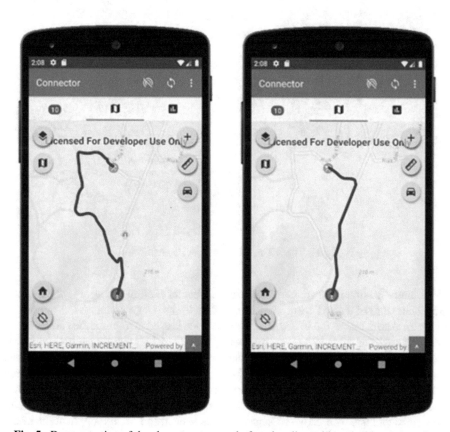

Fig. 5. Demonstration of the closest water supply functionality: with and without obstacles.

4   The CPS-IoT Multi-sensor Node

The role of this node is to provide local field sensor data that can help decision-makers not only assess the circumstances in the field and the state of the firefighting assets but also to outline strategies to mitigate the effects of wildfires. It provides important data to simulate fire propagation according to the weather conditions and detect reignition spots by scanning the region affected by a wildfire during the aftermath analysis.

The presented IoT multi-sensor node has three main operating modes which can provide critical data for generating alerts to ensure both the vehicle and its crew's safety (Alarm mode), acquire thermal data to find potential re-ignition spots in the aftermath of a wildfire (Thermal Mapping mode) and provide local weather data that will help

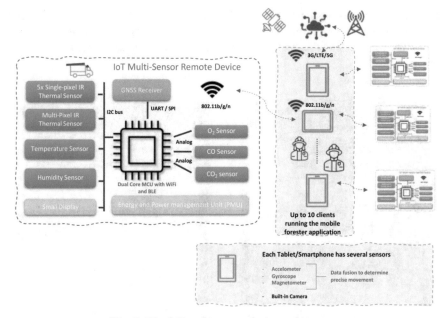

Fig. 6. The IoT multi-sensor device architecture.

obtain more accurate fire spread simulations (Weather Station mode). Figure 6 shows the architecture of the IoT Multi-Sensor Device with its components.

In the Alarm mode, the IoT Multi-Sensor Device is used to monitor the vehicle's surrounding environment and its crew by sensing the CO and O_2 gas concentrations inside and outside the vehicle, the O_2 gas concentrations on the vehicle's engine admission, and the temperatures surrounding the vehicle. A group of single-pixel thermal infrared (IR) sensors is used to monitor the temperatures surrounding the vehicle. Having these multiple sensors equally spaced makes it possible to get a 360° coverage of the vehicle's surroundings. The acquired sensor data is sent to the mobile application where corresponding alerts are generated. A low O_2 gas concentration on the vehicle's engine admission may affect its operability potentially putting the vehicle and even its crew in a dangerous situation. On the other hand, a low O_2 and high CO gas concentrations inside the vehicle's cabin can cause the crew to pass out or even put their lives at risk, therefore it is essential to leverage this system to ensure both humans and equipment safety in an ever dynamic and dangerous scenario such as in a wildfire.

In the Thermal Mapping mode, the IoT Multi-Sensor node is used to acquire thermal data from areas affected by wildfires in the aftermath of these events, to find possible reignition spots. To achieve this, the IoT Multi-Sensor Device is equipped with a 768-pixel thermal IR sensor capable of detecting a 24×32 matrix of spot temperatures to build a thermal image. This data is sent to the mobile application where it is used to generate a colored map that facilitates the identification of hot spots. Upon their detection, firefighters can quickly intervene to avoid a potential reignition.

In the Weather Station mode, the IoT Multi-Sensor node is used to measure weather parameters such as the air temperature and humidity, the concentration of O_2 gas, and the wind direction and speed. This data is sent to the mobile application and can be used to perform more accurate fire spread simulations. By having a local weather station on the wildfire locations, fire spread simulators can use more reliable data that may consider the local microclimate created by extreme wildfires. This will theoretically lead to more accurate predictions of the wildfire's expected trajectory and, simultaneously, determine the risk areas for its spread.

The IoT Multi-Sensor node is built around the ESP32 microcontroller (MCU) [19] to which all the sensors are connected and providing sensor data to connected clients. The ESP32 MCU is configured to work as a web server in the softAP mode. In this mode, it acts as an Access Point (AP) that supports up to 10 clients and provides a JSON-encoded message containing real-time sensor measurements from the sensors onboard. The mobile client application connects to this AP and performs a GET request periodically to its web server that returns the updated JSON message with the sensor's measurements. All the data post-processing is conducted on the mobile application. This device is prepared to be reconfigurable allowing the easy integration of more sensors.

As referred before, the CPS-IoT Multi-Sensor node hosts a temperature and humidity sensor, a GNSS receiver to acquire the device's location, a CO and O_2 sensors to measure gas concentrations, a multi-pixel and 5 single-pixel IR sensors to measure and map the surrounding temperature. The validation of the IoT Multi-Sensor node focused on assessing the reliability of the multi-pixel IR thermal sensor.

This sensor produces 768 temperature values organized into a 24 × 32 matrix that go through an initial pre-processing phase where a non-uniform mean filter is applied to the data that gives greater weight to pixels closer to the center and less weight to the border pixels that are more susceptible to noise, resulting in a more homogeneous image. Furthermore, in this phase the undetermined values are removed by using an algorithm that detects their presence in pixels and replaces those pixel values with the mean value of the surrounding pixels. After the pre-processing phase, the sensor was put to test in a prepared scenario using a controlled fire. Several tests were conducted to know the impact of speed and distance to the heat source in the measurement quality. Initially, measurements were taken to determine the impact of distance in the sensor granularity. As expected, the greater the distance the lesser prominent was the heat source in the resulting image. The second phase of test focused on assessing the impact of both distance and speed on the detection of heat sources.

The results of these tests present on Fig. 7 show that the greater the speed and distance the more significant the impact on the heat source identification accuracy, nevertheless, it demonstrates that the chosen multi-pixel IR thermal sensor performs well under these test conditions. The last component of its validation was to test the connection with the mobile client application that worked seamlessly thus validating this system component.

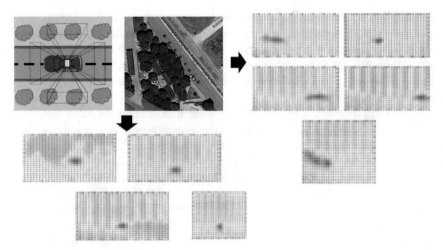

Fig. 7. Experiment conducted at a distance of 20 m from the heat source (a) with no movement, and (b) moving at 30 km/h.

5 Conclusions

A system for effective wildfire firefighting demands the evolution of the simplistic IoT sensor network approach into a Cyber-Physical System with smart data fusion. In addition, given the difficulty of guaranteeing continuous network communication in the field, it is necessary to provide enough processing, sensing and local communication to the remote fire brigade. To respond to the latter requirement, the CPS must reinforce the computing capability at the edge.

In this paper an example Cyber-Physical System is presented which consists on a DSS adapted to the Portuguese wildfire firefighting. Several modules are integrated to support the firefighting operational management and decision making. The system has been validated in a controlled environment, showing the effectiveness of the proposed solution for supporting decision making in a fire suppression context.

The integration of multi-sensor technologies alongside the mobile client application sensors and functionalities has proven to provide major value in leveraging the mobile device's network capabilities and redundancy with the IoT Multi-Sensor node flexibility in adding new sensors that not only allow the user to have access to information in the field but also this data can be used to improve local fire spread simulations. This implementation does not require to have a WSN put in place enabling the flexibility of having a single node already installed in the firefighter's vehicle to which they can connect locally to its network with their mobile device running the mobile client application and get its data.

Acknowledgements. This work was financially supported by FCT (National Foundation of Science and Technology) within the Research Unit CTS – Centre of Technology and Systems, UIDB/00066/2020, and the Project foRESTER (PCIF/SSI/0102/2017 - 400k€ total budget, http://www.forester.pt.

References

1. Nazarenko, A.A., Camarinha-Matos, L.M.: Towards collaborative cyber-physical systems. In: 2017 International Young Engineers Forum (YEF-ECE), pp. 12–17 (2017). https://doi.org/10.1109/YEF-ECE.2017.7935633
2. Ferreira-Leite, F., Ganho, N., Bento-Gonçalves, A., Botelho, F.: Iberian atmospheric dynamics and large forest fires in mainland Portugal. Agric. For. Meteorol. **247**, 551–559 (2017). https://doi.org/10.1016/j.agrformet.2017.08.033
3. Pultar, E., Raubal, M., Cova, T.J., Goodchild, M.F.: Dynamic GIS case studies: wildfire evacuation and volunteered geographic information. Trans. GIS **13**(s1), 85–104 (2009). https://doi.org/10.1111/j.1467-9671.2009.01157.x
4. Smith, A.K., Dragićević, S.: A four-dimensional agent-based model: a case study of forest-fire smoke propagation. Trans. GIS **18**, 715–723 (2019). https://doi.org/10.1111/tgis.12551
5. Sakellariou, S., Tampekis, S., Samara, F., Sfougaris, A., Christopoulou, O.: Review of state-of-the-art decision support systems (DSSs) for prevention and suppression of forest fires. J. Forest. Res. **28**(6), 1107–1117 (2017). https://doi.org/10.1007/s11676-017-0452-1
6. Abedi Gheshlaghi, H., Feizizadeh, B., Blaschke, T., Lakes, T., Tajbar, S.: Forest fire susceptibility modeling using hybrid approaches. Trans. GIS **25**, 1–23 (2020). https://doi.org/10.1111/tgis.12688
7. Kalabokidis, K., et al.: Virtual fire: a web-based GIS platform for forest fire control. Eco. Inform. **16**, 62–69 (2013). https://doi.org/10.1016/j.ecoinf.2013.04.007
8. Kalabokidis, K., Ager, A., Finney, M., Athanasis, N., Palaiologou, P., Vasilakos, C.: AEGIS: a wildfire prevention and management information system. Nat. Hazards Earth Syst. Sci. **16**(3), 643–661 (2016). https://doi.org/10.5194/nhess-16-643-2016
9. Noble, P., Paveglio, T.B.: Exploring adoption of the Wildland fire decision support system: end user perspectives. J. Forest. **118**(2), 154–171 (2020). https://doi.org/10.1093/jofore/fvz070
10. Noonan-Wright, E.K., et al.: Developing the US Wildland fire decision support system. J. Comb. **2011**, 1–15 (2011). https://doi.org/10.1155/2011/168473
11. Curva, J., et al.: Infrared fire alarm for vehicle protection. In: International Young Engineers Forum (YEF-ECE) Costa da Caparica, Portugal, pp. 19−24 (2020). https://doi.org/10.1109/YEF-ECE49388.2020.9171813
12. Abdullah, S., Bertalan, S., Masar, S., Coskun, A., Kale, I.: A wireless sensor network for early forest fire detection and monitoring as a decision factor in the context of a complex integrated emergency response system. In: 2017 IEEE Workshop on Environmental, Energy, and Structural Monitoring Systems (EESMS). IEEE (2017)
13. Zhu, Y., Xie, L., Yuan, T.: Monitoring system for forest fire based on wireless sensor network. In: Proceedings of the 10th World Congress on Intelligent Control and Automation. IEEE (2012)
14. Gandia, A., Criado, A., Rallo, M.: El Sistema BOSQUE, Alta Tecnologia en Defensa del Medio Ambiente. DYNA, pp. 34–38, n. 6 (1994)
15. Laurenti, A., Neri, A.: Remote sensing, communications and information technologies for vegetation fire emergencies. In: Proceedings of TIEMEC 1996, Montreal (1996)
16. Girão, P.S., Postolache, O., Pereira, J.M.D.: Data fusion, decision-making, and risk analysis: mathematical tools and techniques. In: Pavese, F., Forbes, A.B. (eds.) Data Modeling for Metrology and Testing in Measurement Science, pp. 1–50. Birkhäuser Boston, Boston (2009). https://doi.org/10.1007/978-0-8176-4804-6_7
17. ArcGIS Developers: ArcGIS Runtime API for Android (2021). https://developers.arcgis.com/android/. Accessed 18 June 2021

18. Comissão Técnica Independente: Análise e apuramento dos factos relativos aos incêndios que ocorreram em Pedrógão Grande, Castanheira de Pera, Ansião, Alvaiázere, Figueiró dos Vinhos, Arganil, Góis, Penela, Pampilhosa da Serra, Oleiros e Sertã, entre 17 e 24 de junho de 2017 (2017). https://www.parlamento.pt/Documents/2017/Outubro/Relat%C3%B3rioCTI_VF%20.pdf. Accessed 18 June 2021
19. Espressif Systems: ESP32-WROOM-32 Datasheet, Ver. 3.1 (2021). https://www.espressif.com/sites/default/files/documentation/esp32-wroom-32_datasheet_en.pdf. Accessed 18 June 2021

Drones as Sound Sensors
for Energy-Based Acoustic Tracking
on Wildfire Environments

Sérgio D. Correia[1,2]([✉]), João Fé[1,2], Slavisa Tomic[1], and Marko Beko[1,3]

[1] COPELABS, Universidade Lusófona de Humanidades e Tecnologias,
1749-024 Lisbon, Portugal
[2] VALORIZA, Instituto Politécnico de Portalegre,
Campus Politécnico n.10, 7300-555 Portalegre, Portugal
`scorreia@ipportalegre.pt`
[3] Instituto de Telecominicações, Instituto Superior Técnico, Universidade de Lisboa,
1049-001 Lisbon, Portugal

Abstract. The present work proposes a method for continuous localization of a moving acoustic source based on energy measurements in the application of detecting/preventing wildfires. The main focus is on the case in which the acoustic sensors are located on a drone, i.e., when they are also in motion. This localization setting is more challenging than the classical one in which the sensors are typically static (anchors) or have slow dynamics compared with the source. The proposed solution consists of an extended Kalman filter (EKF) that deals with non-linearities and singularities in the acoustic observation model, as well as the dynamic trajectory of the sensors. Performed simulations corroborate its feasibility in different noisy environments and illustrate its superiority over techniques that do not consider process states' prior knowledge.

Keywords: Acoustic source tracking · Energy-based localization · Kalman filter · Wildfire detection/Prevention

1 Introduction

The use of Unmanned Aerial Vehicles (UAVs) has gained considerable prominence given their success in simple domestic applications [14] or critical military operations [15]. They find several applications such as border control [2], coast patrol [24], fire perimeter monitoring [23], search and rescue [18], among several other examples that could be mentioned. More than automatizing labor or reducing operational costs in the referred contexts, UAVs can accomplish dangerous tasks for human operators or reach inaccessible regions. With regard to wildfire environments, UAVs can be used for monitoring [21], detection [19] or prediction [20], being increasingly present in a fire-fighting scenario.

© IFIP International Federation for Information Processing 2022
Published by Springer Nature Switzerland AG 2022
L. M. Camarinha-Matos et al. (Eds.): IFIPIoT 2021, IFIP AICT 641, pp. 109–125, 2022.
https://doi.org/10.1007/978-3-030-96466-5_8

From the point of view of communications, sharing, and data management, the *Internet of Things* (IoT) has emerged as an aggregating concept, both in terms of communication networks and in terms of data management and manipulation [1,13,29]. The term IoT does not refer to technology but rather to a general concept that embraces different techniques and ideas, with profound implications for professional activities and life in society. It can be considered as: *an arrangement of interconnected objects, consisting of electronics, software, sensors, and actuators, which handle and transmit information to a wide network infrastructure and between each other.* Thus, IoT brings connectivity, portability, and distributed processing, dramatically increasing the processing capacity and its architectures, allowing the emergence of a whole set of new applications.

Bearing in mind the usage of drones in a fire-fighting scenario and the IoT paradigm, the present work considers performing an energy-based acoustic localization as an add-on to existing architectures that employ drones for fire-fighting support. The new feature uses communication capabilities already in place to send acoustic information to an edge or centralized data processing stage. The sound location information may therefore be forwarded to rescue teams available in the terrain. However, the present problem introduces certain complexity given that both the acoustic source and the sensors (or microphones) are in motion. Furthermore, it is considered that the trajectory of the drones, and therefore the location of the acoustic sensors, are not controlled by the location platform, preventing, for instance, the creation of an ideal path for the acquisition of location data.

To address the motion problem and account for the highly non-linear decay model of the acoustic energy, an Extended Kalman Filter (EKF) is envisioned and implemented. The locations of the acoustic sensors (or anchors that are usually assumed known) will consist of a provided discretized path along the search-space. Several simulation conditions are created concerning the signal-noise-ratio (SNR) of the measures and the number of available drones in the range of the sound source. With those conditions, it is intended to demonstrate that acoustic energy can be a reliable measure to accomplish sound localization, retaining the advantages of being of a simple acquisition technique (it does not require complex additional hardware).

It is worth mentioning that the proposed scenarios configure a problem that, to the best of authors' knowledge, has not been considered in the scientific literature, which is: besides the dynamics of the acoustic yet moving target and the intrinsic simplicity of employing acoustic energy measures, the sensors are also mobile. Thus, the proposed solution can be seen to support computer vision systems at locations obstructed by smoke screens or dense vegetation, detection of help requests, or tracking of physical means.

The remainder of this work is organized as follows. Section 2 summarizes previous related work, and Sect. 3 formulates and characterizes the energy-based acoustic localization problem on the wildfire scenario. Section 4 describes the proposed methodology, while Sect. 5 presents and discusses simulation results. Finally, Sect. 6 concludes the work.

2 Related Work

2.1 UAVs for Wildfire Detection, Prevention and Monitoring

Considering the past few years, several solutions based on data acquisition provided by UAVs have been proposed for wildfire prevention, prediction, and monitoring. Sensing capacity based on weather sensors data (temperature, humidity, CO, or CO_2) are used to feed certain prediction model which in turn is processed, proving alerts for early detection or for analyzing the fire front evolution [22]. In such cases, the drones act as nodes in a wireless sensor network, and the IoT paradigm is applied to process the information on the edge of the network or in cloud environments [27]. The use of cameras for fire detection is one of the most used techniques. Nevertheless, the image sensor needs to have a visual line-of-sight towards the monitored zone. In an already started fire, both dense vegetation and smoke will prevent visibility to the actors in this scenario, such as firefighters, fire trucks, or even civilians that may need rescuing. In such situations, the possibility of acoustic sensing and consequent localization can be a significant advantage for rescue operations and ground support, for instance, locating people who yell for help. The work presented in [31] considers the problem of controlling the drone's path based on sound localization performed through an array of several microphones, monopolizing the drone's action and weighing the structure and energy consumption with multiple hardware. The use of microphone arrays is a well established technique to obtain directional data to triangulate the source position through sound, with the inconvenience being the requirement for multiple sensors distributed in the body of the drone [30].

The present work stands out with the methods proposed in the literature because it requires only one sound sensor in each drone, obtaining the necessary information for the positioning system by associating sources originating in multiple drones. This way, drones that are already assigned to patrol and rescue missions can easily be supplemented with an acoustic location functionality without significant changes in their structure.

2.2 Acoustic Localization

The localization of an acoustic source has been mainly addressed through range-based methods, where a measure translated into distance is acquired. While works considering time [26] or angle [16] have shown good performance results in terms of the localization error, those methods rely on high precision hardware for timing purposes, or they have to be equipped with an array of microphones, considerably increasing the complexity of the sensors. Considering the present application scenario, i.e., the fact that the necessary parts have to be applied in a moving drone with limited weight and electric power, these methodologies might not be the best solution. As an alternative, the acoustic energy measurement presents itself as an efficient solution, which allows for location of a sound source with light hardware resources and low computational complexity [6,9,10].

Since it was first proposed [12], the energy-based acoustic problem was solved through deterministic approaches [17]. From weighted least-squares, which the

performance is degraded in noisy environments [3], to methods based on semidefinite programming [4], or second-order cone programming [5], that rely on approximating the original problem into a convex optimization one, has demonstrated
robust results, even in noisy environments. More recently, solutions that depend
on metaheuristic approaches, namely on swarm optimization [7,8], showed that,
through intelligent initialization of an initial candidate population, swarm optimization methods could present concurrent results but with low computational
complexity. That is, those methodologies would be adequate to run on embedded
processors, attaining a solution with low latency [9]. The fact that the mentioned
algorithms were tested and evaluated on several different embedded processors [9]
motivated us to use them here as a benchmark for comparison with the proposed
methodology. To this end, Elephant Herding optimization and a weighted least
squares approach (WLS) are used to determine individual solutions considering,
at each time instant, the known position of the drone and its measures in those
exact moments.

3   Problem Formulation and Characterization

The problem envisioned implies to determine a set of positions $x_{t\in\{1,...,T\}} \in \mathbb{R}^2$
(the extrapolation to $\mathbb{R}^3$ is straightforward) of a sound source over some interval
T. As to the acoustic sensors, N drones with pre-determined paths fly over the
search space acquiring the acoustic signals. Both the target and the drone's
path are represented in Fig. 1, where the red dashed line represents the acoustic
source movement over the search-space (represented as a firetruck). The target's
trajectory performs several changes in its direction to analyze response of the
proposed algorithm.

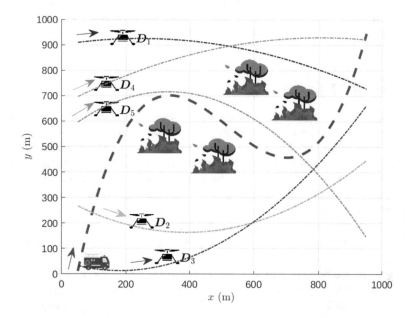

Fig. 1. Drones and target trajectories over the search-space (Color figure online)

The search-space is considered as a square with sides of 1 km, that is, $x \in [0, 1000]$ m and $y \in [0, 1000]$ m in Cartesian space. Also, $N = 5$ drone trajectories (labelled as D_1 to D_5) are shown to create situations of crossing between the trajectories of the drones and the trajectory of the acoustic source. While position control of drones could be considered to improve error in the localization process as in [25], in this case, it would imply subverting the main function of drones. Thus, it is considered that the trajectory is determined as a function of the evolution of the fire front, control of the availability of means, avoidance of smoke columns, etc. The drone trajectories are here considered as parametric equations of time $t \in [50, 950]$ s as:

$$
\begin{cases}
D_1(x,y) = (t, -4 \cdot 10^{-4} \cdot t^2 + 0,2 \cdot t + 900) \\
D_2(x,y) = (t, +9 \cdot 10^{-4} \cdot t^2 - 0,7 \cdot t + 300) \\
D_3(x,y) = (t, +11 \cdot 10^{-4} \cdot t^2 - 0,4 \cdot t + 50) \\
D_4(x,y) = (t, -4 \cdot 10^{-4} \cdot t^2 + 0,65 \cdot t + 665) \\
D_5(x,y) = (t, -15 \cdot 10^{-4} \cdot t^2 + 1,0 \cdot t + 550)
\end{cases}
\tag{1}
$$

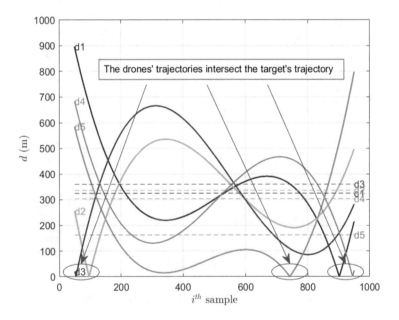

Fig. 2. Drones to target distance over time

To characterize the problem in more detail, namely in terms of the distance between the sensors and the target, Fig. 2 shows the evolution of the distance between each sensor and the target (solid lines), and their mean value over the considered time interval (dashed lines). As it can be seen, there are five intersections between trajectories ($d_i = 0$), several drones fly at distances greater than 500 m (on the XY horizontal plane), and their mean value is around 350 m.

The obtained energy measure at the ith sensor drone D_i is modeled as follows, according to [12]

$$y_i^t = \frac{g_i P_d}{\|x_t - D_i\|^\beta} + \epsilon_i^t, \text{ for } \quad i = 1, 2, \dots, N, \tag{2}$$

where y_i^t is the energy acquired by sensor i at time t, g_i is the sensor gain, P_d is the transmitted power at a reference distance d, β is a decay propagation factor dependent on environment conditions (equal to 2 in free space [4]), x_t is the unknown acoustic source position at instant t, D_i is the position of the sensor i, and $\epsilon_i^t \sim \mathcal{N}(0, \sigma_\epsilon^2)$ is considered as a random zero-mean Gaussian noise, for each link i and time t. For the sake of simplicity, σ_ϵ^2 is considered constant over time and at each sensor link but will be adjusted regarding distance to touch upon the SNR considered at 1 m.

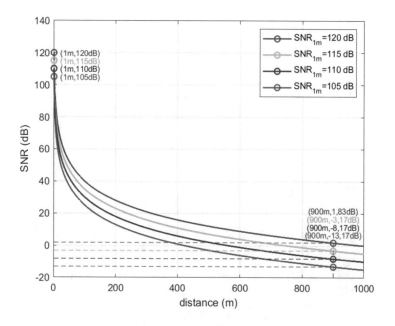

Fig. 3. Considered SNRs function of the distance

With regard to the measurement noise, the energy observations y_i^t are corrupted with an SNR of $(105, 110, 115, 120)$ dB at a reference distance of 1 m. It should be pointed out that, maintaining the SNR constant over the search space (and not the noise level), and highlighting that the energy decays at a rate of $1/d^2$, the true SNR at a given distance is indeed much lower due to the high area of the search-space. Figure 3 shows the decay of the SNR considering its reference value at $1\,\mathrm{m}$. For a distance measurement of $900\,\mathrm{m}$, as with D_1 (see Fig. 2), when considering an SNR_{1m} of $105\,\mathrm{dB}$, its equivalent SNR at $900\,\mathrm{m}$ will be approximately $-13\,\mathrm{dB}$. This situation implies that, given the dimensions of the search-space, noise assumes very significant values for points far from the acoustic source. For the mean values of Fig. 2 ($\approx 350\,\mathrm{m}$), the SNR assume values between $0\,\mathrm{dB}$ and $20\,\mathrm{dB}$.

Lastly, a set of $M_c = 10.000$ measures are generated and corrupted for each instant t through the parametric equation (3) (red dashed line on Fig. 1), being the simulations carried out over M_c Monte Carlo runs.

$$x_{(x,y)} = (t, 10^{-5} \cdot (t - 520)^3 - (t - 300) + 800), \quad \text{for} \quad t \in [50, 950] \quad (3)$$

4   the Proposed Methodology

The Bayesian theory, which integrates information given by observations with prior knowledge, extracted from some target motion model, is one of the major tools applied when considering target tracking [11, 28]. In the present situation, since the measurement model is non-linear, an EKF is employed. To this end, let $\boldsymbol{\theta}_t = [\boldsymbol{x}_t^T, \boldsymbol{v}_t^T]^T$ denote the target state at some instant t, with $\boldsymbol{v}_t \in \mathbb{R}^2$ denoting the target velocity at time instant t (as mentioned, the generalization to $\mathbb{R}^3$ is straightforward). When considering a constant velocity motion model, a state transition matrix $\boldsymbol{S}$ can be defined through (4), in such a way that the state $\boldsymbol{\theta}_{t+1}$ is obtained from $\boldsymbol{\theta}_t$. The term $\boldsymbol{r}_t$ represents the noise perturbations and follows a Gaussian distribution with zero-mean and covariance $\boldsymbol{Q}$, i.e., $\boldsymbol{r}_t \sim \mathcal{N}(\boldsymbol{0}, \boldsymbol{Q})$.

$$\boldsymbol{\theta}_{t+1} = \boldsymbol{S}\boldsymbol{\theta}_t + \boldsymbol{r}_t \quad (4)$$

The matrices $\boldsymbol{S}$ and $\boldsymbol{Q}$ are defined as:

$$\boldsymbol{S} = \begin{bmatrix} 1 & 0 & \Delta & 0 \\ 0 & 1 & 0 & \Delta \\ 0 & 0 & 1 & 0 \\ 0 & 0 & 0 & 1 \end{bmatrix}, \quad \boldsymbol{Q} = q \begin{bmatrix} \frac{\Delta^3}{3} & 0 & \frac{\Delta^2}{2} & 0 \\ 0 & \frac{\Delta^3}{3} & 0 & \frac{\Delta^2}{2} \\ \frac{\Delta^2}{2} & 0 & \Delta & 0 \\ 0 & \frac{\Delta^2}{2} & 0 & \Delta \end{bmatrix}, \quad (5)$$

where q denotes the state process noise intensity [28].

A measurement $\boldsymbol{z}_t$ of the state $\boldsymbol{\theta}_t$ is made according to $\boldsymbol{z}_t = \boldsymbol{h}(\boldsymbol{\theta}_t) + \boldsymbol{\epsilon}_t$, where the $\boldsymbol{z}_t$ corresponds to the measured energies $\boldsymbol{y}^t$ and $\boldsymbol{\epsilon}_t \sim \mathcal{N}(\boldsymbol{0}, \boldsymbol{R})$ the measurement noise, with $\boldsymbol{R}$ being a covariance matrix composed by the energies variance σ_ϵ^2:

$$\boldsymbol{R} = \begin{bmatrix} \sigma_\epsilon^2 & & \\ & \ddots & \\ & & \sigma_\epsilon^2 \end{bmatrix} \in \mathbb{R}^{N \times N}, \quad (6)$$

and the observation model $\boldsymbol{h}(\boldsymbol{\theta}_t)$ set as:

$$h_i(\boldsymbol{\theta}_t) = \frac{g_i P_d}{\|\boldsymbol{\theta}_{t_{1:2}} - \boldsymbol{D}_i\|^2}, \quad \text{for} \quad i = 1, 2, \ldots, N. \quad (7)$$

Since the EKF approximates the non-linear model by its first-order Taylor series expansion, the Jacobian matrix of (7) with respect to $\boldsymbol{\theta}_t$ is defined as:

$$\mathbf{J}_h = \frac{\partial \boldsymbol{h}}{\partial \boldsymbol{\theta}_t} = \begin{bmatrix} \dfrac{-2g_1 P_d(\boldsymbol{\theta}_{t_1} - \boldsymbol{s}_{1,x})}{\|\boldsymbol{\theta}_{t_{1:2}} - \boldsymbol{s}_1\|^4} & \dfrac{-2g_1 P_d(\boldsymbol{\theta}_{t_2} - \boldsymbol{s}_{1,y})}{\|\boldsymbol{\theta}_{t_{1:2}} - \boldsymbol{s}_1\|^4} & 0 & 0 \\ \vdots & \vdots & \vdots & \vdots \\ \dfrac{-2g_N P_d(\boldsymbol{\theta}_{t_1} - \boldsymbol{s}_{N,x})}{\|\boldsymbol{\theta}_{t_{1:2}} - \boldsymbol{s}_N\|^4} & \dfrac{-2g_N P_d(\boldsymbol{\theta}_{t_2} - \boldsymbol{s}_{N,y})}{\|\boldsymbol{\theta}_{t_{1:2}} - \boldsymbol{s}_N\|^4} & 0 & 0 \end{bmatrix}. \qquad (8)$$

Then, the EKF can be implemented as shown in Algorithm 1, where two issues are beyond the standard EKF, that is the calculation of the initial state $\hat{\boldsymbol{\theta}}_{1|1}$, and the treatment of trajectory intersections.

Algorithm 1. The proposed extended Kalman filter

Require: $\boldsymbol{Q}$, $\boldsymbol{S}$, $\boldsymbol{R}$
1: **Starting State** $(t = 1)$:
2:    $\hat{\boldsymbol{x}}_t \leftarrow$ solve (9) for $\boldsymbol{y}^t$ via iEHO [7]
3:    $\hat{\boldsymbol{\theta}}_{t|t} = [\hat{\boldsymbol{x}}_t^T, 0, 0]^T$ ▷ Set unknown velocity to $\boldsymbol{0}$
4:    $\hat{\boldsymbol{P}}_{t|t} = \boldsymbol{I}_4$
5: **for** $t = 2, 3, \ldots, T$ **do**
6:    $i = \arg\max_{i \in \{1, \ldots, N\}} y_i^t$
7:    **if** $y_i^t > \xi$ **then**
8:       $\hat{\boldsymbol{\theta}}_{t|t} = [\boldsymbol{D}_i, [\hat{\boldsymbol{\theta}}_{t|t}]_{3:4}^T]^T$ ▷ A high energy measure means the source is most probably close to the drone that acquired this measurement
9:    **else**
10:      **Prediction:**
11:         $\hat{\boldsymbol{\theta}}_{t|t-1} = \boldsymbol{S}\hat{\boldsymbol{\theta}}_{t-1|t-1}$
12:         $\hat{\boldsymbol{P}}_{t|t-1} = \boldsymbol{S}\hat{\boldsymbol{P}}_{t-1|t-1}\boldsymbol{S}^T + \boldsymbol{Q}$
13:      **Update:**
14:         $\boldsymbol{H}_t = \mathbf{J}_h(\hat{\boldsymbol{\theta}}_{t|t-1})$
15:         $\boldsymbol{K} = \hat{\boldsymbol{P}}_{t|t-1}\boldsymbol{H}_t^T(\boldsymbol{H}_t\hat{\boldsymbol{P}}_{t|t-1}\boldsymbol{H}_t^T + \boldsymbol{R})^{-1}$
16:         $\hat{\boldsymbol{\theta}}_{t|t} = \hat{\boldsymbol{\theta}}_{t|t-1} + \boldsymbol{K}(\boldsymbol{y}^t - \boldsymbol{h}(\hat{\boldsymbol{\theta}}_{t|t-1}))$
17:         $\hat{\boldsymbol{P}}_{t|t} = (\boldsymbol{I}_4 - \boldsymbol{K}\boldsymbol{H}_t)\hat{\boldsymbol{P}}_{t|t-1}$
18:    **end if**
19: **end for**

With regard to the filter implementation details the filter's initialization is performed by solving a WLS problem, considering the initial point measurements only and a metaheuristic approach (further explanations in Eq. 9). Also, the problem is treated when the drone trajectory crosses the target trajectory, which may imply singularities in the decay of the acoustic model. Due to its linear approximations, the EKF becomes unstable when the order of energy measures increases abruptly (which happens when a drone gets close to the acoustic target). To prevent the EKF from diverging, a special condition is evaluated before each iteration of the filter. This condition tests if any of the measured energies at the current time instant is greater than a threshold ξ. If it evaluates to true that EKF iteration is passed over, and instead the estimated position of the source is updated to the position of the drone that measured the high energy, while the estimated velocity and the process covariance matrix remain unchanged. Considering the energy decay model, one can see that, for a high threshold ξ, estimating the source current position as the current position of the drone will not be too erroneous. In particular, considering a threshold $\xi = 300$, $g_i = 100$ and $P = 20$, the estimated position of the acoustic source is assumed as the position of the drone $\boldsymbol{D}_i$ whenever the drone is at an estimated distance $\tilde{d} = \sqrt{\frac{g_i P}{y_i}} \approx 2.58\,\text{m}$ or less from the target source (meaning that the expected tracking error during that time is equal or less to 2.58 m).

With the purpose of evaluating and comparing the performance of the proposed methodology, a WLS approach is defined as (and summarized in Algorithm 2):

$$\hat{\boldsymbol{x}}_t = \arg\min_{\boldsymbol{x}_t} \sum_{i=1}^{N} w_i^t \left(y_i^t - \frac{g_i P_d}{\|\boldsymbol{x}_t - \boldsymbol{D}_i\|^2} \right)^2, \tag{9}$$

where weight, $w_i^t = \dfrac{\tilde{d}_i^{t^{-1}}}{\sum_{i=1}^{N} \left(\tilde{d}_i^{t^{-1}} \right)}$ (with $\tilde{d}_i^t = \sqrt{\frac{g_i P_d}{y_i^t}}$), imputes more importance to energies measured by closer sensors (based on the distance estimate). The estimator (9) is highly non-convex, non-linear, and non-continuous with singularities at $\boldsymbol{D}_i$, making gradient-based optimizers likely to converge to local optimums. However, when employing metaheuristics to solve the Algorithm 2, in particular the Improved Elephant Herding Optimizer (iEHO), it is possible to obtain good results for acoustic source localization problem [7,9].

Algorithm 2. Series of T localizations by WLS

1: **for** $t = 1, 2, \ldots, T$ **do**
2:     $\hat{\boldsymbol{x}}_t \leftarrow$ solve (9) for $\boldsymbol{y}^t$ via iEHO [7]
3: **end for**

It's worth remembering that the drone trajectories $(D_{(x_i,y_i)})$ are predetermined based on features related to the wildfire dynamics. Those would have the purpose of collecting information for the fire front prediction, providing communications links for ground teams, etc. Bottom line, the trajectories are not controlled by the acoustic localization system; instead, they are distributed among the space, to cover the wildfire environment, independent of the current location of the acoustic source, and with no information about its maneuvers.

5   Results and Discussion

To validate the proposed method and evaluate its performances, several simulations were carried on both the EKF algorithm and the WLS counterpart.

The results shown in this section include the performances of the methods considering three typologies for the sensors drone, that is $N \in \{3, 4, 5\}$, four different SNRs $(120, 115, 110, 105)$ dB, $q = 0, 6 \, \mathrm{m}^2/\mathrm{s}^3$, $\Delta = 1 \, \mathrm{s}$, each evaluated for $Mc = 10.000$ runs. The model parameters were $P = 20$, $g_i = 100$ (for $i = 1, \ldots, N$), and $\beta = 2$. The simulations were performed using MATLAB® R2020b, on a machine with an AMD Ryzen™ 3 3100 quad-core processor at 3.6 GHz, with 16 GB of RAM, and Ubuntu 18.04.4 LTS (Linux kernel 5.4.0) operating system.

The results are made up of two sets of metrics. Figures 5, 7, and 9 plot the mean error (distance between the real and estimated target position) over the Mc runs for $N = 3$, $N = 4$, and $N = 5$ respectively. The dashed constant line and the value overlapping the graph correspond to the plot's mean over the all trajectory. Additionally, Figs. 4, 6, and 8 represents the mean trajectory obtained over the Mc runs. The shaded areas in Figs. 4, 6, and 8 illustrate the standard deviation of the trajectory for the M_c runs. This area is the union of T ellipses, where half the width of the tth ellipse is equal to the standard deviation (of M_c runs) in x axis of the tth point of the trajectory. Also, half the height of the ellipse is equal to the standard deviation in y axis of the tth point of the trajectory, and the center of the ellipse is at the tth point of the mean trajectory. These figures also present the drones' trajectories (dashed lines) to seek correlations with the shape of the graph. Finally, Table 1 resumes the overall mean error for the considered scenarios.

Table 1. Summary of the mean error (ME) obtained for the overall trajectories.

N (number of drones)	SNR_{1m} (dB)	ME_{WLS} (m)	ME_{EKF} (m)
3	105	91,499	53,170
	110	65,215	30,893
	115	45,752	29,053
	120	34,272	26,900
4	105	42,473	27,938
	110	34,491	24,758
	115	30,483	24,737
	120	25,097	20,298
5	105	20,215	20,254
	110	15,605	15,733
	115	12,518	11,638
	120	9,744	8,532

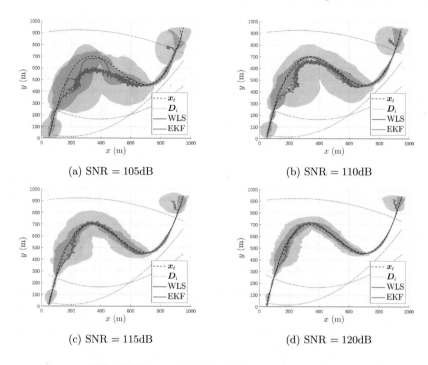

Fig. 4. Mean trajectory of M_c runs for $N = 3$.

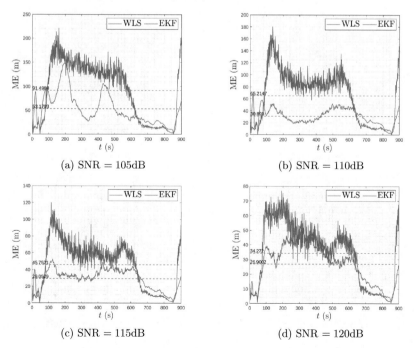

Fig. 5. Mean error of M_c runs for $N = 3$.

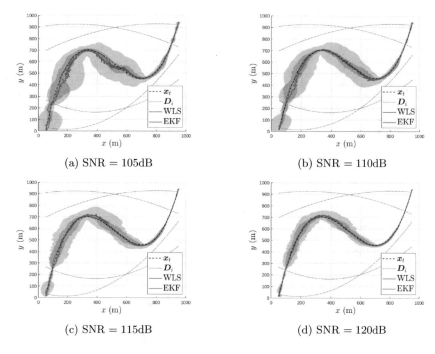

(a) SNR = 105dB   (b) SNR = 110dB

(c) SNR = 115dB   (d) SNR = 120dB

Fig. 6. Mean trajectory of M_c runs for $N = 4$.

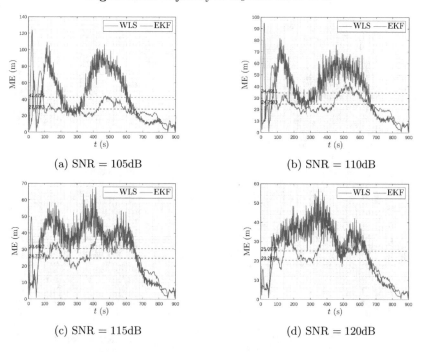

(a) SNR = 105dB   (b) SNR = 110dB

(c) SNR = 115dB   (d) SNR = 120dB

Fig. 7. Mean error of M_c runs for $N = 4$.

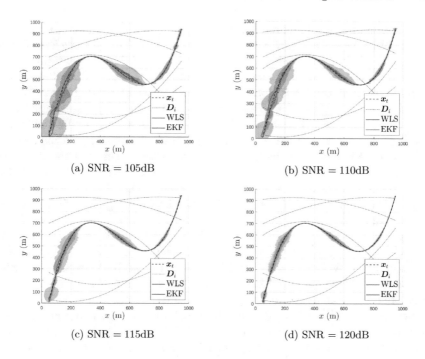

(a) SNR = 105dB

(b) SNR = 110dB

(c) SNR = 115dB

(d) SNR = 120dB

Fig. 8. Mean trajectory of M_c runs for $N = 5$.

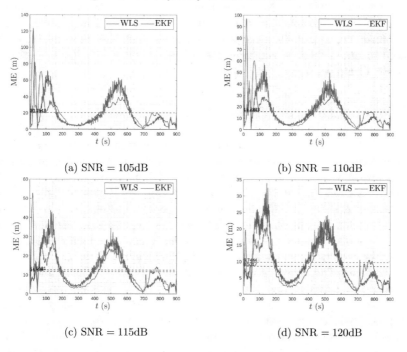

(a) SNR = 105dB

(b) SNR = 110dB

(c) SNR = 115dB

(d) SNR = 120dB

Fig. 9. Mean error of M_c runs for $N = 5$.

When considering the overall results presented in Table 1 one can see that when performing the acoustic measurements with $N = 3$ drones, the EKF implies a reduction of about 40% when compared with the WLS implementation. When considering the error over the trajectory path (Fig. 5), besides the first instants of the path until the EKF does not establishes useful prior information, the obtained error is always lower. Nevertheless, when considering the error deviation (see Fig. 4), it is pretty highlighted that the EKF has a much stable and reliable overall path. Another evidence that can be extracted from Fig. 4 is the behavior of the proposed scheme for the trajectories intersections, that is when the drones intersect the target trajectory, the error is minimal, a situation that is also valid when trajectories approach each other ($750\,\mathrm{s} < t < 850\,\mathrm{s}$). The same analysis can be performed when considering $N = 4$ sensor drones (Figs. 6 and 7), although the reduction is somewhat less significant, reaching values in the order of 25%. Finally, when considering $N = 5$ sensor drones, the overall decline is marginal; meanwhile, Fig. 8 demonstrates that the deviation is much higher for the WLS implementation. When considering Fig. 9, one can see that the moment when EKF has a higher error that EKF is in the first moments of the path. It should be pointed out that although the position is initialized with the WLS method, the velocity is initialized with $[0,0]^T$, that is, without considering any previous information of the system dynamics (line 3 of Algorithm 1). As a concluding remark, in the worst-case scenario, when $N = 3$ and the SNR is 105 dB, a mean error over the trajectory of about 50 m is obtained when considering a search-space of $1000 \times 1000\,\mathrm{m}^2$. Not forgetting that, for these conditions, the mean distance of the sensors reaches 350 m, which would imply a local SNR of about 3 dB. Moreover, by simply enlarging the drone's fleet, the mean overall error is reduced to about 28 m in the same conditions ($SNR = 105\,\mathrm{dB}$), resulting in a reduction of almost 50%.

6   Conclusions and Future Work

In this work, the problem of tracking a moving acoustic source was addressed based on energy measurements, which are considered to be acquired by microphones positioned on drones, and thus, also with some moving dynamics. The proposed methodology is based on implementing an Extended Kalman Filter that, besides dealing with the measurement model non-linearity, also deals with the trajectories intersections, avoiding the filter divergence. Simulations performed over different sets of number of drone sensors and different SNR corrupting the energy measures show the effectiveness, stability, and repeatability of the method. These results were also compared with a WLS implementation that does not consider the prior knowledge given by the motion model as a well-known and accepted benchmark that validates the credibility of the solutions presented. The present work establishes the energy-based acoustic source localization strategy, which brings simplicity to physical implementation and processing level when placed alongside with its counterparts. Ultimately, the present work proposed an EKF methodology for acoustic localization validated with results that demonstrates its effectiveness and reliability. It can be concluded that using energy-based measurements to perform the localization of a moving target can be considered as an add-on to current wildfire platforms.

As future work, the analysis of fusion techniques that make use of the estimated location to govern the movement of the sensor drones, contributing to reduction of the estimation error without jeopardizing its primary function on the wildfire scenario will be considered. Also, to enhance the credibility of the present work, it is important to extend the developed experiments to real-world scenarios.

Acknowledgments. This research was funded by Fundação para a Ciência e a Tecnologia under Projects UIDB/04111/2020 and foRESTER PCIF/SSI/0102/ 2017; and Instituto Lusófono de Investigação e Desenvolvimento (ILIND) under Project COFAC/ILIND/COPELABS/1/2020.

References

1. Aggarwal, C.C., Ashish, N., Sheth, A.: The Internet of Things: a survey from the data-centric perspective. In: Aggarwal, C. (ed.) Managing and Mining Sensor Data, pp. 383–428. Springer, Boston (2012). https://doi.org/10.1007/978-1-4614-6309-2_12
2. Bassoli, R., Sacchi, C., Granelli, F., Ashkenazi, I.: A virtualized border control system based on UAVs: design and energy efficiency considerations. In: 2019 IEEE Aerospace Conference (2019). https://doi.org/10.1109/aero.2019.8742142
3. Beck, A., Stoica, P., Li, J.: Exact and approximate solutions of source localization problems. IEEE Trans. Signal Process. **56**(5), 1770–1778 (2008)
4. Beko, M.: Energy-based localization in wireless sensor networks using semidefinite relaxation. In: 2011 IEEE Wireless Communications and Networking Conference (2011). https://doi.org/10.1109/wcnc.2011.5779361
5. Beko, M.: Energy-based localization in wireless sensor networks using second-order cone programming relaxation. Wireless Pers. Commun. **77**(3), 1847–1857 (2014). https://doi.org/10.1007/s11277-014-1612-7
6. Correia, S.D., Beko, M., Cruz, L.A.D.S., Tomic, S.: Implementation and validation of elephant herding optimization algorithm for acoustic localization. In: 2018 26th Telecommunications Forum (TELFOR) (2018). https://doi.org/10.1109/telfor.2018.8611919
7. Correia, S.D., Beko, M., Tomic, S., Cruz, L.A.D.S.: Energy-based acoustic localization by improved elephant herding optimization. IEEE Access **8**, 28548–28559 (2020). https://doi.org/10.1109/access.2020.2971787
8. Correia, S., Beko, M., Cruz, L., Tomic, S.: Elephant herding optimization for energy-based localization (2018). https://doi.org/10.20944/preprints201807.0051.v1
9. Correia, S., Fé, J., Tomic, S., Beko, M.: Development of a test-bench for evaluating the embedded implementation of the improved elephant herding optimization algorithm applied to energy-based acoustic localization. Computers **9**(4), 87 (2020). https://doi.org/10.3390/computers9040087
10. Correia, S.D., Tomic, S., Beko, M.: A feed-forward neural network approach for energy-based acoustic source localization. J. Sens. Actuator Netw. **10**(2), 29 (2021). https://doi.org/10.3390/jsan10020029

11. Fe, J., Correia, S.D., Tomic, S., Beko, M.: Kalman filtering for tracking a moving acoustic source based on energy measurements. In: 2021 International Conference on Electrical, Computer, Communications and Mechatronics Engineering (ICEC-CME) (2021). https://doi.org/10.1109/iceccme52200.2021.9590919

12. Hu, Y.H., Li, D.: Energy based collaborative source localization using acoustic micro-sensor array. In: 2002 IEEE Workshop on Multimedia Signal Processing (2002). https://doi.org/10.1109/mmsp.2002.1203323

13. Khalil, N., Abid, M.R., Benhaddou, D., Gerndt, M.: Wireless sensors networks for Internet of Things. In: 2014 IEEE Ninth International Conference on Intelligent Sensors, Sensor Networks and Information Processing (ISSNIP) (2014). https://doi.org/10.1109/issnip.2014.6827681

14. Kim, S.H.: Choice model based analysis of consumer preference for drone delivery service. J. Air Transp. Manag. **84**, 101785 (2020). https://doi.org/10.1016/j.jairtraman.2020.101785

15. Ko, Y., Kim, J., Duguma, D.G., Astillo, P.V., You, I., Pau, G.: Drone secure communication protocol for future sensitive applications in military zone. Sensors **21**(6), 2057 (2021). https://doi.org/10.3390/s21062057

16. Kraljevic, L., Russo, M., Stella, M., Sikora, M.: Free-field TDOA-AOA sound source localization using three soundfield microphones. IEEE Access **8**, 87749–87761 (2020). https://doi.org/10.1109/access.2020.2993076

17. Meng, W., Xiao, W.: Energy-based acoustic source localization methods: a survey. Sensors **17**(2), 376 (2017). https://doi.org/10.3390/s17020376

18. Mishra, B., Garg, D., Narang, P., Mishra, V.: Drone-surveillance for search and rescue in natural disaster. Comput. Commun. **156**, 1–10 (2020). https://doi.org/10.1016/j.comcom.2020.03.012

19. Park, M., Tran, D.Q., Jung, D., Park, S.: Wildfire-detection method using DenseNet and CycleGAN data augmentation-based remote camera imagery. Remote Sens. **12**(22), 3715 (2020). https://doi.org/10.3390/rs12223715

20. Radke, D., Hessler, A., Ellsworth, D.: FireCast: leveraging deep learning to predict wildfire spread. In: Proceedings of the Twenty-Eighth International Joint Conference on Artificial Intelligence (2019). https://doi.org/10.24963/ijcai.2019/636

21. Rashid, M.T., Zhang, D., Wang, D.: Poster abstract: a computational model-driven hybrid social media and drone-based wildfire monitoring framework. In: IEEE INFOCOM 2020 - IEEE Conference on Computer Communications Workshops (INFOCOM WKSHPS) (2020). https://doi.org/10.1109/infocomwkshps50562.2020.9162586

22. Sahal, R., Alsamhi, S.H., Breslin, J.G., Ali, M.I.: Industry 4.0 towards forestry 4.0: fire detection use case. Sensors **21**(3), 694 (2021). https://doi.org/10.3390/s21030694

23. Simões, D., Rodrigues, A., Reis, A.B., Sargento, S.: Forest fire monitoring through a network of aerial drones and sensors. In: 2020 IEEE International Conference on Pervasive Computing and Communications Workshops (PerCom Workshops) (2020). https://doi.org/10.1109/percomworkshops48775.2020.9156137

24. Stokes, D., Apps, K., Butcher, P.A., Weiler, B., Luke, H., Colefax, A.P.: Beach-user perceptions and attitudes towards drone surveillance as a shark-bite mitigation tool. Mar. Policy **120**, 104127 (2020). https://doi.org/10.1016/j.marpol.2020.104127

25. Strumberger, I., Bacanin, N., Tomic, S., Beko, M., Tuba, M.: Static drone placement by elephant herding optimization algorithm. In: 2017 25th Telecommunication Forum (TELFOR) (2017). https://doi.org/10.1109/telfor.2017.8249469

26. Sun, S., Zhao, C., Zheng, C., Zhao, C., Wang, Y.: High-precision underwater acoustical localization of the black box based on an improved TDOA algorithm. IEEE Geosci. Remote Sens. Lett. **18**(8), 1317–1321 (2021). https://doi.org/10.1109/lgrs.2020.3002169

27. Sungheetha, A., Rajesh Sharma, R.: Real time monitoring and fire detection using Internet of Things and cloud based drones. J. Soft Comput. Paradigm **2**(3), 168–174 (2020). https://doi.org/10.36548/jscp.2020.3.004

28. Tomic, S., Beko, M., Dinis, R., Tuba, M., Bacanin, N.: Bayesian methodology for target tracking using combined RSS and AoA measurements. Phys. Commun. **25**, 158–166 (2017). https://doi.org/10.1016/j.phycom.2017.10.005

29. Vikash, Mishra, L., Varma, S.: Middleware technologies for smart wireless sensor networks towards Internet of Things: a comparative review. Wirel. Pers. Commun. **116**(3), 1539–1574 (2020). https://doi.org/10.1007/s11277-020-07748-7

30. Wakabayashi, M., Okuno, H.G., Kumon, M.: Multiple sound source position estimation by drone audition based on data association between sound source localization and identification. IEEE Robot. Autom. Lett. **5**(2), 782–789 (2020). https://doi.org/10.1109/lra.2020.2965417

31. Yamada, T., Itoyama, K., Nishida, K., Nakadai, K.: Sound source tracking by drones with microphone arrays. In: 2020 IEEE/SICE International Symposium on System Integration (SII) (2020). https://doi.org/10.1109/sii46433.2020.9026185

IoT for Smart Health

cStick: A Calm Stick for Fall Prediction, Detection and Control in the IoMT Framework

Laavanya Rachakonda[1] , Saraju P. Mohanty[2(✉)] , and Elias Kougianos[3]

[1] Department of Computer Science, University of North Carolina Wilmington,
Wilmington, USA
rachakondal@uncw.edu
[2] Department of Computer Science and Engineering, University of North Texas, Denton, USA
saraju.mohanty@unt.edu
[3] Department of Electrical Engineering, University of North Texas, Denton, USA
elias.kougianos@unt.edu

Abstract. Falls are constant threats to older adults and can minimize their ability to live independently. To help mitigate the occurrences and effects of such unfortunate accidents, it is imperative to find an accurate, reliable, robust and convenient solution to make life easier for elder adults who may have visual or hearing impairments. In order to reduce such occurrences, a calm stick, cStick is proposed. cStick is an IoT (Internet of Things) enabled system which has a capability to predict falls before their occurrence, to warn the user that there may be an incident of fall, to detect falls and also provide control remedies to reduce their impact. cStick monitors the location of the user, the physiological changes that occur when a person is about to fall and also monitors the surroundings the user is in when having an incident of fall. Based on the changes in the monitored parameters, the decision of fall i.e., a prediction, warning or detection of fall is made with an accuracy of approximately 95%. Control mechanisms to reduce the impact of the fall along with connection capabilities to the help unit are provided with the cStick system.

Keywords: Smart Healthcare · Healthcare Cyber-Physical System (H-CPS) · Internet of Medical Things (IoMT) · Fall detection · Fall prediction · Elderly falls · Visually impaired · Hearing impairment · IoT-edge computing

1 Introduction

Falls are accidents that come with age. Every year, 37.3 million falls are recorded from the elderly, 65 years and above. As a matter of fact, one among four older people falls each year but less than half tell their doctor [4,30]. The probability of having multiple falls increases after having the first fall [21]. Every 11 s, there is an older person being treated for an incident of fall [1]. Statistics indicate that fall incidence rates have increased by 31% from 2007 to 2016 and the rate is expected to grow in the future [3].

The occurrences and causes of falls are many. 67% of falls do not happen from a height but happen when a person trips or slips. Ill-fitting clothes and shoes can also be a

© IFIP International Federation for Information Processing 2022
Published by Springer Nature Switzerland AG 2022
L. M. Camarinha-Matos et al. (Eds.): IFIPIoT 2021, IFIP AICT 641, pp. 129–145, 2022.
https://doi.org/10.1007/978-3-030-96466-5_9

130   L. Rachakonda et al.

reason for the older person to fall [8]. Hearing impairments in older adults cause three times the risk of an accidental fall than other older adults [18]. Medical conditions, sedatives and antidepressants such as Parkinson's disease, insomnia, sedation, and obesity also contribute to the increased risk of falling in older adults [7,17]. Isolation and physical inactivity due to the pandemic also has an effect on the increased risk of falling in older adults [23,24].

The impact of falls on the elderly human body is very high. Falls can cause broken bones, wrists, arms, ankles and hips. In 2014, 29 million older adults received injuries from falls. 95% of the cases involving falls lead to hip fractures [1]. In 2013, 50% of the cases involving falls resulted in traumatic brain injuries in older adults [31]. In 2016 alone, there were 29,668 deaths in older adults caused due to falls [13].

In order to reduce such accidents, cStick, a calm stick to monitor falls in older adults is proposed. cStick has been designed in such a way that it can assist both visually and hearing impaired older adults. cStick has an ability to not only detect falls but to also predict the incident of fall so as to reduce their occurrences. cStick can monitor the surroundings, warn the user if there was a previous fall detected at a certain location, and update the location and its surroundings to the user. The device prototype of the proposed cStick is represented in Fig. 1.

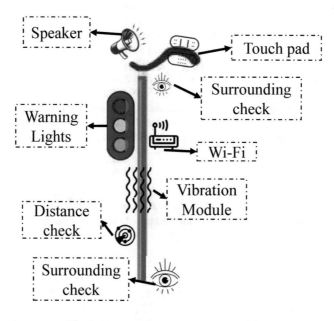

Fig. 1. Proposed device prototype of cStick.

cStick ia a state-of-the-art device in the IoMT framework. IoMT stands for Internet of Medical Things and it is a subset of Internet of Things (IoT). IoT is defined as the network of devices which are connected and are capable to transfer information as they have a unique IP addresses [19]. When the fundamentals, tools, techniques and concepts of such applications and devices with Internet capabilities are related to healthcare domains, the IoT is known as the IoMT [27]. There are many applications ranging from Smart Healthcare, Smart Transportation, Smart Supply Chain, Posture Recognition, Smart cities, etc., that involve the IoT and the IoMT [20].

cStick is an IoMT-enabled edge computing device as it has the capabilities to process and analyze the information at the user end and store the information at the cloud end. Applications or devices proposed in this framework require little to no human intervention [19]. The IoMT framework has many components as represented in Fig. 2 [27].

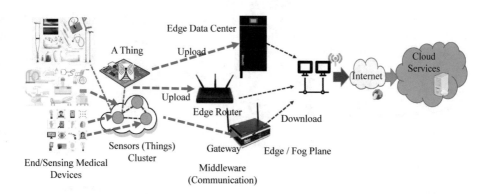

Fig. 2. IoMT framework used in cStick.

Edge computing is defined as a distributed computing paradigm that allows data processing and analysis done at, or near the source of the data, i.e., closer to the user. With edge computing, the dependency on the cloud to process and analyze the data can be reduced. Major advantages of edge computing include reduction in latency or delay which means data can be real-time; reduction in the bandwidth utilization, therefore less network traffic; reduction in total costs, increase in application efficiency, and increase in the security and privacy aspects of the devices [11]. The edge computing paradigm is represented through Fig. 3.

The main motivation for cStick is to provide real-time data analysis on the status of older adults in terms of falls, to constantly protect them, to reduce the incidents of fall, to provide instant support and help in the event of a fall and to propose a system that works for all elders, even with visual and hearing impairments.

The organization of the paper is as follows: Sect. 2 provides the state-of-the-art literature and marketable products for elderly healthcare followed by issues in these. Section 3 provides the novel contributions that are proposed through cStick and how it provides an excellent solution to all the missing aspects. Section 4 provides a detailed understanding of the physiological parameters considered in cStick. Section 5 provides a representation of the architectural flow used for fall prediction and detection in cStick. Section 6 describes the design process involved in cStick for fall prediction, detection and control. Section 7 is comprised of the implementation and validation of the

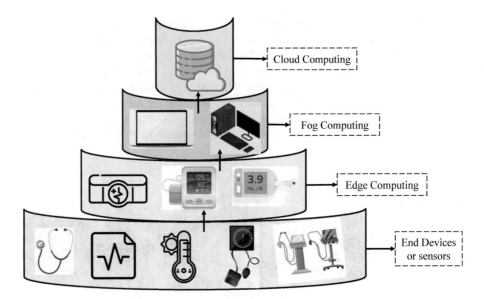

Fig. 3. IoMT-edge computing paradigm used in cStick.

IoMT-Edge computing proposed in cStick followed by conclusions and future directions of this research in Sect. 8.

2   Related Prior Research

Though there is a good number of wearables in the market that provide care for older adults, most of them only focus on fall detection and not prediction. Some wearables proposed are able to detect trips and slips but not specifically fall. Also most of them use only accelerometers as the physiological feature and need the user to request help after a fall. A detailed presentation of these works is provided in Table 1. Some of the major disadvantages of these wearables are the generation of false positives and false negatives which can cause unnecessary alerts, monthly maintenance charges and privacy concerns.

Some works which detect falls in elderly are provided in Table 2. These articles only detect falls with no fall prediction. Also, most of them only consider a single physiological signal for monitoring falls which lacks in efficiency of the system proposed.

2.1   Major Issues with the Existing Solutions

Some of the major issues with the existing solutions are:

- There is no unified detection as there are not many physiological signal data that are being considered to make the decision of fall.
- There are no fall prediction mechanisms or strategies included.

Table 1. Wearable products for elderly healthcare.

Wearable	Activity	Physiological data	Prediction	Detection	Drawback
Owlytics [22]	Walk, trip and slip	Accelerometer	Partially Yes	Yes	Users need to manually request for help. It only uses one physiological signal to detect falls
Smart watch [2]	Physical activity	Accelerometer	No	Yes	It uses only accelerometers, does not work on low thresholds like double carpet, bathroom, hardwood floors. The user must manually select the option SOS and as a result it fails if the person is unconscious. Users may remain on the floor with no help for long hours
Vayyar home [15]	Bathroom activity monitoring	Radars	No	Yes	Location constraint as its mounted on a wall inside bathroom. User needs to manually request help by talking to the device. Connectivity issues may arise
Hip hope [16]	Physical activity	Accelerometer	No	Yes	The location of the wearable placement can be an inconvenience. Malfunction of the device will have additional injuries for hips as its located around hips

- Most of them are location constrained and can only be used at a specific location.
- Users need to manually or verbally request help upon falls and this can be an issue if the user is unconscious.
- Wearables or the device prototypes proposed may be inconvenient for the users to wear.
- Generation of false positives and negatives can be higher due to which unnecessary alerts can be generated.
- Cost for the installation and maintenance can be higher as most need monthly subscriptions.

3   Novel Contributions

cStick is designed to provide constant care for older adults by continuously monitoring the physiological parameters while a person is walking. It has IoT capabilities and it can be a part of any network or device [26]. The novel contributions that are proposed through cStick are:

Table 2. Research contributions for elderly healthcare

Name	Prototype	Activities	Sensors	Prediction	Detection	Accuracy
Han et al. [12]	No	Walk, sit, fall, lean	Accelerometer, gyroscope	Partially yes	Yes	No.
Pongthanisorn et al. [25]	No	Sleeping positions	Piezoelectric and weight	No	Yes	No.
Engel et al. [9]	No	Walk, trip, stumble, fall	Accelerometer	No	Yes	94.
Razmara et al. [28]	No	Questionnaire	None	No	Yes	90

– Accounting for multiple physiological signal data to analyze the decision of falls.
– Continuous data monitoring to predict the occurrences of falls in order to reduce the number of accidents.
– Continuous surrounding monitoring to allow the users to understand the environment in order to reduce tripping and injuries.
– Continuous monitoring of general health signals so as to have to a detailed understanding on the causes of the fall.
– Location tracking of the user to not only provide immediate support but also to notify the user with a warning.
– Ability to have two-way communication with the device, when needed.
– Assisting visually impaired and hearing impaired elders by incorporating audio and touch response systems, respectively.
– Having a capability to connect to any wearable or health monitoring device to provide more adaptable elder fall monitoring systems.

4   Physiological Parameters Considered in cStick

There are many physiological changes that occur inside a human body throughout the course of the day. Not all signals have a defined relationship with falls. For example, though body temperature and sweat change according to the actions done by the human being, these changes are discarded as there are may be external reasons such as weather, environment etc., which can cause fluctuations in them [26]. So here are the physiological parameters considered to analyze falls in cStick. Upon careful consideration, cStick is designed in a way that it can monitor:

4.1   Grasping Pressure

When a person is about to fall or losing strength, the tendency to hold surroundings - be people or objects, increases. Based on this, cStick monitors the grasping pressure that is applied on the cane. The individual baselines for each individual can be different, so cStick monitors sudden changes in the squeezing force.

4.2   Dietary Habits

cStick monitors the blood sugar levels of the older adults. The total occurrences of falls can be linked with low sugar levels (hypoglycemia). When the sugar levels are below 70mg/dL the chances of having falls increases as the older adults may feel weak, tired, anxious, shaky, or suffer strokes and unconsciousness [10].

4.3   Posture

The posture of the human body tells a lot about its orientation. If there is a leaning in any direction, the chances of losing the balance are high. Such scenarios can lead to side and back falls causing injuries to hips or the head.

4.4   Blood Oxygen Levels

Older adults have lower saturation levels than younger adults. Oxygen saturation levels about 95% are considered normal for older adults. Lower levels may cause shortness of breathe, asthma, excess sweating, low heart rate and sometimes leads to unconsciousness in older adults [14].

4.5   Irregular Heart Beats per Minute

Cardiac output decreases linearly at a rate of about 1% per year in normal subjects past the third decade [5]. The resting supine diastolic blood pressure for younger men was 66 ± 6 and 62 ± 8 for older men and higher heart rates can result in shortness of breathe, fatigue, stroke and unconsciousness [6].

4.6   Surroundings of the User

Surroundings have a larger impact on the human body when a fall occurs. Monitoring the surroundings helps to reduce the impact of falls. cStick is designed in such a way that it can detect the reason behind the accident of fall. Surrounding objects, human beings or any other moving or non-moving things are continuously monitored to eliminate the accidents of falls.

4.7   Location of the User

The location of the user plays a very important role as it allows notification of the user to stay alert. Warning the user about a previously occurred fall will make him aware of the surroundings. Also, location tracking helps to provide required help without the user asking for it.

A schematic representation of cStick is represented in Fig. 4. Here, the Edge-data analyzed and the decision of fall are sent to the doctor and/or caregivers using the IoMT.

5   Architectural Flow for Fall Prediction and Detection in cStick

The architectural flow of the proposed system begins with the data collection from the wearable sensors. The data from the stick is compared and analyzed to make the decision of fall or a prediction of a fall. This decision is provided to the user using fall response mechanisms which are both compatible for visually or hearing impairment elders and are described in the next sections. The architectural flow is represented in Fig. 5.

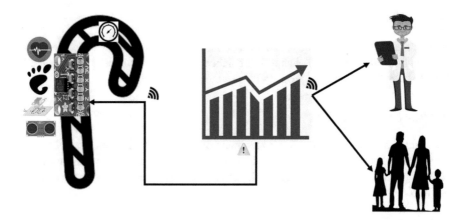

Fig. 4. Schematic representation of cStick.

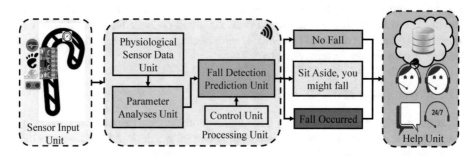

Fig. 5. Architectural view of cStick.

5.1 Physiological Sensor Data Unit

The physiological parameters that are considered in designing the cStick are explained in Sect. 4. In this section the detailed presentation of the sensors which are used to analyze the falls and predict the possible falls is discussed.

Accelerometer. The accelerometer sensor parameter in cStick is used to measure the non-gravitational or linear acceleration. The accelerometer is located inside the stick and is designed to respond to the vibrations associated with any movement. The microscopic crystals that undergo stress when in vibration help in providing a voltage which is generated as a reading on any acceleration. When there is a movement in human body, the axes of accelerometer x,y and z are continuously changing. When a 3-g spike in the y axis is noticed, it means that the person is sitting down. If the g-force of the y axis exceeds ± 3 g's, the accelerometer would pass the threshold to detect a fall.

Gyroscope. In cStick a gyroscope sensor parameter is used to detect the changes in the orientation of the human body. The gyroscope is used to measure the rate of rotation around a particular axis with which the direction of the fall can be determined. For example, if the person is about to or has fallen in front, towards the back or side.

Heart Rate Variability. In cStick the heart rate variability is considered to measure sudden changes in the breaths per minute as a sudden change in the heart rate is abnormal [29]. According to [6], the maximum heart rate in older adults is lower (at around 162 ± 9 beats/min) than the maximum heart rate in younger men (191 ± 11 beats/min).

Blood Sugar Levels. Blood sugar levels are very important in older adults and can have significant role in detecting falls, as discussed in Sect. 4. Hypoglycemia and hyperglycemia have significant effects on the strength, cognitive ability and heart rates in older adults and so their continuous monitoring is provided in cStick.

Blood Oxygen Saturation (SpO_2) Levels. Continuous monitoring of $SpØ_2$ levels is provided in cStick as hypoxemia or low blood oxygen levels creates shortness of breath, excessive sweating, low heart rate and even unconsciousness in older adults [14].

5.2 Parameter Analysis Unit

The relationship between the sensor parameters to the falls in older adults is discussed here. As explained in Sects. 4 and 5.1, the distance of the user to the nearest object, the ±3-g for the y axis from the accelerometer which is the threshold, the gyroscope reading to indicate the direction of fall, the sugar levels of the user, sudden spike in heart rate, the duration of pressure or squeeze applied on the stick and the blood oxygen levels are considered to make the decision of the falls. The parameter ranges for the decisions of prediction and detection are represented in Table 3.

Table 3. Parameter range descriptions for fall prediction and detection in cStick.

Distance	Pressure	HRV	Sugar levels	SpO_2 levels	Accelerometer	Decisions
>50 cm	Small	60–90 bpm	70–80 mg/dL	>90	<Threshold	No fall. Happy walking!
<30 cm	Medium	90–105 bpm	30–70 mg/dL	80–90	>Threshold	Take a break, you tripped!
<10 cm	Large	>105 bpm	<30 mg/dL or >160 mg/dL	<80	>Threshold	Definite fall. Help is on the way!

5.3 Fall Prediction and Detection Unit

The decision of falls is made from the analysis represented in Table 3. Prediction of the fall is defined as a mechanism to let the user know that the user might have an accident and taking a break might be good for him/her. Detection is stating that there has been a definite accident of fall and the user needs assistance.

5.4   Control Unit

As there is continuous monitoring of the vital signal data in cStick, any other additional cause an older person may fall is also taken care of. This includes monitoring the heart rate, sugar levels and blood oxygen levels. If there is anyone of these that are causing the user to loose cognitive ability, strength or even consciousness, cStick will be able to help the user by warning the user to take a break, in other words by predicting the user that there may be an accident.

In addition, as the location of the user along with the surroundings are also monitored, the chances of having falls or any other accidents can also be reduced.

6   Design Flow for Fall Prediction and Detection in cStick

The design flow of the working principle involved in cStick is represented with the Algorithm 1.

The buzzer, vibrator and microphone attached are activated depending not only on the decision of the fall but also when there is an abnormal reading in the vital signals. The location of the user will be updated throughout the time period the user is using the stick. The design flow of cStick is also represented in Fig. 6.

7   Implementation and Validation for Fall Prediction and Detection in cStick

7.1   Physiological Data Acquisition

For the implementation and validation in cStick, a dataset of 9670 samples based on Table 3 was used. For the baseline and as a validation the data from [32] has been taken. Here the decision of the fall was done based on the 14 volunteers who participated in the study.

7.2   Machine Learning Model for Edge Computing Used in cStick

The well shuffled dataset with 6 features and 3 classes in the label was trained in TensorFlow. The 6 features here are: Heart rate variability, accelerometer, blood oxygen levels, sugar levels, pressure applied on the stick and distance from the nearest object. The classes for the label i.e., for the decision are no fall detected, a fall is predicted i.e., the user has tripped or slipped and a fall has detected i.e., a definite fall. The scatter plot of two of the features considered in cStick is represented in Fig. 7.

Algorithm 1. Working Principle for Fall Prediction and Detection in cStick.

1: Declare and initialize the input variables d for distance, h for HRV, sl for sugar levels, s for SpO$_2$ to zero.

2: Declare and initialize the output variables b for buzzer, v for vibrator and l for location to zero.

3: Declare string variables decision of the fall d, p for pressure, m for microphone or speaker and a for accelerometer to zero.

4: **while** $p \neq 0$ **do**

5:     Start monitoring and gathering physiological signal data which are a, h, sl, s and l.

6:     **if** $d > 50$ cm && $p ==$ 'small' && $60 > h < 90$ && $70 > sl < 80$ && $s > 90$ && $a <$ 'Threshold' **then**

7:         $d =$ 'No fall. Happy walking!'.

8:         $l = 1$.

9:     **else if** $d < 30$ cm && $p ==$ 'medium' && $90 > h < 105$ && $30 > sl < 70$ && $80 > s < 90$ && $a >$ 'Threshold' **then**

10:         $d =$ 'Take a break, you tripped!'.

11:         $m =$ 'Take a break, you tripped!'.

12:         $b = 1$ && $v = 1$ && $l = 1$.

13:     **else if** $d < 10$ cm && $p ==$ 'Large' && $h > 105$ && $sl < 30$ && $sl > 160$ && $s < 80$ && $a >$ 'Threshold' **then**

14:         $d =$ 'Definite fall. Help is on the way!'.

15:         $m =$ 'Fall detected, help is on the way!'.

16:         $b = 2$ && $v = 2$ && $l = 1$.

17:     **end if**

18:     **if** $p == 0$ **then**

19:         Stop monitoring and gathering physiological signal data.

20:     **else**

21:         Repeat steps from 5 through 12.

22:     **end if**

23: **end while**

24: Repeat the steps from 4 through 18 whenever a user is using cStick.

The model that is used in cStick to define the relationship between the features and the label is a fully connected neural network or dense model. Here, a linear stack of layers with 6 nodes in the input layer, two dense layers with 20 neurons each and three nodes in the output layer are considered. The rectified linear function is used as an activation function for the hidden layers and the sigmoid function is used for the output layer. 200 epochs are provided with batch size of 32 and 0.01 learning rate for the model.

The predictions of the model without training and predictions of the model after the training are represented through Fig. 8.

With loss and accuracy as the metrics and a stochastic gradient descent algorithm as the optimizer, 7736 samples for training and 1934 samples for testing, the model has produced 96.67% accuracy, as shown in Fig. 9. The software verified implementation is implemented on IoMT-Edge computing platform in the following sections.

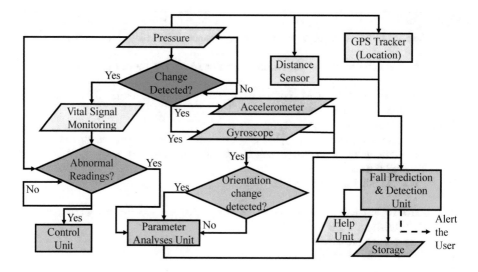

Fig. 6. Design flow of cStick.

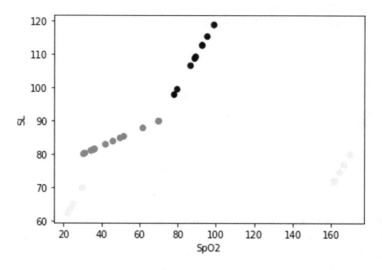

Fig. 7. Scatter plot of features in cStick.

Prediction: [2 2 2 2 2 2 0 2 0 2 2 2 0 0 0 2 2 2 2 2 0 2 2 0 2 2 2 2 2 2 2 2]
Labels: [1 2 1 1 2 0 0 1 0 2 1 1 0 0 0 2 2 0 0 1 0 2 1 0 1 0 1 1 2 1 1 0]

[[1, 1], [2, 2], [0, 0], [1, 1], [1, 1],[1, 1], [0, 0], [2, 2],[1, 1], [2, 2],[2, 2], [0, 0], [2, 2], [1, 1], [1, 1], [0, 0], [1, 1], [0, 0], [0, 0], [2, 2], [0, 0], [1, 1], [2, 2], [1, 2], [1, 1], [1, 1], [0, 0], [1, 1], [2, 2], [1, 1]]

Fig. 8. Predictions before and after training in cStick.

Training Metrics

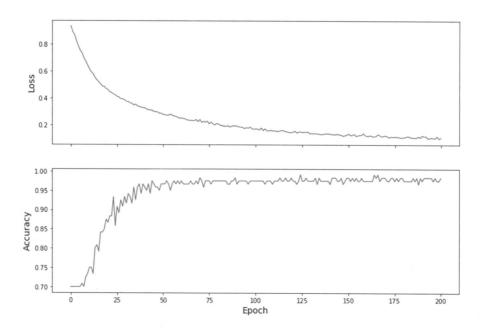

Fig. 9. Loss and accuracy obtained in cStick.

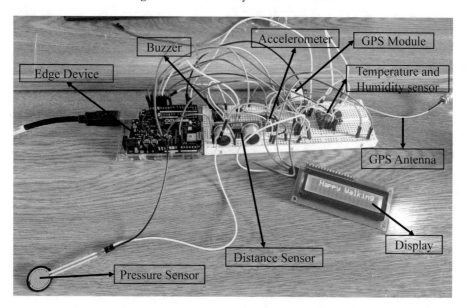

Fig. 10. Real-time IoMT-edge implementation in cStick.

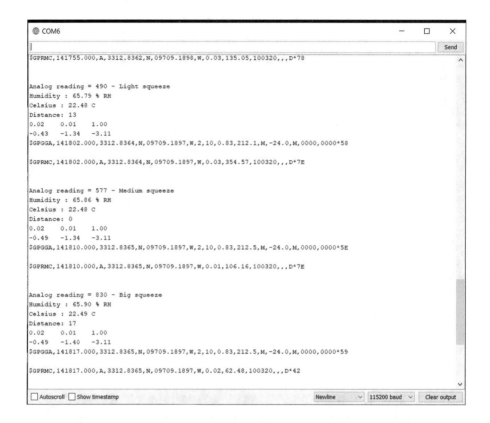

Fig. 11. Serial monitor display in cStick.

7.3   Real-Time IoMT-Edge Computing Validation in cStick

For the IoMT-Edge computing, a controller has been chosen with real time sensor data from various sensors which monitor the required parameters considered in cStick, as discussed in Sect. 4. The Edge Computing setup is represented in Fig. 10.

The location of the user is also validated in cStick along with the conceptual validation as shown in Fig. 12.

The serial monitor display of the sensors along with the dataset data is represented in Fig. 11. Here, the squeeze or the pressure applied by the user on the stick, distance from the nearest object or person, heart rate variability, location of the user, sugar levels, blood oxygen levels are continuously monitored and the buzzer with various voltage levels and a speaker are provided as output sources.

A brief comparison with existing research is presented in Table 4.

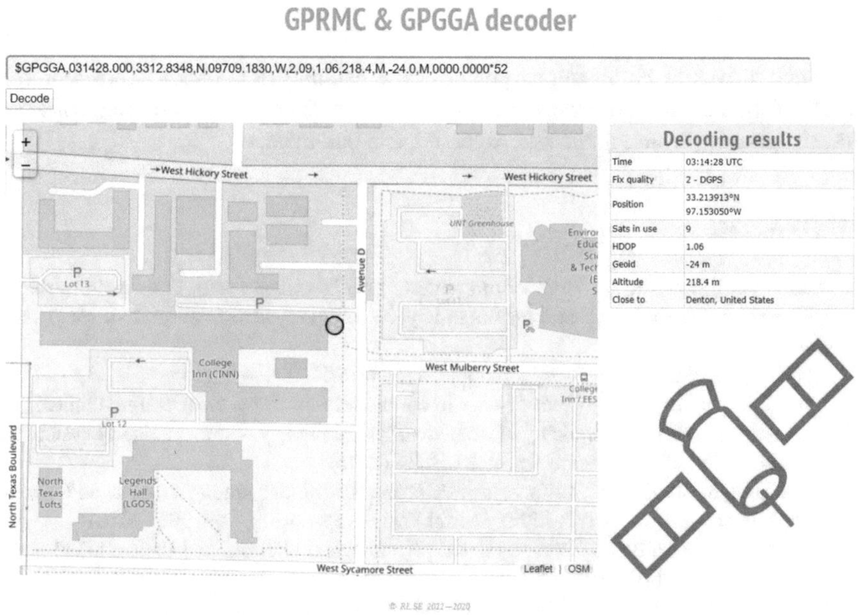

Fig. 12. User location validation in cStick.

Table 4. Comparison with the state-of-the-art research.

Name	Prototype	Activities	Sensors	Prediction	Detection	Accuracy
Han et al. [12]	No	Walk, sit, fall, lean	Accelerometer, gyroscope	Partially yes	Yes	No.
Pongthanisorn et al. [25]	No	Sleeping positions	Piezoelectric and weight	No	Yes	No.
Engel et al. [9]	No	Walk, trip, stumble, fall	Accelerometer	No	Yes	94%.
Razmara et al. [28]	No	Questionnaire	None	No	Yes	90%.
cStick (current paper)	Yes, a calm stick	Walking - Vital signal monitoring	Accelerometer, HRV, Pressure, Sugar levels, SpO2, Gyroscope	Yes	Yes	96.67%.

8 Conclusions and Future Research

8.1 Conclusions

Elderly care requires utmost attention with the technological developments happening day by day. Keeping that in mind, a cStick, also known as calm stick, is proposed with which the users are not only provided with a fall detection monitoring device but also a fall prediction device with an accuracy of approximately 96.67%. cStick also monitors the vital signals of the older adults and this allows in the early detection of accidents including falls. It has a capability of connecting to any smart or IoMT device to enhance its performance. cStick can also be used by visually or hearing impaired older adults as it has autonomous control mechanisms.

8.2   Future Research

As cStick strives to be an improvement in the existing technology and research for elderly healthcare, in future work more focus will be placed on considering many other vital signals and physiological and psychological parameters.

References

1. Alshammari, S.A., et al.: Falls among elderly and its relation with their health problems and surrounding environmental factors in Riyadh. J. Family Community Med. **25**(1), 29–34 (2018)
2. Apple: Apple Watch. https://support.apple.com/en-us/HT208944
3. Avin, K.G., et al.: Management of falls in community-dwelling older adults: clinical guidance statement from the academy of geriatric physical therapy of the american physical therapy association. Phys. Therapy **95**(6), 815–834 (2015)
4. Bergen, G., Stevens, M.R., Burns, E.R.: Falls and fall injuries among adults aged 65 years - United States, 2014. MMWR Morb. Mortal Wkly. Rep. **65**(37), 993–998 (2016)
5. Boss, G.R., Seegmiller, J.E.: Age-related physiological changes and their clinical significance. W. J. Med. (1981)
6. Christou, D.D., Seals, D.R.: Decreased maximal heart rate with aging is related to reduced beta-adrenergic responsiveness but is largely explained by a reduction in intrinsic heart rate. J. Appl. Physiol. **105**(1), 24–29 (2008). https://doi.org/10.1152/japplphysiol.90401.2008
7. Dionyssiotis, Y.: Analyzing the problem of falls among older people. Int. J. Gen. Med. **5**, 805–813 (2012)
8. Edelman, M.M.S., Ficorelli, C.T.: Keeping older adults safe at home. Nursing **42**(1), 65–66 (2012)
9. Engel, W., Ding, W.: Reliable and practical fall prediction using artificial neural network. In: 13th International Conference on Natural Computation, Fuzzy Systems and Knowledge Discovery (ICNC-FSKD). pp. 1867–1871 (2017). https://doi.org/10.1109/FSKD.2017.8393052
10. Gregg, E.W., et al.: Diabetes and incidence of functional disability in older women. Diabetes Care **25**(1), 61–7 (2002)
11. Hamdan, S., Ayyash, M., Almajali, S.: Edge-Computing architectures for internet of things applications: a survey. Sensors (Basel) **20**(22), 6411–6463 (2020)
12. Han, H., Ma, X., Oyama, K.: Towards detecting and predicting fall events in elderly care using bidirectional electromyographic sensor network. In: IEEE/ACIS 15th International Conference on Computer and Information Science (ICIS), pp. 1–6 (2016). https://doi.org/10.1109/ICIS.2016.7550897
13. Hartholt, K.A., Lee, R., Burns, E.R., van Beeck, E.F.: Mortality from falls among US adults aged 75 years or older, 2000–2016. JAMA **321**(21), 2131–2133 (2019)
14. Hjalmarsen, A., Hykkerud, D.L.: Severe nocturnal hypoxaemia in geriatric inpatients. Age Ageing **37**(5), 526–529 (2008)
15. Home, V.: Vayyar Walabot (2020), https://vayyar.com/
16. Hope, H.: Hip-Hope^{TM} smart wearable hip protector using cutting-edge technology and design (2020), https://www.hip-hope.com/
17. Immonen, M., et al.: Association between Chronic Diseases and falls among a Sample of Older People in Finland. BMC Geriatr. **20**(225), 1–12 (2020)
18. Lin, F.R., Ferrucci., L.: Hearing loss and falls among older adults in the United States. Arch. Int. Med. **172**(4), 369–371 (2012)

19. Mohanty, S.P., Choppali, U., Kougianos, E.: Everything you wanted to know about smart cities: the internet of things is the backbone. IEEE Consum. Electr. Mag. **5**(3), 60–70 (2016). https://doi.org/10.1109/MCE.2016.2556879

20. Nižetić, S., Šolić, P., López Artaza, D., Patrono, L.: Internet of Things (IoT): opportunities, issues and challenges towards a smart and sustainable future. J. Clean. Prod. **274**(122877), 1–33 (2020)

21. O'Loughlin, J.L., Robitaille, Y., Boivin, J.F., Suissa, S.: Incidence of and risk factors for falls and injurious falls among the community-dwelling elderly. Am. J. Epidemiol. **137**(3), 342–354 (1993)

22. Owlytics: Owlytics Healthcare. (2020). https://www.owlytics.com/

23. Paulo, H., Pelicionia, S.R.L.: COVID-19 will severely impact older people's lives, and in many more ways than you think! Braz J. Phys. Ther. **24**(4), 293–294 (2020)

24. Pohl, J., Cochrane, B.B., Schepp, K.G., Woods, N.F.: Falls and the social isolation of older adults in the national health and aging trends study. Innov. Aging **1**(1), 268–269 (2017)

25. Pongthanisorn, G., Viriyavit, W., Prakayapan, T., Deepaisam, S., Somlertlamvanich, V.: ECS: elderly care system for fall and bedsore prevention using non-constraint sensor. In: International Electronics Symposium (IES), pp. 340–344 (2020). https://doi.org/10.1109/IES50839.2020.9231781

26. Rachakonda, L., Sharma, A., Mohanty, S.P., Kougianos, E.: Good-eye: a combined computer-vision and physiological-sensor based device for full-proof prediction and detection of fall of adults. **574**, 273–288 (2019)

27. Rachakonda, L., Bapatla, A.K., Mohanty, S.P., Kougianos, E.: SaYoPillow: blockchain-integrated privacy-assured IoMT framework for stress management considering sleeping habits. IEEE Trans. Consum. Electr. **67**(1), 20–29 (2021). https://doi.org/10.1109/TCE.2020.3043683

28. Razmara, J., Zaboli, M.H., Hassankhani, H.: Elderly fall risk prediction based on a physiological profile approach using artificial neural networks. Health Inform. J. **24**, 410–418 (2018)

29. Steimer, T.: The biology of fear- and anxiety-related behaviors. Dialog. Clin. Neurosci. **4**(3), 231–249 (2002)

30. Stevens, J.A., et al.: Gender differences in seeking care for falls in the aged medicare population. Am. J. Prev. Med. **43**(1), 59–62 (2012)

31. Taylor, C.A., Bell, J.M., Breiding, M.J., Xu, L.: Traumatic brain injury-related emergency department visits, hospitalizations, and deaths - United States, 2007 and 2013. MMWR Surveill. Summ. **66**(9), 1–16 (2017)

32. Özdemir, A.T., Barshan, B.: Detecting falls with wearable sensors using machine learning techniques. Sensors **14**(6), 10691–10708 (2014). https://doi.org/10.3390/s140610691, https://www.mdpi.com/1424-8220/14/6/10691

Hardware/Software Co-Design of a Low-Power IoT Fall Detection Device

Dimitrios Karagiannis[1(✉)], Ilias Maglogiannis[2], Konstantina S. Nikita[1], and Panayiotis Tsanakas[1]

[1] School of Electrical and Computer Engineering, National Technical University of Athens, Zografou, Greece
dkaragiannis@biosim.ntua.gr
[2] Department of Digital Systems, University of Piraeus, Piraeus, Greece

Abstract. Falls can cause severe injuries to elder people. Many studies have been conducted in order to develop devices that improve the recognition of fall events, while very few have demonstrated approaches for the minimization of their power consumption. We propose a hardware/software co-design of an Internet of Things (IoT) fall detection device that takes advantage of accelerometer's embedded functionalities and enables its interrupt-driven operation while the rest of the circuit is in shutdown mode. In contrast with most low power fall detection devices, the proposed device supports Wi-Fi connectivity that enables ubiquitous use and real-time remote fall events monitoring through cloud services, without the need of external equipment or a local server. The device integrates a vibration motor and a cancelation button, which notify the detection of a fall event and waits for Patient's response, while the implementation of battery monitoring mechanism enables continuous device use.

Keywords: Fall detection · Low power · Internet of Things · IoT · Hardware/Software co-design · Accelerometer

1 Introduction

Falls are a major issue for elderly people as they are very common and their prevention can reduce the admissions to nursing homes [1]. Moreover, falls due to seizures and nonepileptic events in an epilepsy monitoring unit (EMU) especially inside bathrooms can harm patients and solutions such as a ceiling lift system has demonstrated significant improvement [2]. Devices that can prevent or detect falls have been developed during the past years with different approaches and improvements concerning the used connectivity protocols with the server; the power consumption management; or the integration of machine learning techniques.

Some approaches for fall detection integrate the use of more sensors than just an accelerometer. In [3–5] researchers proposed systems using barometric pressure measurements, and T. De Quadros et al. [6] designed a wrist worn fall detection device using gyroscope and magnetometer, in addition to accelerometer. MPU6050 sensor has also been used, as it can provide both accelerometer and gyroscope measurements [7, 8].

Fall detection devices have been tested in different places, like aforementioned wrist or chest and with different communication technologies such as Bluetooth, Zigbee or Wi-Fi. W. Zhuang et al. [9] have developed a smart button system placed on the chest that collects accelerometer data and send them over Bluetooth low energy to an Android mobile. In [10] a microcontroller establishes Wi-Fi connection with the server and reports fall events and battery status. Yuan et al. [11] proposed a wrist-worn wearable as a ZigBee End Device that connects to a base station in order to communicate with cellular networks. A ZigBee server can further process sensors data in order to evaluate the fall detection [7, 8].

Fall detection devices should be easy to carry and operate for many hours without the need of recharging, as it can interrupt continuous monitoring, and discourage their use. Researchers have investigated various techniques in order to lower power consumption and provide a long-lasting battery operation [12], usually applying interrupt-driven algorithms [4, 8]. In [11] a wrist-worn wearable device utilizes interrupt signals generated by the accelerometer, that lead to less data processing and, therefore, lower power consumption. J. He et al. [7] developed an interrupt-driven device that is placed in the back neck area of a wearable vest and can operate continuously for more than 30 h with a 600 mAh battery. C. Wang et al. [5] reduced the power consumption using both hardware- and firmware-based approaches, enabling an estimated battery life (450 mAh capacity) of 664.9 usage days with an average current of 28.2 μA, using the ADXL362 accelerometer that is more power efficient compared with the ADXL345, which is frequently used in fall detection devices. In order to lower power consumption, an algorithm that changes sampling rate dynamically, according to fall indication, has been proposed [3].

Fall events can be evaluated with different techniques, like processing the sensors data with a Kalman Filter and kNN Algorithm [7], using a SVM classification algorithm [9], or using a Fall Detection Convolutional Neural Network (FD-CNN) [8]. Machine learning methods demonstrated advantages compared to threshold-based [6].

Post Fall actions are important for immediate response to patient's condition. In [13] the accelerometer is connected with a microcontroller and a module that provides GPS/GSM service in order to send SMS in case of a fall. The device will vibrate and the patient can withdraw the alarm with a button. In [14] a hardware fall detection system has been designed that can enable an alarm and activate a mechanism in order to protect the patient. There are also commercial products with cellular connection capabilities that include fall detection and many other features - not essential for elder people - but the battery life is limited [15].

We propose an Internet of Things (IoT) fall detection device that is placed on the chest using an innovative co-design of hardware and software, to achieve low power consumption. Whereas many aforementioned devices are low power, they use a ZigBee network that requires a local server to be fully functional. Our proposed device supports serverless operation using Wi-Fi, which is broadly available and doesn't require any external equipment for most of the patients. Newer mobile phones enable Wi-Fi hotspot using the existing cellular connectivity, which provides ubiquitous internet access. Although Wi-Fi communication is useful, it requires high power consumption that makes it not suitable for a fall detection device. In order to solve this issue, we propose a hardware architecture that enables the operation only of the accelerometer, where the rest of the circuit is in shutdown mode consuming negligible energy. Our fall detection device has very low power consumption during patient's every day activities, but in case of a fall event it turns into high power mode. Moreover, we integrated battery undervoltage detection and protection mechanisms in order to ensure continuous device operation. The device incorporates a cancelation mechanism, through a button and a vibration motor, that notifies the patient in case of a fall event detection. Although patient's immobility after a fall is usually verified with accelerometer measurements, instead in the proposed device a Cancelation button is used, which can help the detection of cases where the patient is moving after fall, because of pain and injuries or epileptic seizures.

This paper is organized as follows: Sect. 2 describes the Fall Detection basic principles and Sect. 3 demonstrates the platform architecture, the hardware of the proposed device and the algorithm it utilizes during operation and after a fall event. Section 4 evaluates the device's power consumption and Sect. 5 is the Discussion, where the Conclusion is in Sect. 6.

2 Fall Detection Basic Principles

For our experiment we used ADXL345, an ultralow power accelerometer from Analog Devices that can provide 3-axis acceleration with up to 13 bit resolution and $\pm$ 16g range [16]. ADXL345 can map different functions to two interrupt pins (INT1 and INT2) with user defined thresholds: single and double tap; free-fall; activity and inactivity sensing. Interrupts enable the fall detection without any processing by the main microcontroller, as the acceleration data are processed by the accelerometer separately.

Free fall interrupt has two user defined thresholds: THRESH_FF and TIME_FF and is set when acceleration for all axes is less than the value stored in THRESH_FF register for more time than the value stored in TIME_FF register [16]. The first phase of a Fall is always the "Weightlessness" where the vector sum of the accelerations from all axes tends to 0 g, in contrast with all other motions like sitting or walking [17]. Our system takes advantage of the "Weightlessness" phase, which is essential for fall, and activates the Free Fall interrupt.

3 Platform Architecture

3.1 Platform Overview

The fall detection device operates in an ultralow power consumption state where the microcontroller and its peripherals are in shutdown mode. ADXL345 operates normally until Patient's fall. Then it activates the FREE_FALL interrupt that turns on the microcontroller and the Vibration motor, in order to notify Patient that he/she has to interact and press a button that is integrated on the device. If there is not a Patient response, the microcontroller connects through Wi-Fi to Cloud services and notifies the Physician about the emergency. If the Patient presses the button the device returns to the ultralow power state (Fig. 1).

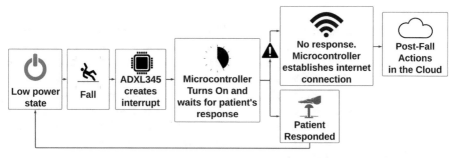

Fig. 1. Platform overview[1]

3.2 Device Hardware Architecture

The device consists of a 3D printed enclosure and a custom PCB with: (i) an accelerometer, (ii) a microcontroller, (iii) two Voltage Regulators, (iv) two Voltage Detectors, (v) a Vibration Motor module, (vi) a Button for interaction with the Patient, (vii) other peripherals (LED, buttons) for microcontroller programming and debugging. The hardware is divided in four sections with different functionalities (A–D) that will be analyzed separately (Fig. 2).

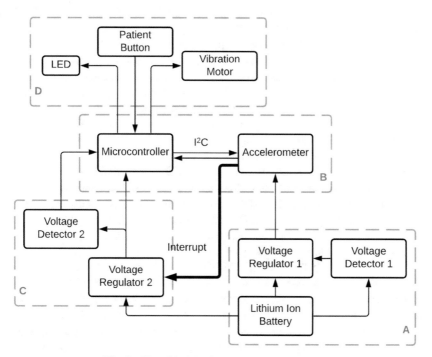

Fig. 2. Simplified device hardware architecture

---

[1] Figure 1, 2, 4, 5, 7 created in Lucidchart. Available: www.lucidchart.com.

Accelerometer Powering Circuit and Battery Undervoltage Protection (A). The power source is a high-density rechargeable lithium-ion battery with 3400 mAh capacity, 3.6 V nominal and 4.2 V maximum voltage. The accelerometer we used is ADXL345 that operates from 2.0 V to 3.6 V [16]. In order to regulate the battery voltage, as voltage regulator 1 the TPS70633DRVR is selected, because it has ultra-low quiescent current (1 μA) and enable (EN) pin that controls its shutdown or active state. Although we use lithium-ion battery that has integrated protection circuit with cutoff voltage at 2.5 V, we added one more protection layer. As voltage detector 1 we selected STM1061N26WX6F that monitors battery voltage and in case it falls below 2.6 V it outputs low. This output is connected with enable (EN) pin of voltage regulator 1 and (when it is low) the regulator will turn into shutdown mode. Moreover, we added capacitors that add stability and better performance to the regulator. Section A (Fig. 2) of the circuit is used only for the accelerometer's operation.

Accelerometer and Microcontroller I^{2}C Communication (B). ESP32-WROOM-32 is a low-cost microcontroller module that supports Wi-Fi, Bluetooth, BLE connectivity and operates at ~3.3 V. It communicates with ADXL345 accelerometer with I^{2}C protocol using the necessary pull-up resistors and 2 pins (SDA, SCL). ADXL345 interrupt pin 1 (INT1) that is used as the FREE_FALL interrupt is not connected with ESP32.

Microcontroller Powering Circuit and Battery Voltage Monitoring (C). The afore-mentioned low-dropout voltage regulator 1 (TPS70633DRVR) powers only ADXL345 accelerometer but not the ESP32-WROOM-32 (ESP32) module. It can provide max current of 150 mA, where ESP32 module needs minimum 500 mA. As Voltage Regula-tor 2, TLV75533PDBVR is selected because it can provide 500 mA to ESP32 and has low dropout voltage that enables stable 3.3 V output even when the battery voltage is decreasing. Also, it supports enable (EN) pin that controls its operational or shutdown state. ADXL345 FREE_FALL Interrupt (INT1) is connected to EN pin of voltage reg-ulator 2 (bold line in Fig. 2). When INT1 is low (i.e. no fall event), Voltage Regulator 2 is in shutdown mode and everything that is powered from it, is turned off. Thus, we succeed an ultralow power consumption under usual circumstances.

After fall detection, accelerometer's FREE_FALL interrupt (INT1) is activated and becomes High, as enable (EN) pin of Voltage Regulator 2. Thus, Voltage Regulator 2 turns on and powers the ESP32 module in order to run the fall detection algorithm. At the end of ESP32 actions, through I2C communication, ESP32 clears ADXL345 INT1 interrupt after reading INT_SOURCE register, that leads to the shutdown of Voltage Regulator 2 and the return to the previous operation.

Voltage Detector 2 (STM1061N31W6F) monitors the output of Voltage Regulator 2 and in case the Voltage is under 3.1 V, it sets the connected Pin of ESP32 Low. Every time ESP32 is turned on, this pin is checked. If it is Low, battery low voltage indication is sent to the Cloud, so Patient will be notified by his/her Physician (who monitors the Cloud) in order to charge the battery and be protected without stopping the functional fall detection device. ESP32 operation will not stop immediately if the battery is below 3.1 V, but after becoming lower than 2.6 V (as described in section A). Though, it is recommended to immediately recharge the battery, as voltage below 3.0 V is not recommended for ESP32 operation [18].

Interaction Components (LED, Vibration Motor and Button) (D). We added a vibration motor module, a LED, and a tactile switch as a Cancelation button. In case of a fall detection, the LED turns on and the motor notifies the Patient so he/she can press the button and deactivate the emergency algorithm. Finally, a SPDT switch, two extra tactile buttons and pin headers are added for easier programming and debugging of the circuit.

3.3 3D Printed Enclosure

The designed hardware and a Li-ion battery of 3400 mAh with integrated protection circuit are placed inside an enclosure that protects and stabilizes the circuit. Also, it provides an easy way to use a cord and hang it around the Patient's neck. The enclosure is 3D printed with PLA filament (Fig. 3).

Fig. 3. 3D printed enclosure, 18650 Li-ion battery and hardware of the fall detection device. The areas with the red frame are used for easier programming of the device but they can be skipped, if we would like to minimize the PCB size. (Color figure online)

3.4 Device Operation Algorithm

Figure 4 demonstrates the Fall event confirmation from the moment of initial detection until the emergency signal that is sent to the Cloud:

(A) The microcontroller (ESP32) and its peripherals are in shutdown mode without consuming power. The accelerometer on the other hand, is in Active mode, operates normally and the FREE_FALL interrupt parameters have been set during the first device operation. During Patient's daily activities, only the accelerometer is running and the rest of the system is waiting for the FREE_FALL interrupt. After fall detection, the interrupt enables Voltage Regulator 2 that is responsible for ESP32 powering.

(B) Fall has already been detected, so ESP32 waits for Patient's response. We have set Vibration for 5 s, followed by 5 s of ESP32 inaction. The Pin connected to the Cancelation Button has already been set as an interrupt pin that can stop Vibration Motor or ESP32 inaction immediately after it is pressed. Vibration reminds Patient that the fall detection algorithm has been activated and a button press is required in order to cancel the emergency. If the Patient does not respond after 10 consecutive cycles of vibration - waiting, ESP32 will proceed to an emergency signal. Even if ADXL345 accelerometer supports inactivity interruption or we can read its acceleration measurements that should indicate Patient's immobility, we use the Cancelation button. Thus, the fall detection algorithm will not be confused by a Patient that has fallen and is moving but is injured and unable to stand up or call for help.

(C) If the battery is exhausted - and therefore Voltage Detector 2 is activated - ESP32 updates a variable that will be used during Cloud connection in order to notify the Physician.

(D) Patient has not responded by pressing the Cancelation button for 100 s (5 s of Vibration and 5 s of waiting for 10 times), thus ESP32 will establish a Wi-Fi connection to the Cloud services where it reports the fall. If the Patient has pressed the Cancelation button, and the Battery is not low, ESP32 resets FREE_FALL interrupt, which in turn disables Voltage Regulator 2 and turns off ESP32. ADXL345 accelerometer continues to operate, in order to detect another possible fall. In case of low battery voltage, even if the Patient responded, ESP32 will connect to the Cloud to update the battery level indication.

3.5 Post-Fall Algorithm

In the previous section we demonstrated the fall detection algorithm that confirms or discards the interrupt signal caused by the accelerometer. After confirmation - and/or battery's low voltage – the microcontroller (ESP32) establishes Wi-Fi connection in order to proceed to the post fall algorithm (Fig. 5). During ESP32 programming we have defined credentials (SSID and password) for Patient's home router and mobile phone Wi-Fi hotspot, which will enable mobile data sharing. Wi-Fi hotspot will provide ubiquitous internet connection even outside of Patient's home.

ESP32 starts by trying to establish connection with the Patient's home router and in case it does not succeed, it tries to connect with the mobile phone's Wi-Fi hotspot. Then, it connects to Adafruit IO, a Cloud service that enables data storing and visualization [19]. In Adafruit IO we created two feeds: one for fall detection and one for battery low voltage indication. These feeds are connected and visualized to a simplified Dashboard that updates in real-time, which the Physician can remotely monitor through the Adafruit IO platform (Fig. 6). Using IFTTT Gmail service, we created a trigger that monitors Adafruit IO data feeds and whenever a fall is recorded, an email is sent to up to 20 recipients. Thus, not only the Physician can remotely and in real-time monitor the Patient, but Patient's relatives also will be alerted in an emergency case. IFTTT ("If This Then That") is a trigger-action programming model that has gained popularity [20] and can be used to further expand our platform with more emergency actions after fall event.

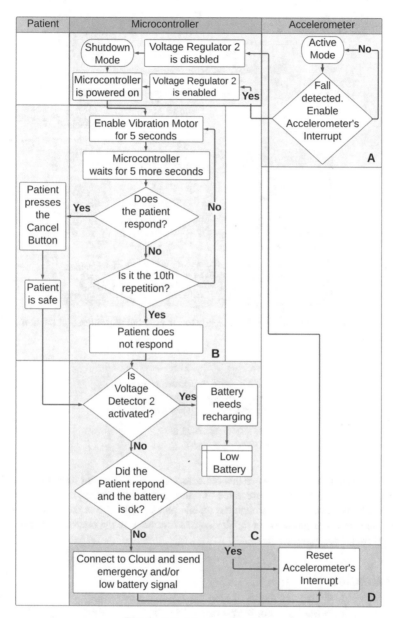

Fig. 4. Fall detection algorithm

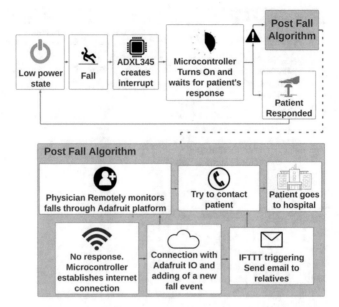

Fig. 5. After fall confirmation, ESP32 proceeds to the post fall algorithm and the connection to Cloud services.

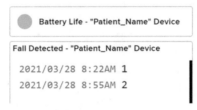

Fig. 6. If the battery voltage is lower that the cutoff, the green indicator turns red. The second block monitors fall detections, where value "1" indicates that the Patient's device is connected through the home network, "2" through the mobile phone, and "3" that the Patient is safe (the Cancelation button was pressed) but the device was connected to the platform to report that the battery is low. (Color figure online)

4   Evaluation

In order to evaluate the power consumption of the device, we simulated a fall event and measured the current with an INA219 current monitor. INA219 was placed in series with the circuit at the high side of voltage (at battery's positive terminal) as demonstrated in Fig. 7. An Arduino UNO communicates with I^2C protocol with INA219 and logs power consumption measurements (Figs. 8 and 9).

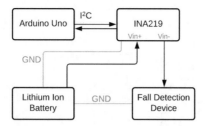

Fig. 7. Experimental design used for the fall detection device power consumption evaluation, before, during and after the fall event.

Figures 8 and 9 demonstrate the current measurements using INA219 during a fall event simulation. At the beginning (before the fall) the values are around zero or negative because the current is very low and INA219 is unable to measure it, so we used a multimeter. The measured current was ~50.5 µA. In order to accomplish this current we set ADXL345 to low power mode and the Output Data Rate to 25 Hz, which is achieved by decimating a common sampling frequency [16]. FREE_FALL interrupt is not affected by lower Output Data Rates because its operation is based on undecimated data. Using a 3400 mAh battery in an ideal scenario where the Patient has no falls at all and there are no interruptions generated from the accelerometer, the device can operate for around 2805 days or 7.69 years without recharging [21]. The current during vibration is ~100 mA and during 5 s of waiting is ~55 mA. For easier demonstration, instead of 10 cycles of vibration-waiting, according to the presented fall detection algorithm, we programmed one cycle for the simulation. During Wi-Fi connection the peak current is 433.92 mA, which is multiple times the low power state current, so the connection with

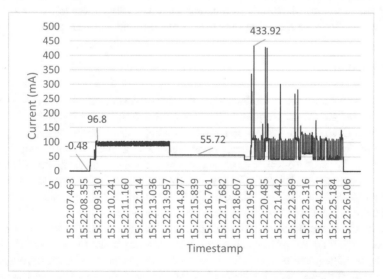

Fig. 8. Current measurements using INA219 during a fall event simulation. The battery voltage is 3.84 V.

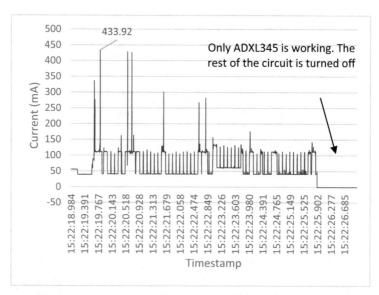

Fig. 9. Current measurements during Wi-Fi connection enlarged. After the end of the fall detection algorithm the device returns to low power state with current 50.5 μA.

the Cloud services occurs only in emergency circumstances (i.e. confirmed fall or low battery voltage). If the Patient responds during the fall detection algorithm by pressing the button and the battery level is not low, the device will return to low power state without Wi-Fi connection. Moreover, we evaluated the device response when power source voltage was less than 3.1 V but more than 2.6 V that led to change of green battery indication in Adafruit IO to red, and when the voltage was less than 2.6 V that set the whole circuit in shutdown mode (measured current was ~1.2 μA).

5   Discussion

The demonstrated fall detection device enables low power consumption, supports server-less operation and doesn't require any infrastructure (other than Wi-Fi connection) or a SIM card. Even though Wi-Fi connectivity is a high-power consumption process that would quickly drain the battery, the proposed device consumes 50.5 μA, when there is no fall event. We used a 3400 mAh battery that in an ideal scenario with no fall detection at all could operate the device for 7.69 years. Even if the actual battery life is much less, the device could be easily maintained by the Patient with rare charges and provide more working hours compared to existing commercial solutions [15].

Furthermore, we incorporated a mechanism that checks battery level and protects the Patient from an unreported fall event due to an insufficiently powered device, by updating the battery status in the cloud. A second protection mechanism shuts down the whole circuit if the battery level is very low. Moreover, the integration of a Cancelation button enables the Patient to reject a false fall detection that makes the device return to the previous low power operation. In cases such as an epileptic seizure - that the Patient is moving after fall but is unable to press the Cancelation button - our device will make a more reliable detection, compared to other approaches that wait for a motionless Patient. With IFTTT we provided an easy way to add extra services, like the notification of other people that the Patient is unsafe, which is already integrated.

Although more experimental data from fall events would be useful in fine tuning the accelerometer's FREE_FALL interrupt parameters and the fall detection algorithm that takes place after microcontroller's activation, the demonstrated low power hardware design works independently. Totally different algorithms and techniques can be applied to the proposed hardware, while the power consumption before the fall detection will be the same.

The device could be further optimized for real-world applications with size and weight reduction. Despite the fact the battery that was used provides a lot of energy, it adds a lot of extra weight and size, while the consumption is very low, thus enabling the use of a smaller one. Also, some PCB components, which demonstrated in Fig. 3, could be removed as they are used for easier development. So, a future smaller version of the device will be easier to use, hanged around the neck or embedded in the Patient's clothes, compared to a smart watch, which he/she is not used to and must wear continuously. Furthermore, there are accelerometers more power efficient than ADXL345 that could reduce the consumption additionally. Also, we can further test our device in order to detect more complex fall events, like a slow fall and improve the cancelation mechanism to include cases where the Patient pressed the Cancelation button but could not stand up afterwards (for example by repeating the vibration-waiting cycles after a few minutes). Finally, instead of just notify other people in case of a fall event using IFTTT email service, we can develop a mobile app to locate the person who is closer and make him/her responsible to visit the Patient.

6 Conclusion

In this paper, we demonstrated a hardware and software co-designed fall detection device that achieves low power operation utilizing accelerometer's interrupt-based embedded functionalities, whereas the rest of the circuit is in shutdown mode, consuming negligible energy. The proposed IoT device can establish Wi-Fi connectivity to implement post-fall actions using Cloud services, without the need of external equipment or a local server, in contrary with other low-power approaches. The integration of a Cancelation button allows a Patient to declare that he/she is safe, while helps the detection of a fallen Patient who is in danger but not immobile. Mechanisms check low battery voltage or depletion, enabling continuous protection against fall events.

Acknowledgment. This research has been co-financed by the European Regional Development Fund of the European Union and Greek national funds through the Operational Program Competitiveness, Entrepreneurship, and Innovation, under the call RESEARCH – CREATE – INNOVATE (project code: T1EDK-02506).

References

1. Tinetti, M.E., Williams, C.S.: Falls, injuries due to falls, and the risk of admission to a nursing home. N. Engl. J. Med. **337**, 1279–1284 (1997). https://doi.org/10.1056/NEJM199710303371806

2. Spritzer, S.D., et al.: Fall prevention and bathroom safety in the epilepsy monitoring unit. Epilepsy Behav. **48**, 75–78 (2015). https://doi.org/10.1016/j.yebeh.2015.05.026

3. Wang C, et al.: A low-power fall detection algorithm based on triaxial acceleration and barometric pressure. In: 2014 36th Annual International Conference of the IEEE Engineering in Medicine and Biology Society, pp. 570–573 (2014). https://doi.org/10.1109/EMBC.2014.6943655

4. Wang, C., et al.: A low-power fall detector balancing sensitivity and false alarm rate. IEEE J. Biomed. Heal Inform. **22**, 1929–1937 (2018). https://doi.org/10.1109/JBHI.2017.2778271

5. Wang, C., et al.: Low-power fall detector using triaxial accelerometry and barometric pressure sensing. IEEE Trans. Ind. Inform. **12**, 2302–2311 (2016). https://doi.org/10.1109/TII.2016.2587761

6. de Quadros, T., Lazzaretti, A.E., Schneider, F.K.: A movement decomposition and machine learning-based fall detection system using wrist wearable device. IEEE Sens. J. **18**, 5082–5089 (2018). https://doi.org/10.1109/JSEN.2018.2829815

7. He, J., Zhang, Z., Yu, W.: Interrupt-driven fall detection system realized via a Kalman filter and kNN algorithm. In: 2018 IEEE SmartWorld, Ubiquitous Intelligence & Computing, Advanced & Trusted Computing, Scalable Computing & Communications, Cloud & Big Data Computing, Internet of People and Smart City Innovation (SmartWorld/SCALCOM/UIC/ATC/CBDCom/IOP/SCI), pp 579–584 (2018). https://doi.org/10.1109/SmartWorld.2018.00120

8. He, J., Zhang, Z., Wang, X., Yang, S.: A low power fall sensing technology based on FD-CNN. IEEE Sens. J. **19**, 5110–5118 (2019). https://doi.org/10.1109/JSEN.2019.2903482

9. Zhuang, W., et al.: A novel wearable smart button system for fall detection. In: AIP Conference Proceedings, p. 020075 (2017). https://doi.org/10.1063/1.4982440

10. López, A., Pérez, D., Ferrero, F.J., Postolache, O.: A Real-time algorithm to detect falls in the elderly. In: 2018 IEEE International Symposium on Medical Measurements and Applications (MeMeA), pp 1–5 (2018). https://doi.org/10.1109/MeMeA.2018.8438747

11. Yuan, J., Tan, K.K., Lee, T.H., Koh, G.C.H.: Power-efficient interrupt-driven algorithms for fall detection and classification of activities of daily living. IEEE Sens. J. **15**, 1377–1387 (2015). https://doi.org/10.1109/JSEN.2014.2357035

12. Ren, L., Peng, Y.: Research of fall detection and fall prevention technologies: a systematic review. IEEE Access **7**, 77702–77722 (2019). https://doi.org/10.1109/ACCESS.2019.2922708

13. Wu, F., Zhao, H., Zhao, Y., Zhong, H.: Development of a wearable-sensor-based fall detection system. Int. J. Telemed. Appl. **2015**, 1–11 (2015). https://doi.org/10.1155/2015/576364

14. Xiuping, Y., Jia-Nan, L., Zuhua, F.: Hardware design of fall detection system based on ADXL345 sensor. In: 2015 8th International Conference on Intelligent Computation Technology and Automation (ICICTA), pp 446–449 (2015). https://doi.org/10.1109/ICICTA.2015.117

15. Apple Watch - Battery - Apple. https://www.apple.com/watch/battery/. Accessed 24 Feb 2021

16. Analog Devices ADXL345 Datasheet. https://www.analog.com/media/en/technical-documentation/data-sheets/ADXL345.pdf. Accessed 10 Jun 2021

17. Jia, N.: Detecting human falls with a 3-axis digital accelerometer. Analog Dialogue **43**, 3–9 (2009)

18. Espressif Systems: ESP32-WROOM-32 Datasheet (2021). https://www.espressif.com/sites/default/files/documentation/esp32-wroom-32_datasheet_en.pdf. Accessed 10 Jun 2021
19. What is Adafruit IO? | Welcome to Adafruit IO | Adafruit Learning System. https://learn.adafruit.com/welcome-to-adafruit-io/what-is-adafruit-io. Accessed 24 Feb 2021
20. Ur, B., et al.: Trigger-action programming in the wild: an analysis of 200,000 IFTTT recipes. In: Proceedings of the 2016 CHI Conference on Human Factors in Computing Systems. Association for Computing Machinery, New York, NY, USA, pp. 3227–3231 (2016). https://doi.org/10.1145/2858036.2858556
21. Battery Life Calculator | DigiKey Electronics. https://www.digikey.com/en/resources/conversion-calculators/conversion-calculator-battery-life. Accessed 31 Mar 2021

Security

ReOPUF: Relaxation Oscillator Physical Unclonable Function for Reliable Key Generation in IoT Security

Raveendra Podeti[1]([✉]), Srihari Rao Patri[1], Srinivas Katkoori[2], and Muralidhar Pullakandam[1]

[1] ECE Department, National Institute of Technology Warangal, Warangal 506004, Telangana, India
raveendra466@student.nitw.ac.in, {patri,pmurali}@nitw.ac.in
[2] CSE Department, University of South Florida, Tampa, FL 33620, USA
katkoori@usf.edu

Abstract. Physical Unclonable Function (PUF) has emerged as a hardware security block designed with low-cost and key generation for IC identification and authentication. The process variations being uncontrollable, they can be exploited as PUF that could generate unique identifiers representing robust keys. Arbiter-based PUFs work on the principle of the conventional delay-based approach realized between two symmetrical engaged paths. On the other hand, oscillator-based PUFs work on frequency differences among a group of identical oscillators arranged in a specific pattern. In this paper, a novel PUF is proposed based on Relaxation Oscillator PUF (ReOPUF) topology for device identification and authentication that can produce unique, unpredictable, and reliable keys to improve the robustness against the supply voltage and temperature variations. The ReOPUF is designed to generate a 4.4 MHz frequency that is suitable for powering IoT sub-systems including sensors while protecting them from malicious attacks. Based on Monte Carlo simulations, the reliability of PUF responses has been improved from 95.33% for the regular Ring Oscillator (RO) PUF to 99.19% for the proposed ReOPUF over a temperature range of $-40\,^{\circ}\mathrm{C}$ to $+120\,^{\circ}\mathrm{C}$ with $\pm10\%$ fluctuations in supply voltage. Moreover, it achieves a good uniqueness result of 49.22%, diffuseness of 49.52%, and worst-case reliability of 97.41% over a range of $10\,^{\circ}\mathrm{C}$ to $85\,^{\circ}\mathrm{C}$, and 10% fluctuations in supply voltage. Thus, we report significant improvement over previous works.

Keywords: Hardware security · Internet-of-Things (IoT) · PUF · Process variations · Reliability · Arbiter PUF · RO PUF

1 Introduction

The design of secure electronic systems is very important so that they can store sensitive information as well as communicate securely with the authorized

L. M. Camarinha-Matos et al. (Eds.): IFIPIoT 2021, IFIP AICT 641, pp. 163–179, 2022.
https://doi.org/10.1007/978-3-030-96466-5_11

devices. The rapid down scaling in feature sizes of Integrated Circuits (ICs) has exponentially improved computing power of processors which require robust security mechanisms [1]. Currently, the secure device authentication and data integration is provided by incorporating cryptographic functions implemented as hardware blocks [4]. The secret key is stored in non-volatile memory such as erasable programmable read-only memories which is vulnerable to invasive or non-invasive attacks. Physical Unclonable Function (PUFs) [2,3,5] emerged as robust security primitives to generate volatile security keys based on the inherent random manufacturing Process Variations (PVs) [6]. It offers a strong volatile key generation and storage to make the system tamper-resistant. When a PUF is fed with a challenge, it generates unique responses based on the physical characteristics of the silicon and is an alternative to the conventional digital signature mechanism.

A group of identical PUF cells with the same manufacturing process leverage the physical properties of each cell and generate a device-specific fingerprint or key [7]. PUF can be used in several applications such as device authentication or identification, key generation for encryption, and pseudo-noise random number generation [8,9]. The uniqueness and randomness are the unpredictable features of a PUF that makes it resistant to security attacks. PUFs are only uncertain in power-up conditions when side-channel or power analysis attacks are performed. To make a strong PUF the key generation must stable and reliable which means the key should not change over time. Several PUF topologies have been proposed to improve reliability in the past decade, such as Arbiter PUF, Ring Oscillator (RO) PUF, SRAM PUF, etc. Among them, Arbiter PUFs [10] are very complex and generate strong challenge and response pairs [11,12], whereas, RO PUFs are less complex and easy to design.

As mobile electronic gadgets become more widespread, day-to-day business (financial transactions, document exchange, health data, etc.) is done through integrated circuits. Thus, it is essential to incorporate strong security to ensure data privacy and trust [1]. PUFs serve as key generators for cryptographic devices to provide secure communication in an untrusted environment [7]. Security in data is generally raised through data sharing or distribution of the keys generated through key generators. The main characteristics of the key generated by a PUF are its randomness and uniqueness due to PVs. The key should be unaffected due to temperature and supply voltage variations and must be resistant to side-channel attacks.

RO PUFs [12,13] are most popular due to their security, simplicity, ease of implementation, and evaluation. However, the main disadvantage of RO PUFs is poor response generation with temperature and supply voltage variations [14,15]. Therefore, the reliability is enhanced by selecting a strong RO pair from 1-out of n-RO pairs, which has the maximum frequency distance from n-pairs. Multi-level supply voltage powered RO PUF are proposed to select the highest reliable voltage configuration [16]. The feedback-based supply voltage control can improve the reliability better than the conventional RO PUFs [17]. A temperature-aware RO PUF with different RO pairs can generate reliable bits against temperature variations [18, 19]. The temperature sensitivity is the major drawback in RO PUFs and can be reduced by applying a negative temperature coefficient of resistance to the inverters with two source feedback resistors. However, to achieve high reliability, a lightweight hybrid RO PUF was proposed with high thermal stability against supply voltage variation [15]. The security can be further strengthened when the system is designed with machine learning [21] based schemes for IoT edge node security.

To this end, we make the following contributions:

- We propose a new Relaxation Oscillator PUF design which we refer to as ReOPUF. The ReOs in ReOPUF is designed to explicitly produce the low frequency i.e., 4.4 MHz suitable for IoT sensor node security.
- The respective PUF quality metrics are evaluated and analyzed for the proposed PUF to demonstrate the high reliability in key generation.
- We perform extensive simulations (in 65 nm CMOS technology) to compare the proposed PUF with conventional RO PUFs in terms of PUF quality metrics with respect to supply voltage and temperature variations. We evaluate two more quality metrics, namely, Diffuseness (D) and Uniformity (u). We compare the strong CRP generation of the proposed ReOPUF with that of arbiter PUF. Further, we perform the entropy and correlation analysis.

The rest of the paper is organized as follows. Section 2 motivates the IoT authentication with PUFs. Section 3 surveys related research regarding existing PUFs and their reliability measurement with PUF quality metrics in response key generation. Section 4 proposes the methodology to achieve high uniqueness and reliability to enhance the security of IoT devices. Section 5 reports the simulation results, evaluates PUF quality metrics and, compares the proposed design with other PUFs. Section 6 presents a detailed security evaluation. Finally, Sect. 7 concludes the paper.

2   IoT Node Authentication with PUFs - Motivation

With the increasing demands on strong security, key generation and device authentication became the most challenging design concerns, particularly for IoT-enabled devices. Traditional security mechanisms that store keys in erasable programmable memories and use them with standard cryptographic algorithms suffer from power limitations. To implement information encryption and authentication, the tamper-resistant devices are equipped with countermeasures to defeat different types of physical attacks. Severe limitations on resources such as memory, CPU and battery power make classical cryptographic solutions unaffordable. Therefore, PUF has become a relatively simple and fast alternative for security.

PUFs are promising hardware security primitives to produce device-dependent challenge-response pairs based on unclonable properties and thus are suitable for reliable key generation [1]. The keys generated by PUFs are more resilient to malicious attacks from physical tampering. Figure 1 shows the

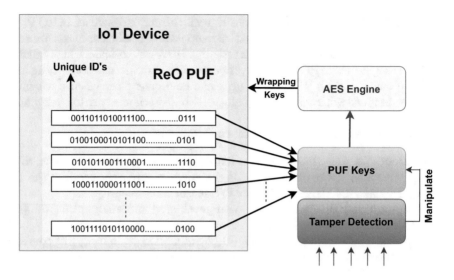

Fig. 1. PUF for IoT enabled devices

security concept of IoT-enabled devices. An IoT device equipped with ReOPUF generates PUF key as a unique ID and is shared through a gateway with the Cloud server. PUF keys are acquired by the Advanced Encryption Standard (AES) engine in the Cloud that can be employed to identify and authorize an IoT device. For example, consider an IoT-enabled sensor node in the field that senses the temperature or moisture data continuously upload the data to the Cloud at regular intervals. This data can be protected in the Cloud by encrypting it with PUF keys generated by ReOPUF. Therefore, due to the uniqueness and reliability of the ReOPUF, the sensor node can be authenticated.

3   Related Research

In this section, we briefly summarize the existing PUF topologies and their quality metrics to generate CRPs for device identification or authentication.

3.1   Ring Oscillator PUF

Figure 2 shows a conventional Ring Oscillator (RO) PUF for key generation [11]. It consists of N identically designed ROs (RO1, RO2, ..., RON), two multiplexers, two counters, and one comparator. Each RO oscillates at different frequency due to manufacturing process variations, even though ROs are designed with an equal number of inverter stages [12]. An N-bit multiplexer can select a pair of frequencies generated from the RO stage based on the challenge input (through selection lines). The counters are used to get the count of the pulses obtained from the MUX stage. The difference in the pulses between the two counters is verified by the comparator and a response is generated. For example, if Counter 1 output is greater than that of Counter 2 then a '1' is generated, otherwise, a '0'. In this manner, an N-bit key can be obtained from an N copies of RO PUF.

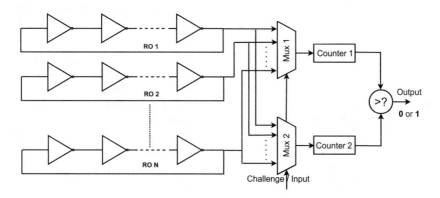

Fig. 2. Ring Oscillator PUF

3.2   Arbiter PUF

Figure 3 shows a basic arbiter PUF. It consists of switch components (SCs) and arbiter block to route the input signal and to perform the arbitration process for earlier response detection respectively [9]. Input and a random challenge are simultaneously fed to the switching components (multiplexers). Based on the delay of the paths the arbiter will detect early rising edge as the response. The mechanism of delay-based PUF is to introduce a race condition between two equally designed delay paths and the faster path will determine the output.

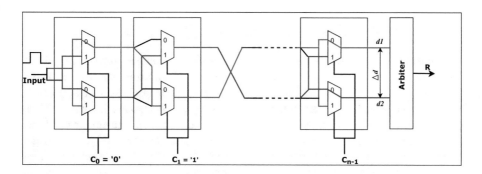

Fig. 3. Arbiter PUF

The circuit accepts of n-bit input challenge 'C' and computes 1-bit response 'R' based on the contention between two symmetrical paths based on relative delay difference ($\Delta d = d1 - d2$). The delay of the input is determined by the two-path processing of multiplexers (MUXs). Formally, the SCs are designed with 2×1 MUXs and properly tuned to get the precise delay (d) as a response. The delays are generally considered as PVs in APUFs, such as produced by the placement of a different combination of transistor arrangements in MUXs to produce certain delays at SCs. The MUXs will active the straight path if the selection (challenge) C_i is '0' and crossed when C_i is '1'. Likewise, MUX stages acting as SCs can create a pair of delay paths that can be selected with challenge input. The output is evaluated for a particular input while a rising signal is fed to both paths at the same time. The two signals race through the delay paths and the arbiter circuit (generally use D Flip-flop) catches the signal which comes earlier. The arbiter determines which rising edge arrives first and sets its output to '0' or '1' depending on the winner. For example, if a 16-bit input is given with a pre-defined challenge, an output '1' is produced if path1 is arrived early otherwise '0' is produced for path2.

3.3   PUF Quality Metrics

The quality of a PUF is measured using three major metrics, namely, *Uniqueness*, *Randomness*, and *Reliability* [20]. Uniqueness measures how different PUF instances can generate different responses when the same challenge is applied. The average inter-chip Hamming Distance (HD) calculated between the obtained responses should ideally be 50%. Randomness is the measure of unpredictability of responses from a PUF. For a good PUF design, the generation of response bits '1's and '0's should be distributed equally i.e., 50%. Reliability of a PUF determines how efficiently a PUF can generate the same response at different operating conditions for a given challenge. It is considered as intra-HD and should ideally be 0%.

4   Proposed Relaxation Oscillator PUF (ReOPUF)

An oscillator is a circuit that generates a repetitive waveform of fixed amplitude and frequency without any external input signal. Oscillators are used in radio, television, computer, and communications. Relaxation Oscillator (ReO) shown in Fig. 4 is specifically preferred for low-frequency applications such as waveform generators, triggering circuits, etc. ReO is considered as a non-linear oscillator that can generate a periodic non-sinusoidal waveform (either voltage or current) at its output such as a square wave, triangular wave, etc. It is also called a non-sinusoidal waveform generator. ReOs do not require external components and are easily implemented in CMOS technology. In addition, ReOs are capable of producing sustained square wave oscillations determined by the time constant RC even though the frequency accuracy is restricted by the tolerances of on-chip capacitors and resistors. ReOs consume less current and power to generate jitter less clock generation.

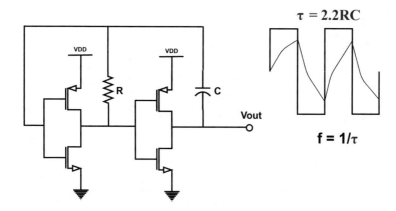

Fig. 4. Basic Relaxation Oscillator

A major drawback of ReO is its susceptibility to process and temperature variations. By the use of polysilicon resistors and the utilization of electron mobility in a MOS transistor offers an accurate frequency reference subjected to achieve fewer process variations and frequency stability over temperature. Most of the reported oscillators suffer from external components, reliability, and excessive power consumption and are not suitable for low-frequency applications requiring long battery lifetime.

The circuit can be designed with an energy storing device such as a capacitor or inductor which charges and discharges continuously to produce a cycle regarding a pre-determined threshold voltage. The frequency (f) or period (t) of oscillation with ReO is determined by the time constant $(\tau = 2.2RC)$ of the capacitive or inductive circuit. Likewise, the frequency is calculated for the basic ReO is $f = 1/\tau$ i.e., 4.4 MHz. ReOs are widely used to produce internal clock signals in several low frequency digital circuits. ReOs are also found in applications of thyristor triggering circuits, oscilloscopes, etc.

ReOPUF is a hardware PUF that exploits PVs occurring in the silicon manufacturing process to produce reliable keys. The random number extracted via ReOPUF is unique and unclonable that can be used as a silicon "fingerprint" for a wide range of security purposes, including encryption, identification, authentication, and security key generation.

Figure 5 shows a Relaxation Oscillator (ReO) PUF consists of 'N' identical ReOs (ReO1, ReO2, ...ReON), two n-bit multiplexers (MUXs), two counters, and a comparator. Each ReO generates a unique frequency when fed with different challenges or inputs. The frequency of 4.4 MHz is specially designed and generated for IoT sensor node applications. The MUXs can produce nonidentical frequencies due to the process variations of the device, even though they are designed with the same device characteristics. The challenge or input applied to both MUXs selects one pair of ReO the frequency difference of which will determine the output. The obtained frequency difference in terms of 1-bit

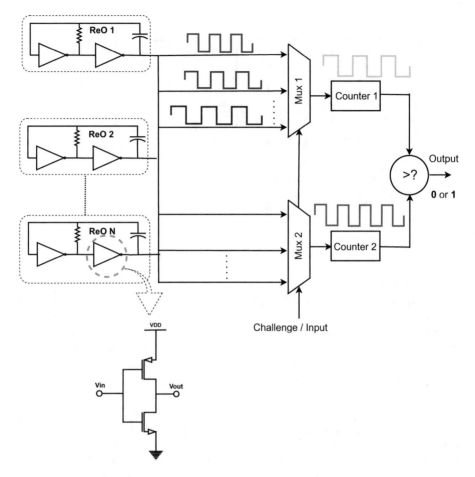

Fig. 5. Proposed Relaxation Oscillator (ReO) PUF

response (either 0 s or 1 s) is considered for key generation. The counter can help to count the number of oscillations of selected ReO pairs processed from MUXs in a fixed time interval. The pulse counts from the counters are compared with the comparator, which gives the response '0' or '1'.

5   Experimental Results

The proposed ReOPUF circuit is implemented in UMC 65 nm technology and simulated with Cadence Spectre. To perform characterization of 50 different PUFs, 100 runs of Monte-Carlo simulations are performed. During simulation, intra-die and inter-die PVs are generated to evaluate the responses. Each 32-stage ReOPUF becomes active with the 5-bit challenge or input (C_0 to C_4) and is evaluated under the nominal operating conditions of 27 °C and 1.2 V supply voltage.

5.1   Evaluation of PUF Quality Metrics

The performance of the ReOPUF is measured and evaluated with the following metrics [20] as defined by National Institute of Standards and Technology (NIST).

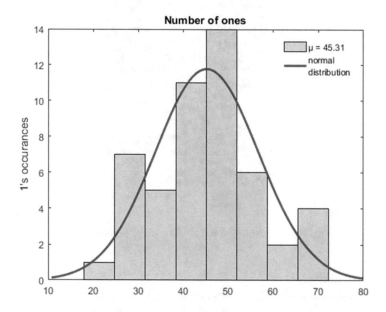

Fig. 6. Uniformity of ReOPUF - distribution of 1 s

5.1.1   Uniformity (u)

Uniformity is the measure of distribution of '1 s' and '0 s' in the response vector $R_{i,j}$ and is defined as

$$Uniformity = \frac{1}{n} \sum_{j=1}^{n} R_{i,j} \times 100\% \tag{1}$$

where, $R_{i,j}$ is the jth binary bit of an n-bit response for an ith input. An ideal PUF should have equal probabilities for '1' and '0' in response, i.e., 50%. We evaluate the 32-bit responses from 50 ReOPUF instances at nominal operating condition i.e., 27 °C, 1.2 V is shown in Fig. 6. The distribution of 1's and 0's generated by the ReOPUF is shown in Fig. 7 as a pixel distribution with a white pixel interpreted as a '1' and a black pixel as a '0'. The probability of generating 1 s is 45.31%, which indicates that ReOPUF output is not predictable and it is hard to attack.

Fig. 7. Uniformity of ReOPUF - pixel representation

5.1.2 Diffuseness (D)

Diffuseness (shown in Fig. 8) is the degree of variation observed in same ReOPUF with different challenges applied nominally. It can be measured by calculating the mean of Hamming Distance (HD) from the response vectors obtained as 49.53%. It is defined as

$$Diffuseness = \frac{2}{l(l-1)} \times \sum_{i=1}^{l-1} \sum_{j=j+1}^{l} \frac{HD(R_i, R_j)}{n} \times 100\% \qquad (2)$$

where 'l' represents randomly selected response vector from CRP space. R_i and R_j are two different n-bit response vectors obtained from two different challenges.

5.1.3 Uniqueness (U)

The randomness in different PUF responses reflects the performance in terms of uniqueness. Ideally, the probability of each response (i.e., '0' or '1') generated by identical PUFs with the same challenge should be 50%. Uniqueness (shown in Fig. 9) measures inter-chip variation among different ReOPUF instances implemented with same challenge. It can be calculated with inter-chip hamming distance (inter-HD) 49.22% as shown below

$$Uniqueness = \frac{2}{m(m-1)} \times \sum_{i=1}^{m-1} \sum_{j=j+1}^{m} \frac{HD(R_i, R_j)}{n} \times 100\% \qquad (3)$$

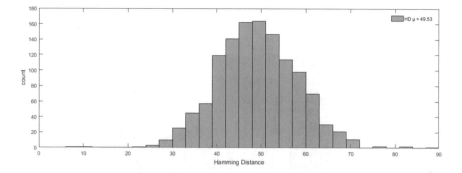

Fig. 8. Diffuseness of ReOPUF

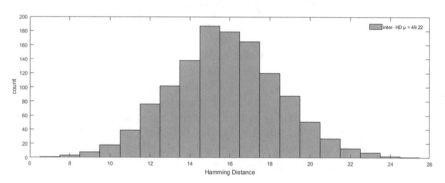

Fig. 9. Uniqueness of ReOPUF

where R_i and R_j are two different n-bit response vectors obtained from same challenge and 'm' represents different ReOPUF instances with same challenge.

5.1.4   Reliability (R)

A PUF should generate the same response in any state for the same challenge applied. Unfortunately, the variations in the supply voltage or temperature can change the behavior of the IC in the form of circuit delay and lead to unpredicted responses. Therefore, the same response bits should be produced at different operating conditions.

Reliability is measured by *intra-HD*, which is performed between two n-bit response vectors generated from the same PUF instances with the same challenges. Ideally, it should be close to 0% for an environment-friendly PUF and can be calculated as follows.

$$intra\text{-}HD = \frac{1}{m} \times \sum_{t=1}^{m} \frac{\mathrm{HD}(R_{i,ref}, R_{i,t})}{n} \times 100\% \qquad (4)$$

$$Reliability = 100 - (intra\text{-}HD) \qquad (5)$$

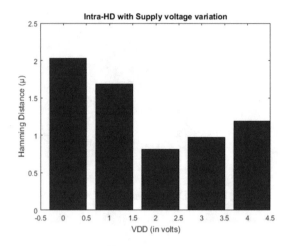

Fig. 10. Reliability of ReOPUF with VDD variation

where 'm' represents some measured trials applied on ReOPUF instances with the same challenge. $R_{i,ref}$ is the reference response measured at normal operating conditions (27 °C and 1.2 V), $R_{i,t}$ is the tth measured response at a different operating conditions. We measure the reliability of the 32-bit responses from 50 ReOPUF instances in different operating conditions.

The average reliability calculated from 50 ReOPUF responses over commercial range (0 °C to 85 °C) is 99.31% at 27 °C as shown in Fig. 11, and the worst-case reliability is 97.19% at 0 °C. A supply voltage variation up to ±10% VDD is applied to the ReOPUF as shown in Fig. 10. The corresponding reliability is 99.19% at 1.2 V, and the worst-case reliability is 97.97%. In addition, over the industrial range (−40 °C to 100 °C) the reliability is 97.41%. Table 1 presents the comparison of different PUF designs with ReOPUF. Table 2 shows the ReOPUF analysis with different temperatures.

6   Security Evaluation of the Proposed PUF

PUFs are specifically proposed for security applications that can withstand attacks under various threat models [21]. A PUF uses a CRP mechanism derived from inbuilt process variations performed by the ICs. Invasive attacks (such as reverse engineering attacks) may alter the physical properties of the device resulted in breaching of CRPs. However, PUF-based systems may be susceptible to two threat models such as PUF for authentication and PUF for secret key generation. If a PUF is used for authentication, the attacker can perform different trials to extract valid CRPs which can be used to crack the PUF function. If it is a secret key generation the attacker can concentrate on the PUF response pairs by exploiting the PUF weakness. In this section, we evaluate the security of PUF by performing the entropy analysis on the responses.

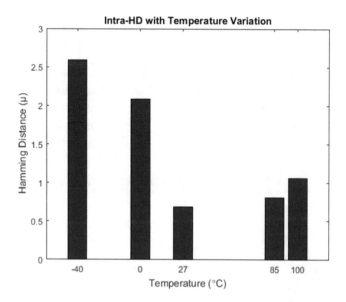

Fig. 11. Reliability of ReOPUF temperature variation

Table 1. Comparison of metrics of different PUF designs (t = temperature variation and v = supply voltage variation)

References	Technology	U (ideal 50%)	R (ideal 100%)
Liu *et al.* [18]	40 nm	49.97%	95.88%
Yuan *et al.* [15]	65 nm	50.42%	97.28%^{t}, 96.30%^{v}
Sauvagya *et al.* [19]	90 nm	46.22%	95.89%
G Edward *et al.* [10]	90 nm	46.14%	99.52%
Tauhidur *et al.* [17]	90 nm	47%	96.91%
This work	**65 nm**	**49.22%**	**97.41%^{t}, 97.97%^{v}**

6.1 Entropy Analysis

Entropy can be used as a measure of unpredictability of a response key from PUFs, though the uncertainty from process variations is unmeasurable [22]. For example, a 32-bit key that is uniformly and randomly generated has 32 bits of entropy. It also takes (ignoring actual computing) $2^{32} - 1$ guesses to break by brute force. Entropy fails to capture the number of guesses required if the possible keys are not chosen uniformly. Entropy is measured for ReOPUF generated 32-bit response when varying with different temperature and supply voltage variations as shown in Figs. 12 and 13. From the analysis, we assure that the ReOPUF responses offer high uncertainty and high average information carried out for communication. It is observed that at different temperatures the entropy varies from 2.39 to 2.48, while at different supply voltages it varies from 2.41 to 2.44.

Table 2. ReOPUF quality metrics at different temperatures

	−40 °C	0 °C	85 °C	100 °C
Intra-HD Temp (%)	97.41	97.91	99.19	98.94
Intra-HD Vdd (%)	97.97	98.31	99.03	98.81
Inter-HD (%)	85.74	94.25	81.89	78.36
Diffuseness (%)	46.27	49.32	48.79	48.03
Uniformity (%)	40.26	45.21	44.35	43.36

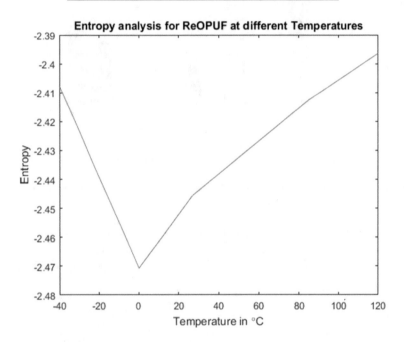

Fig. 12. Entropy of ReOPUF with temperature variation

6.2 Correlation Coefficient Analysis

The correlation coefficient is calculated for every PUF instance to determine if there is any correlation among the PUF cells [23]. If zero correlation is attained, then there is no such dependency exists among PUF cells. In the occurrence of −1 or +1 attainment there exists a linear dependency among the PUF cells i.e., weakly dependent (−1) or strongly dependent (+1) based on the CRPs generated by PUFs. For this test, 32 PUF cells are used. Pairwise, the covariance of two cells is divided by the product of their standard deviations as shown:

$$\rho(X,Y) = \frac{E[(X - \mu X)(Y - \mu Y)]}{\sigma_x \sigma_y} \tag{6}$$

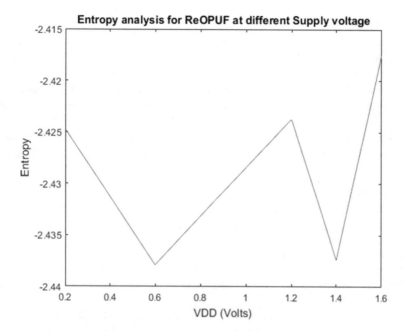

Fig. 13. Entropy of ReOPUF with supply voltage variation

where ρ is defined as the correlation coefficient of two independent variables X and Y, μ and σ represent mean and standard deviation of the independent responses obtained from the PUFs respectively. A positive (negative) value of ρ indicates a positive (negative) correlation between the two variables. The higher (lower) the value of ρ stronger the positive (negative) correlation. The closer this value lies to zero the weaker the relationship between the two PUF cells. The obtained ρ for ReOPUF falls between 1.57 to 2.59 states that the responses are strongly correlated to the respective challenges and the uncertainty becomes the matter of reliability in security evaluation.

6.3   Power Analysis of ReOPUF

We measure the power consumption of the single-stage implementation of ReOPUF and RO-PUF as shown in Table 3. For 32-bit key implementations, the estimated average powers of ReOPUF and RO-PUF are 3.79 mW and 15 mW respectively.

Table 3. Power comparison for different PUFs

	RO-PUF	ReOPUF
Power (single PUF instance) (in μW)	497.53	118.42
Power (32 PUF instances) (in mW)	15	3.79

7   Conclusion

In this paper, we have introduced a relaxation oscillator-based PUF mechanism with the advantage that challenges fed through simple oscillation can achieve more reliability than any other oscillator PUFs. The experimental evaluation of ReOPUF shows the uniqueness and reliability of 49.22% and 97.97% respectively, which is better than that of the previous works. ReOPUF significantly improves upon the previous ROPUF designs, and has the potential to be the basis for CRPs based identification and authentication applications designed for IoT.

References

1. Babaei, A., Schiele, G.: Physical unclonable functions in the internet of things: state of the art and open challenges. Sensors **19**(14), 3208 (2019)
2. Challa, R.P., Islam, S.A., Katkoori, S.: An SR flip-flop based physical unclonable functions for hardware security. In: Proceedings of 2019 IEEE 62nd International Midwest Symposium on Circuits and Systems (MWSCAS), Dallas, TX, USA, pp. 574–577 (2019)
3. Govindaraj, R., Ghosh, S., Katkoori, S.: Design, analysis and application of embedded resistive RAM based strong arbiter PUF. IEEE Trans. Dependable Secure Comput. **17**(6), 1232–1242 (2020)
4. Potkonjak, M., Goudar, V.: Public physical unclonable functions. Proc. IEEE **102**(8), 1142–1156 (2014)
5. Liang, W., Liao, B., Long, J., Jiang, Y., Peng, L.: Study on PUF based secure protection for IC design. Microprocess. Microsyst. **45**, 56–66 (2016)
6. Abu-Rahma, M.H., Anis, M.: Variability in VLSI circuits: sources and design considerations. In: 2007 IEEE International Symposium on Circuits and Systems, pp. 3215–3218. IEEE, May 2007
7. Lee, J.W., Lim, D., Gassend, B., Suh, G.E., Van Dijk, M., Devadas, S.: A technique to build a secret key in integrated circuits for identification and authentication applications. In: 2004 Symposium on VLSI Circuits. Digest of Technical Papers (IEEE Cat. No. 04CH37525), pp. 176–179. IEEE, June 2004
8. Lim, D., Lee, J.W., Gassend, B., Suh, G.E., Van Dijk, M., Devadas, S.: Extracting secret keys from integrated circuits. IEEE Trans. Very Large Scale Integr. (VLSI) Syst. **13**(10), 1200–1205 (2005)
9. O'donnell, C.W., Suh, G.E., Devadas, S.: PUF-based random number generation. In: MIT CSAIL CSG Technical Memo, vol. 481 (2004)
10. Suh, G.E., Devadas, S.: Physical unclonable functions for device authentication and secret key generation. In: 2007 44th ACM/IEEE Design Automation Conference, pp. 9–14. IEEE, June 2007
11. Bernard, F., Fischer, V., Costea, C., Fouquet, R.: Implementation of ring-oscillators-based physical unclonable functions with independent bits in the response. Int. J. Reconfig. Comput. **2012** (2012)
12. Gao, M., Lai, K., Qu, G.: A highly flexible ring oscillator PUF. In: Proceedings of the 51st Annual Design Automation Conference, pp. 1–6, June 2014
13. Avaroğlu, E.: The implementation of ring oscillator based PUF designs in Field Programmable Gate Arrays using of different challenge. Phys. A **546**, 124291 (2020)

14. Tao, S., Dubrova, E.: MVL-PUFs: multiple-valued logic physical unclonable functions. Int. J. Circuit Theory Appl. **45**(2), 292–304 (2017)
15. Cao, Y., Zhang, L., Chang, C.H., Chen, S.: A low-power hybrid RO PUF with improved thermal stability for lightweight applications. IEEE Trans. Comput. Aided Des. Integr. Circuits Syst. **34**(7), 1143–1147 (2015)
16. Mansouri, S.S., Dubrova, E.: Ring oscillator physical unclonable function with multi level supply voltages. In: 2012 IEEE 30th International Conference on Computer Design (ICCD), pp. 520–521. IEEE, September 2012
17. Rahman, M.T., Forte, D., Fahrny, J., Tehranipoor, M.: ARO-PUF: an aging-resistant ring oscillator PUF design. In: 2014 Design, Automation & Test in Europe Conference & Exhibition (DATE), pp. 1–6. IEEE, March 2014
18. Liu, C.Q., Cao, Y., Chang, C.H.: ACRO-PUF: a low-power, reliable and aging-resilient current starved inverter-based ring oscillator physical unclonable function. IEEE Trans. Circuits Syst. I Regul. Pap. **64**(12), 3138–3149 (2017)
19. Sahoo, S.R., Kumar, S., Mahapatra, K., Swain, A.: A novel aging tolerant RO-PUF for low power application. In: 2016 IEEE International Symposium on Nanoelectronic and Information Systems (iNIS), pp. 187–192. IEEE, December 2016
20. Maiti, A., Gunreddy, V., Schaumont, P.: A systematic method to evaluate and compare the performance of physical unclonable functions. In: Athanas, P., Pnevmatikatos, D., Sklavos, N. (eds.) Embedded Systems Design with FPGAs, pp. 245–267. Springer, New York (2013). https://doi.org/10.1007/978-1-4614-1362-2_11
21. Laguduva, V., Islam, S.A., Aakur, S., Katkoori, S., Karam, R.: Machine learning based IoT edge node security attack and countermeasures. In: 2019 IEEE Computer Society Annual Symposium on VLSI (ISVLSI), pp. 670–675. IEEE, July 2019
22. Van Den Berg, R.: Entropy analysis of physical unclonable functions. MSc. thesis, Dept. Math. Comput. Sci., Eindhoven Univ. Technol., Eindhoven (2012)
23. Lin, L., Holcomb, D., Krishnappa, D.K., Shabadi, P., Burleson, W.: Low-power sub-threshold design of secure physical unclonable functions. In: Proceedings of the 16th ACM/IEEE International Symposium on Low Power Electronics and Design, pp. 43–48, August 2010

Cyber-Physical Application for the Safety and Security Enforcement in Oil and Gas Transportation

Nicola Zingirian(✉) ⓘ

DEI - University of Padova, 35131 Padova, Italy
nicola.zingirian@unipd.it

Abstract. The paper presents an innovative mobile application enabling the security and safety inspectors of Oil & Gas Transportation to receive in their car all the real-time data necessary to drive them to the visual evidence of the truck driver's unsafe or dishonest activities. The application works on the top of an IoT platform managing a sensor network installed on over 3,000 tank trucks. The paper presents the application domain, the architecture, the implementation, and the experiments, also reporting a set of quantitative experimental results that validate the application effectiveness. The results also qualify the application as one of the first cases of real-time Cyber-Physical Systems for Logistics and Transportation Safety and Security validated for the measured impact on the operations, and not just in terms of scenarios or technology potentials.

Keywords: Road safety · Transportation security · IoT · Real application

1   Introduction

The paper presents an innovative mobile application developed on top of an Oil & Gas Transportation Internet of Things (IoT) platform based on a sensor network installed on over 3,000 tank trucks [21]. The use case refers to detectives who receive in their car all the real-time data necessary i) to chase and approach a truck secretly, and ii) to wait for the right time to come out of hiding in such a way to get the eye witnessed evidence of the truck driver's incorrect or dishonest actions against the safety or the security.

To better understand the critical mission of this application, it deserves to analyze the application scenario. The Oil & Gas Transportation domain is a very critical process, as it handles massive amounts of highly flammable, explosive, and pollutant fuels, mostly delivered in urban areas, where the exposure to disasters is very high [11]. Moreover, fuels are unfortunately subject to theft, being an easily salable value in illegal markets [4]. Finally, public authorities keep the fuel supply chains under special surveillance, as a large part of the transported value is represented by taxes and excise duties, so that every product loss also corresponds to tax evasion.

Furthermore, Oil & Gas Logistics and Transportation, like any other large-scale supply chain, are characterized by continuous and capillary deliveries over nationwide

© IFIP International Federation for Information Processing 2022
Published by Springer Nature Switzerland AG 2022
L. M. Camarinha-Matos et al. (Eds.): IFIPIoT 2021, IFIP AICT 641, pp. 180–196, 2022.
https://doi.org/10.1007/978-3-030-96466-5_12

retail networks. Considering that the stock levels are often kept low because of cash shortages, the supply imposes frequent small deliveries to the same reservoirs. This context makes the surveillance also very time-critical, as it should not interfere with the trip efficiency.

Over time, this scenario has made it very convenient to centrally monitor the tankers transporting fuels in real-time, to supervise i) the proper safety procedure execution, ii) the efficient product transportation and delivery, and, above all, iii) the product integrity against the product theft. Our research group, following up an EU-funded project [10], established a University Spin-off company that, in tight connection with the Department of Information Engineering, has created and is managing the IoT platform that today is used by all the major Italian oil companies as well as other companies in other countries.

The new application presented in this paper has been designed and recently deployed on the top of this monitoring system, to support the enforcement of safety procedures and the safeguarding of the product that is currently under test at the Italiana Petroli, the second-largest Italian oil company, considering that driver's fraud is by far the most severe security problem.

This application addresses the oil company personnel who are referred to as the inspectors. The inspector's role has been traditionally to verify, on the spot, the tanker equipment compliance with the contractual obligations specified in the transportation tenders and the procedural conformity during product loading, driving, and delivering. In recent years, however, the inspector's task has become increasingly focused on the dishonest behavior of the drivers who transport the fuel, because the margin reductions in the oil business has made the product losses, amounting up to several million euros yearly, less and less sustainable. This task is critical, as the product accounting alone is not precise enough to discriminate the product stealing from the metrological system tolerance errors caused by the approximations of mechanical and fluid dynamics models, also including the calculation of thermal volume variations[1].

The application presented in this paper provides the inspectors with clues of illegal driver's operations. After the identification of these drivers, the mobile application first supports the inspectors to chase any selected moving truck, then to approach it, to understand the best moment to come out of the hide, and to register, directly on the spot, every non-conformity found, applying penalties to the transporter and, in severe cases, imposing the removal of the driver.

The rest of the paper presents the state of the art, the architecture, the implementation, and a report of experimental results.

---

[1] Being 0.5% the tolerance accepted by the European Standard Measurement Instrument Directive (MID), the cumulated accepted errors of both the load and the unload measurements, corresponding to a 40,000-L trip is 40 L, i.e., a value of about 60 Euros per trip, including the taxes. For an average of 2 trips per day, that value is more than 2.700 Euro per month, for each truck. Considering a typical 200 trucks fleet working daily for a medium oil company the non-accountable product loss standing within the MID's tolerance corresponds to over 6 million euros per year.

2 State of the Art

The solution presented is in the state of the art of the field automation to support the security and the safety of dangerous good transportation, as well as the state of the art of the Cyber-Physical Systems.

2.1 State of the Art of Tank Truck Automation

During the last two decades the industrial practice has given rise to various electronic devices that today are part of the standard tank truck equipment to counteract operation errors or abuses in fuel delivery. Among these are the Sealed Parcel Delivery System [6] and the automation of the loading and unloading operations [5], embedded in the electronic registers connected to the Metrologic sensors that measure the quantities delivered, based on volume [12], levels [1], mass [16] or flow rate [17] transductors.

These systems, by limiting the user's freedom in the valve actuation to access the product, help to avoid errors and abuses (e.g., product contamination [9], overfill [2]), but unfortunately cannot ultimately solve the security issues. Several system manufacturers have also included a data logging system in their automation systems, also proposed as industrial standards (e.g. [7]) so that service workshops can access the data locally, after authentication, to analyze the operation and the actions performed by the driver.

2.2 Cyber-Physical Systems

The cost of retrieving the data by connecting locally to the tank truck automation systems, as well as the incompleteness of such data, could not keep the security level sufficiently high. During the last decade, such limitations pushed the major oil companies to adopt early IoT and Sensor Networks [21], to

- include further vehicle sensors,
- perform on-board signal processing,
- collect and process all the data in real-time in a cloud platform,
- correlate all the data through expansible and shared logic implemented in the platform,
- make available the information to all transport customers and all the main Oil & Gas haulers to trigger appropriate corrective actions.

This trend has been initially favored by the European regulation for the road transportation of dangerous goods (the ADR, "Accord Dangereux Routier"), as it started requiring, since 2009, the GPS tracking for all vehicles transporting the main dangerous goods categories, including fuels. Unfortunately, this regulation has not evolved further, so that the current ADR-2019 release, despite the IoT and sensor network evolution, is still requiring just a basic Automatic Vehicle Location.

Nevertheless, during the last decade, such regulation limits have not prevented the Oil & Gas Logistics IoT platforms from deploying several new applications addressed to a variety of stakeholders, e.g., Depots and Terminal Managers, Oil Company Managers, Haulers, Haulers' subcontractors, Authorities.

Among the recent applications, the one presented in this paper i) takes advantage, better than the others, of the real time sensor data potential, ii) includes human operators in a Cyber-Physical feedback loop [20] and iii) shows how critical logistics can be secured through Cyber-Physical Systems. We present this application as a contribution to extend the pool of Cyber-Physical System applications, (see e.g. [3] as well as the link [13] to the UC Berkeley Ptolemy project's taxonomy), as current taxonomies do not include the dangerous or critical transportation domain, limiting the main real application categories to Smart grids [14], Healthcare [15], and vehicle mobility [18] and a few others.

3   System Architecture

Figure 1 shows the overview of the System Architecture supporting the application described in this paper. The Vehicle Node manages the sensors installed on the tank trucks. The Data Flow Management Platform receives the messages from the Vehicle Nodes and dispatches data to the applications, adopting the management information received from external Enterprise Resource Planners (ERPs) as dispatching criteria. The applications consume, process and integrate data to provide the users with office and mobile services.

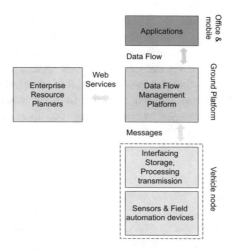

Fig. 1. System architecture overview

3.1   Vehicle Node

The architecture of the sensor network installed on the tank trucks inherits some characteristics of the vehicle telematics, i.e., the Fleet Management Systems (FMS) and of the Automatic Vehicle Location/Management (AVL/M) systems. Such systems periodically store and send the vehicle's GPS coordinates together with data sets including mileage, fuel consumption, working hours, driving, pauses, rests, etc.

Unlike the FMS and AVL/M black boxes, the Vehicle Node is equipped with an onboard remotely programmable microcontroller, capable of interfacing an ever-increasing number of sensors to monitor the transported goods and to support custom signal processing and filtering.

The acquired data are analogic signals, digital inputs, and field device data interfaces such as RS232, RS485, CAN. Table 1 shows the typical sensor network signals interfaced.

Based on the data coming from the various sensors and field devices, the onboard unit generates periodic telemetries, as well as asynchronous events or alarms, each marked with timestamps, geo-coordinates, speed and direction values, plus other attributes such as the identifier of the main vehicle and of another vehicle possibly coupled, the driver identifier, etc. Each sensor connected to each Vehicle Node is accessible as a sensor network node.

The collected signals never include any operator's data entries, except for the loading and unloading pre-sets, manually entered to activate the automated loading and unloading operations. The system, therefore, transparently collects all the information without requiring any manual input. This characteristic derives from security-by-design requirements. Similarly, the configuration of the Vehicle Node equipment itself does not depend on any on-site service operators, but on users authorized by the platform, through a command-based configuration interface.

The data transmission takes place via UDP/IP over GPRS or LTE. For each transmitted message a reply message acknowledges both data reception and information save, matching the sequence numbers. The message payload is AES256-encrypted, using a server-generated key that, at every daily or weekly key update, reconfigures the Vehicle Node through a specific key-change message encrypted by the old key to guarantee both authenticity and confidentiality. From the generation of the message to its availability to Remote applications, each asynchronous message constitutes the basic block of the whole architecture. The Data Flow is the sequence of messages dispatched to the proper modules, and each message is bound to one notification, at every data flow processing block.

The sensor equipment is defined by the contractual standards of the tank trucks that work for the major companies, including AGIP/ENI, Tamoil, Kuwait Petroleum (including Shell Network), Italiana Petroli (formerly Total Erg and API). These contractual standards have been constantly evolving for several years and constitute the driver for continuous system tuning and extension. Among the most recent innovations are the optical fiber-based sealing devices, the electrical continuity detection systems between the vapor recovery lines and the grounding lines, and the availability of RFID seals (Fig. 2).

3.2 Data Flow Management Platform

This platform acts as a ground station receiving all the sensor data from all the Vehicle Nodes, works similarly to the FMS or AVL/M systems, as it generates reports, statistics, maps, tables, and dashboards.

Table 1. Typical tank truck sensor network signal

Sensor	Information	Purpose
Wet leg	Presence of product in the tanker trucks pipes	Check whether pipes are empty after each delivery and filled before the first delivery
Valve	Open or close foot valve state	Check whether the product is accessed not in correspondence with measured deliveries
Hatch open	Open or close unloading station opened	Check whether the unloading station is accessed not in correspondence with measured deliveries
Level	Level of product in the tanker	Check whether the level change not in correspondence with measured deliveries
Loaded product temperature	Temperature of product in the tanker	Calculate the volume difference upon temperature changes between loading and unloading
Unload product temperature	Temperature of product during unloading	
Loading couplers	Opening of the loading couplers	Check whether the couplers are opened not in terminals or depots
EBS	Activation of the anti-roll system	Reports dangerous near miss
Digital tachograph	Driver identity and driver time	Check if the driver corresponds to the authorized person and bind any action to the driver
Electronic measuring	Presets and unloaded volumes, total counters, flow rate, product, delivery ticket number	Bind any actions done on the unloading station to the delivery accounted
Sealing system (SPDSS)	State of the compartments: empty, sealed, broken seal	Compare the information of the Sealing System with the detected driver's activities
Overfill	Overfill detection beyond the safety ullage for each tanker compartment	Incident near-miss
Electrical grounding	Connection of the tanker chassis to the delivery point grounding system	Incident near-miss
Density	Measures the product density in each compartment	Allow precise calculation volume compensation and detects product crossovers

Fig. 2. Vehicle node hardware mounted on a tanker semi-trailer.

However, unlike the FMS and AVL/M systems, it also manages the data as either real-time or deferred streams, called the Data Flow, addressed to various applications, making it possible to feed applications for transport customers, carriers, workshops, and public utility service centers.

This feature is managed by building a bidirectional data flow dispatching layer based on the vehicle attributes and of dynamic data (such as trip plans, geofence, truck operations), also supporting bidirectional communications.

In particular, there are two Data Flow types:

- **Dynamic Data Flow** consists of messages that, according to appropriate dispatch rules, are directly routed to the destination as soon as the Vehicle Node generates and transmits them to the Data Flow Management Platform. These messages are dispatched in cut-through mode as real-time streams, instead of being stored, retrieved, and forwarded.
- **Static Data Flow** consists of pre-processed items derived from the Vehicle Node messages and prepared in advance by the Data Flow manager and dispatched upon the application request. The Static Data Flows appear like database query results, except for the fact the result sets, instead of being built on the fly from the Database fields, are pre-cooked streams that offer much more reactivity than multiple row selections on relational tables.

The main data flow is directly implemented as an incremental Unix file, where newly received and parsed messages are appended. The main data flow is dispatched in real-time to pre-cooked JSON files, after a cleansing filter, each organized by truck, day and company to implement the static data flow. The dynamic dataflows are connected to the main data flow streams, using the Posix inotify services and in-line appropriate filters. This implementation on top of the Posix System calls, being strictly domain-oriented, delivers even more flexibility and performance than document-oriented DBMS, such as the MongoDB.

Figure 3 shows a basic scheme for forwarding Real-Time data flows, which depend on the ownership of the vehicle for directing flows to the haulers and on the trip plans, received from external ERPs for directing flows to the transport customers, i.e., the oil companies. Whereas the transporters are interested in obtaining the operational data of their vehicles, the transport customers, instead, are interested in obtaining real-time data related to the owned goods that are being transported, from the end of the product load up to the subsequent product load.

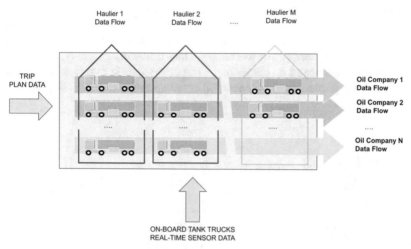

Fig. 3. Differentiated data flows dispatching rules to haulers (colored transparent vertical arrows) and to the oil logistic companies (solid horizontal-colored arrows)

Other criteria used for dispatching the Data Flows are, for example, the proximity of an authorized service operator or the entrance/exit in/out specific geo-fenced areas.

The possibility to forward distinct Data Flows to distinct applications is the key platform feature. Such versatility has made the penetration of the solution extremely pervasive, thus creating a de facto standard in fuel transportation, so far, in Italy, Serbia and in some parts of South Africa.

3.3 Applications

The Applications developed on top of the Data Flow Management Platform cover different processes and include, for instance, travel tracking, electronic waybill documentation, tank truck maintenance, just-in-time truck routing, terminal and depot surveillance.

The application presented in this paper represents a recent successful example of the application supported by dynamic Data Flows.

4 Application Logic

4.1 Office Operations

To analyze the behavior of the drivers, the route and the operations carried out by these drivers are examined in a dashboard showing all the information on a map that is studied by the inspectors (see Fig. 4). To facilitate the investigation, the system generates alarms in correspondence with suspicious situations, avoiding unnecessary human consultation of large data amounts. Table 2 shows a list of alarm logics in use. These logics derive from the human experience and retrospective analysis of the behavior of drivers who have been caught red-handed in their malicious operations. It is worth noticing that the employee's privacy law allows regarding the sensor data as equipment data, not as behavioral data. Therefore, such data can just provide behavior clues, but never as evidence of behaviors. The inspector's role is to understand the clues and to go on the spot and get visual evidence of misbehaviors. Thus, following the analysis of the alarms and of the traces displayed on the map, the inspectors decide to physically pursue the truck to catch the product stealing operation or the operation that does not comply with the regulation.

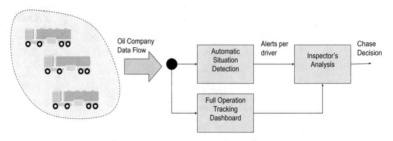

Fig. 4. Office operations supported

Table 2. Alerts

Alert name	Data
Opening of the hatch and or foot valves out of the delivery points	RFID-based opening sensor
Stop during residual product flush	Electronic head data
Opening of the hatch in hauler parking zones	RFID-based opening sensor
Stop in the parking zone before the end of the trip	Trip Plan, geo-coordinates, geo-fenced areas
Opening of the loading coupler out of the loading zone	Namur proximity sensors in loading coupler
Residual product detection after the last delivery	Wet Leg sensors
Delivered quantity discrepancy versus thermic variation	Temperature sensors in chambers, Metrologic delivery quantity

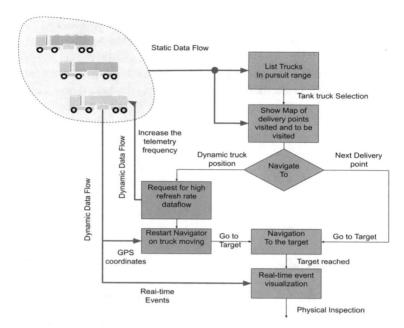

Fig. 5. Diagram of the on-field operations

4.2 On-Field Operations

The On-Field operations are organized as a sequence of steps, illustrated in Fig. 5, and detailed in this section.

- **Trucks Selection:** Before starting the chase, the inspector watches on his/her tablet the list of tank trucks that he/she is authorized to pursue, i.e., those that are currently operating for the oil company for which the investigation is taking place. This information is obtained by getting a filtered Data Flow of the trucks that are executing the trips planned for that customer (see the horizontal path of Fig. 3). The list is sorted by the truck distance and filtered up to a maximum distance radius from the inspector's location and is also represented over a dynamic map in real-time.
- **Trip Progress Information:** When a truck is selected, the current trip information appears on a map, showing the path so far covered, the delivery points already served and the planned delivery points to be reached.
- **Navigation:** The inspector decides whether to follow at the proper distance the moving tank truck, or to wait for it at the next delivery place, according to some criteria including the trip progress information, the inspector location, and the place in which the misbehavior will likely take place, i.e., stopovers vs. delivery places. Following this selection, the navigation starts in static mode, if the target is the delivery place, otherwise, in dynamic mode if the target is the moving truck. If navigation is dynamic, the application continuously receives the geo coordinates and the events transmitted by the truck in dynamic Flow data. To always have fresh information, the application

requires Data Flow Manager to reconfigure the onboard equipment of the tracked tanker, setting a 5 s localization sampling period instead of the 60-s default.

- **Real-Time Event Watching:** As noticed, the critical requirement of the inspector's activity is to appear on the spot at the exact moment when the non-conformity can be unequivocally documented. In this situation, the event messages (e.g., the start of the delivery, vapor recovery interconnection, hatch opening, electronic meter start, or valve opening, or end of the delivery) are the key information to decide when to physically catch the driver in the act of abusing or misusing the equipment.

5   Implementation Notes

The main implementation challenges relate to the on-field operations, as they represent the most critical part of the process.

5.1   Application Interfaces

The application is an Android App including the following control or data interfaces:

- **Data Flow Interfaces:** These data interfaces support the interaction with the Data Flow Management Platform. Both Static and Dynamic Data Flow are interfaced.

  - *Static Data Flow:* The items are prepared as pre-cooked JSON records for the application's download. The client's requests can configure appropriate data filtering logic.
  - *Dynamic Data Flow*: The application receives the messages as WebSocket data frames [8] that are handled asynchronously. The application interface allows configuring appropriate data filtering logic in the service subscription.

- **Navigation Interface:** This control interface opens the Navigation Software and refreshes the target. This interface takes advantage of the Android Intent mechanism. The Sygic navigator has been selected for the possibility of specifying the target in the intent link, also showing acceptable time overheads during the navigation target updates.
- **Location Service Interface:** This data interface allows retrieving the inspector's geo coordinates necessary to select the vehicle within a given distance radius from the inspector, both to limit the truck selection and to estimate the proper refresh navigation rate.

5.2   Application Graphical User Interfaces

The GUIs are handled by Android Activities and Fragments. All the application GUIs, except for the navigation, which is directly managed by the third-party Sygic Software, consists of the following views:

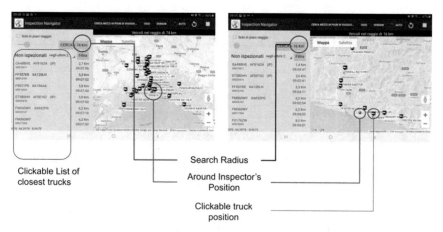

Fig. 6. User's interface for truck list visualization and truck selection

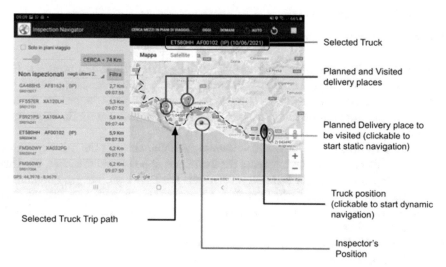

Fig. 7. User's interface for trip visualization and navigation selection

- Clickable Map of the Pursuable trucks over the map: this is a Web View, connected to the static Data Flow (Fig. 6)
- Clickable List of the pursuable trucks as ordered list and radius configuration cursor (Fig. 6)
- Clickable Map view of the selected truck trip (Fig. 7)
- Visualization for incoming dynamic events (Fig. 8)
- Notifications over the Sygic maps implemented as Android Toast

Realtime Sensor Events

Fig. 8. User's interface for real-time event check

5.3 Logic Implementations

The implementation includes the following logic implementation.

- **Selection of the truck according to their distance from the user's position.** This logic is implemented as a filter configuration in the Data Flow Manager, during the application request. Further filters apply to the inspector's identity to restrict the data visualization just to those trucks that are traveling at that moment for the inspector's company.
- **Trip stop coloring.** This logic allows showing red pinpoints for the delivery places already visited, and yellow pinpoints for the places to be visited (See Fig. 7). This logic is implemented in the Data Flow Manager. The Delivery point geo coordinates and status are maintained in the Data Flow Manager. It is worth noticing that the visit of the delivery point is confirmed only after the valve opening signal so that a simple stop in the delivery place does not correspond to a visit.
- **Navigation Updating Logic.** This logic decides when the navigator target needs to be refreshed. Every asynchronous message coming from the Dynamic Data Flow interface wakes up the Navigation Updating logic, to verify whether the vehicle has changed position after the previous localization message, the distance between the user and the chased truck, and the time passed after the last target changes. The algorithm decides whether to trigger a new intent to the navigator or not, weighting the usefulness of the update and the time overhead caused the target change.

6 Experimental Results

6.1 Performance Indicators

This section reports on the performance indicators derived from the analysis of the application logs related to the work of 4 inspectors, pursuing in total 68 tank trucks.

Table 3 reports the number of dynamic and static navigations activated. The balance between static and dynamic navigation changes from user to user, although in general dynamic navigation is the preferred option. The dynamic navigation ran in total 76 times to follow 68 trucks as the chase of most selected trucks took place in one shot.

The average measured chase duration is 28 min, also including the waiting time between the truck approach and the physical intervention. More in detail, Fig. 5 reports the distribution of the measured chase time, showing that 85% of the chases lasted less than one hour. This represents the main key performance index, considering that chasing a single truck without the application, typically took 4 h in the past (Fig. 9).

Table 3. Number of navigations for each inspector (identified by Android ID) in Nov 2019

User (Android id)	Dynamic navigation	Static navigation	Total
16321d9d4efb332a	10	7	17
2dc5b9f48de9422c	59	5	64
32b8b154976f7d26	0	25	25
46c91a52b1345bee	7	1	8
Total	**76**	**38**	**120**

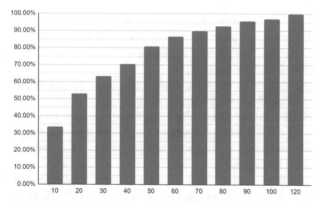

Fig. 9. Chase duration distribution: the y-axis reports the percentage of chases lasting less than the duration reported in the x-axis (minutes).

6.2   Application Impact

The performance has increased the inspector's efficiency. Before adopting this application, each inspector used to complete about 35 inspections per year on average. In 2019, using the application each inspector completed 146 inspections per year, thus increasing the performance by more than 4 times, allowing visiting all the trucks two times per year, on average. In 2019, the system allowed catching 23 cases of illegal products found onboard. Table 4 reports further security and safety non-conformities detected, showing the categories and the relative occurrence of the bad practices.

Table 4. Top detected non-conformities (occurrence rate per inspection)

Checked item	Category	Severity	Non-conformities
Vapor recovery	Safety	High	11.3%
Company physical sealing	Security	Medium	7.1%
Client's livery	Quality	Low	7.0%
Explosion proof tools	Safety	High	6.9%
Correct itinerary execution	Quality/Security	Medium	6.4%
Metrological sealing	Security	High	5.9%
Illegal onboard	Security	High	5.2%
Couplers opening	Security	High	4.5%
Electrical grounding	Safety	High	3.0%

7 Privacy Issues

The compliance of the application to the privacy regulation (GDPR) is based on the following items.

- The transport companies declare their sensor data ownership to the National Privacy Authority, for the exact purposes of asset protection and people safety, appointing the data provider as the data manager.
- The data set is limited to the truck equipment, and does not extend to the driver, differently from the video surveillance.
- The driver identity is associated with the truck, using the tachograph identification card data, as the company has to guarantee to entrust the dangerous freights only to the drivers who are authorized to enter critical facilities are enabled to conduct the truck and are not blacklisted.
- The data related to product location, access, and delivery are exported in real-time to the oil company, which is the product owner. Each data item exported is specified in the contractual clauses.
- During the trip the driver, by his/her job description, has to carefully follow the routes and the schedules, for safety and security reasons, so that any discrepancy, including stops and over speeds, represents potential security or safety threats to be monitored.
- The data are maintained for 5 years, on-line or off-line, in a secure physical IT infrastructure, managed by a ISO 27001-certified provider, making the data remotely accessible to the staff entitled to view and analyse the data.
- The staff is not allowed to share such data to anyone who is not authorized.
- The physical authentication of the data sources is based on the serial numbers of the IoT device and the encryption key that can be changed only remotely by the provider, and on the cross check with serial number of other field devices, such as the electronic measuring system or the sealing system.
- No data processing is allowed to infer personal information of the driver.

8 Concluding Remarks

In addition to the application domain, the key innovative aspect of the application presented in this paper is to guide an organization towards the full reactivity in the anomaly management, by inserting the human operators in the physical process feedback, driving their actions and strategies through sensors' information in real time.

We believe that this type of application represents an emerging context of the Cyber-Physical Security Systems. In fact, while the Cyber-Physical Security is commonly understood as the security against cyber-attacks to the IT platforms managing or controlling physical systems[19], this application suggests extending the Cyber-Physical Security concept to the physical process security enhancement supported by the IT platforms, proving it in the full process, not only in the technologies.

References

1. Boehm, A.: Device for discharging liquid from a tank and method for emptying the residue from a line section, 12 June 2012. U.S. Patent 8,196,904
2. Cadman, G.R., Thiara, J.S., Scully Signal Co: Fluid overfill protection and product identification system (1996). U.S. Patent 5,507,326
3. Chen, H.: Applications of cyber-physical system: a literature review. J. Indust. Integr. Manage. **02**(03), 1750012 (2017). https://doi.org/10.1142/S2424862217500129
4. Cottin, B.: Black gold, black market risk management. Risk. Insur. Manage. Soc. Inc. **56**(8), 12–13 (2009)
5. Dudley, et al.: Control Systems For Liquid Product Delivery Vehicles. Knappco, LLC , Kansas City, MO (US), 29 September 2020. U.S. Patent 10,787,358 B2
6. EN 15208: Tanks for transport of dangerous goods - Sealed parcel delivery systems - Working principles and interface specifications
7. EN 15969: Tanks for transport of dangerous goods - Digital interface for the data transfer between tank vehicle and with stationary facilities (2018)
8. Fette, I., Melnikov, A.: The WebSocket Protocol. RFC 6455, IETF, December 2011. https://doi.org/10.17487/RFC6455
9. FMC Technologies Measurement Solutions, Inc.: Sening® Innovative Tank Truck Systems,. Sening® NoMix Cross-Over Prevention, April 2009
10. Fornasa, M., et al.: VISIONS: a service oriented architecture for remote vehicle inspection. IEEE Intell. Transp. Syst. Conf. **2006**, 163–168 (2006). https://doi.org/10.1109/ITSC.2006.1706736
11. Ghaleh, S., Omidvari, M., Nassiri, P., Momeni, M., Lavasani, S.M.M.: Pattern of safety risk assessment in road fleet transportation of hazardous materials (oil materials). Safety Sci. **116**, 1–12 (2019). https://doi.org/10.1016/j.ssci.2019.02.039
12. Haar, T.: Haar Alfons Maschinenbau GmbH and Co: Method and apparatus for measuring the volume of flowing liquids (1999). U.S. Patent 5,922,969
13. https://ptolemy.berkeley.edu/projects/cps/
14. Jha, A.V., et al.: Smart grid cyber-physical systems: communication technologies, standards and challenges. Wirel. Netw. **27**(4), 2595–2613 (2021). https://doi.org/10.1007/s11276-021-02579-1
15. Jimenez, J.I., Jahankhani, H., Kendzierskyj, S.: Health care in the cyberspace: medical cyber-physical system and digital twin challenges. In: Farsi, M., Daneshkhah, A., Hosseinian-Far, A., Jahankhani, H. (eds.) Digital Twin Technologies and Smart Cities. IT, pp. 79–92. Springer, Cham (2020). https://doi.org/10.1007/978-3-030-18732-3_6

16. O'Banion, T.: Coriolis: the direct approach to mass flow measurement. Chem. Eng. Prog. **109**(3), 41–46 (2013)
17. Olivier, P.D., Shermer, W.P., Nanaji, S.A.: Fuel dispenser fuel flow meter device, system and method, 30 August 2005. U.S. Patent 6,935,191
18. Yanagihara, T., Nawa, K., Chandrasiri, N.P., Oguchi, K.: Cyber physical system for vehicle application. Trans. Inst. Meas. Control. **36**(7), 898–905 (2014)
19. Wells, L.J., Camelio, J.A., Williams, C.B., White, J.: Cyber-physical security challenges in manufacturing systems. Manuf. Lett. **2**(2), 74–77 (2014)
20. Sowe, S.K., Simmon, E., Zettsu, K., de Vaulx, F., Bojanova, I.: Cyber-physical-human systems: putting people in the loop. IT Prof. **18**(1), 10–13 (2016). https://doi.org/10.1109/MITP.2016.14
21. Zingirian, N., Valenti, C.: Sensor clouds for intelligent truck monitoring. In: 2012 IEEE Intelligent Vehicles Symposium, pp. 999–1004 (2012). https://doi.org/10.1109/IVS.2012.6232192. (Author, F.: Article title. Journal 2(5), 99–110 (2016))

A Secure and Efficient Cloud-Connected Body Sensor Network Platform

Myles Keller, Brooks Olney$^{(\boxtimes)}$, and Robert Karam

University of South Florida, Tampa, FL 33620, USA
{myleskeller,brooksolney,rkaram}@usf.edu

Abstract. A Body Sensor Network (BSN) is a system made up of low-power sensor nodes that monitor the wearer's body and surroundings. BSNs have emerged as a prominent technology, largely influenced by the increased health consciousness, widespread availability of wireless-enabled consumer electronics, and growing wireless connectivity infrastructure. In this paper, we present an extensible, cloud-connected BSN platform leveraging lightweight, efficient compression and encryption techniques suitable for edge computing. The platform includes a tunable wavelet-based compression algorithm, suitable for biosignal compression, a lightweight, secure block cipher (SPARX) to encrypt data during transmission, and Amazon Web Services (AWS) connectivity via Message Queuing Telemetry Transport (MQTT). We utilize this platform to evaluate the benefits of compressing sensor data by comparing the delay, power, and energy efficiency on the BSN platform when transmitting encrypted data to the cloud. The tunable compression algorithm efficiently reduces the size of transmitted packets on diverse types of sensor data, with low reconstruction error. When paired with a lightweight block cipher, the combination enables improvements in energy consumption (38%) and energy efficiency (58%) when compared to encryption alone.

Keywords: Body sensor networks · Edge computing · Cryptography · Low power · Cloud storage · Data compression

1 Introduction

Body Sensor Networks (BSNs) have evolved into a groundbreaking technology in the public health sector [1,6,26]. Wearable sensors can provide a convenient, non-invasive option for continuous, real-time sensing of physiological properties such as heart rate, movement, and blood pressure, among others [29]. This information can be useful to healthcare professionals in properly assessing their patients' ailments and care needs and represents a step towards truly personalized healthcare.

BSNs have a considerably easier time connecting to cloud infrastructure now that more products are equipped with wireless access points and most public and

© IFIP International Federation for Information Processing 2022
Published by Springer Nature Switzerland AG 2022
L. M. Camarinha-Matos et al. (Eds.): IFIPIoT 2021, IFIP AICT 641, pp. 197–214, 2022.
https://doi.org/10.1007/978-3-030-96466-5_13

private buildings have some form of Wi-Fi connectivity. Moreover, 5G-enabled devices and infrastructure are becoming more pervasive, enabling communication directly between the bio-sensors and the cloud [15].

While this improved networking infrastructure is undoubtedly beneficial in ensuring that BSN telemetry reaches healthcare providers as quickly and reliably as possible, there are a number of potential security and privacy issues associated with widely available internet connectivity for BSNs. The data broadcast to the cloud from a BSN is often comprised of both the wearer's medical telemetry data as well as data relevant to their perceived surroundings. While this can be useful in healthcare, if this data is compromised, it could reveal sensitive personal information about an individual's health activities, location, and habits. To combat these security and privacy risks, encryption can be implemented on the BSN; however, this can be computationally expensive and power hungry. Most embedded devices which are used in BSN platforms are equipped with small form-factor microcontrollers, which require special algorithms and implementations for cryptographic operations due to their limited available energy and program instruction size. Hence, development of lightweight block ciphers [4,5,30] and their subsequent evaluations on different Internet of Things (IoT) platforms [7,8,19] have been critical in addressing these concerns and enabling many advancements in the areas of IoT and wearable BSNs. Any data pre-processing, such as data compression and encryption, should consume minimal power so as not to intrude on the needs of the embedded network connectivity hardware.

Wi-Fi and 4G connections account for the majority of cloud infrastructure connections and require far more energy than most other wireless communication technologies [17]. Considering that the majority of BSN ecosystems are made up of small, worn or implanted electronics with relatively limited battery capacities, one can appreciate the importance of making all correspondence with the cloud as brief and meaningful as possible. Reducing communication frequency is a realistic strategy for decreasing energy consumption, but it comes at a cost of less frequent updates which is not suitable in all situations, including any instance where real-time decision making is needed, e.g. in a closed-loop treatment system.

In cases where the system is required to communicate in real-time with little to no delay, the system must be transmitting frequently, which consumes a significant amount of power. Therefore, compressing the data before encrypting and delivering it to the cloud may be advantageous. While there are many works which propose different methods of BSN data compression, to the best of our knowledge, there are no other works which present a framework for an extensible BSN while simultaneously evaluating the impact of data compression and encryption on the power consumption of devices in a BSN.

The main contributions of this paper are as follows:

1. We present a customizable BSN platform that integrates AWS connectivity
2. We implement a tunable and efficient compression algorithm suitable for microcontroller implementation to compress signals from the body sensors
3. We integrate a light weight block cipher (SPARX) directly within the BSN to encrypt the user's data prior to transmission

4. We demonstrate the need for local processing by comparing the power consumption of the device with and without data compression and encryption.

We found that the compression algorithm not only effectively and efficiently reduces the packet size for diverse types of sensor data, it also enables us to implement a lightweight block cipher while consuming considerably less energy and reducing the overall processing time. The rest of the paper is structured as follows: in Sect. 2 we provide a background on BSNs, data compression and data encryption. In Sect. 3 we present the methodology of our approach, including the design of the platform itself, the algorithms used for compression and encryption, and the experimental setup. In Sect. 4 we present and discuss the results of our approach. Finally, we conclude in Sect. 5 with future work.

2   Background

In this section, we start by providing a background on BSNs and how they fit into standard IoT architectures. Then, we describe several data encryption and compression techniques designed for use in BSNs.

2.1   Body Sensor Networks

A Body Sensor Network (BSN) is a system made up of low-power sensor nodes that monitor the wearer's body and surroundings. Current research on BSN platforms largely focuses on advancements in wireless connectivity [12,28], evolving network and data security paradigms [22], and development of platform implementations within domains such as the public health sector [21]. For example, Fig. 1 presents a diagram of a BSN containing a variety of connected devices. Each device monitors a different physiological phenomena and reports back to a central point. This central point then relays this information through the cloud or local network for a corresponding application for the user and/or medical professional.

BSNs are commonly composed of a variety of devices. This has motivated research efforts towards multi-sensor data fusion enabled systems for merging the functionality of these sensors into one seamless platform [12,14,21]. Sensor fusion typically focuses on using multiple different sensors (or the same sensor) at different locations with different amounts of spatial coverage and thus sensor fidelity. High quality sensor fusion can greatly improve the usability of the BSN application. However, fusion approaches introduce a number of processing complexities and may require additional sensor communication – resulting in information and performance losses [12].

The sensors themselves may be non-invasive wearables such as smart watches, or more invasive implantable devices which are designed to monitor internal physiological signals. To be minimally invasive, implantable devices are designed to be as small as possible and, consequently, have small batteries, and must operate very conservatively. This alone is a strong motivation to minimize the computational overhead in these devices to prolong their lifetime [16].

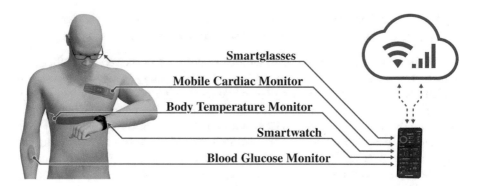

Fig. 1. Example of a Body Sensor Network (BSN) consisting of multiple wired/wireless sensors, surgically implanted or worn on the body, used for physiological monitoring, personalized medical treatment, and/or closed-loop control of integrated subsystems.

Wireless sensors that compose the BSN are the fundamental building blocks of the system, with several different layers of data pre-processing and application design built to support them. As described by Gravina et al. [13], the typical system architecture of a BSN consists of two to four of the following layers:

- *Body* - programmable sensors either wearable by the user or safely implanted
- *Mobile* - smartphones, smartwatches, and tablets which have an interactive graphical interface for monitoring and maintaining the hardware devices
- *Edge* - optional intermediate layer which may subside between the body sensors and mobile applications or other devices
- *Cloud* - optimal for offloading complex computations and data storage. And is also often integrated with the mobile and/or edge layer(s).

The specific platform architecture used by this work is described in detail in Sect. 3, but broadly, we use body sensors with a user-friendly, browser-based front-end, accessible from an authorized mobile device. This front-end allows the user to monitor sensor data in a real-time, but is optional, as the BSN supports direct-to-cloud upload capabilities.

2.2 Data Privacy and Security

In BSN platforms, proper data privacy and security methods must be in place to ensure integrity of the system and privacy of the user. Considering that the devices are monitoring and transmitting sensitive location and physiological information about a user, an attacker may want to gain unauthorized access to this data for their own illicit means. To this end, many different lightweight block ciphers have been proposed that can be used to encrypt sensitive data by general purpose microcontrollers and microprocessors which commonly exist within these hardware platforms [18,25]. Aside from the encryption algorithms themselves, there have also been several advancements which propose different optimizations to data privacy in BSNs in general [23]. For example, the authors in [24] propose a *selective encryption* scheme for electrocardiogram data which uses supervised machine learning to determine the most important parts of the signals to encrypt. Doing so can minimize the amount of data that has to be encrypted, and even filter out a great deal of data.

2.3   Data Compression

Naturally, because sensors are often configured to operate in real-time, they may generate a large amount of data. This presents two main problems: 1) the device itself must transmit more data and thus consumes more power, and 2) extra storage (e.g. in the cloud) may be required for the accumulated data. In recent years, researchers have investigated different methods of data compression specifically geared toward BSNs and the types of data they sense [3, 10, 11]. In [3] the authors presented a lossless transform-based technique leveraging the Discrete Wavelet Transform (DWT) extended with Lagrange polynomial interpolation. They evaluated their framework on multiple different sensors – temperature, pressure, gyroscope, accelerometer – and demonstrated they could compress the data anywhere from 30% to 92%, depending on the sensor type. Though promising, the authors do not present an encoding which would enable recovery of the data. In [11] the authors proposed a compression algorithm which consists of both lossy and lossless compression stages, using prediction on the receiver to modulate transmission rates while leveraging lossless coding techniques when sending update data. In our use case, we employ a fully-defined compression algorithm on a sensor node within the BSN, which can be easily tuned with a single parameter for a given sensor type.

3   Methodology

In this section, we describe the features of our BSN platform, including component devices and capabilities. We then discuss the methods used to compress, encrypt, and publish the sensor data. Finally, we outline the experimental setup.

3.1   Platform Design

The platform used in this work is an extensible, programmable node environment that enables rapid prototyping and development of wearable technology through robust visual feedback and efficient use of BSN software and hardware. While the platform functions independent of any external internet or computer connection, it is configured by default to communicate through a WebSocket connection via WiFi or USB with a browser-based, real-time multimodal visualizer.

The physical counterpart to the platform consists of off-the-shelf microcontrollers (ESP32) flashed with custom firmware allowing it to communicate on the BSN platform. Each microcontroller can assume one of two roles: *controller* or *node*. Nodes serve as physical hubs for sensor hardware to interface with,

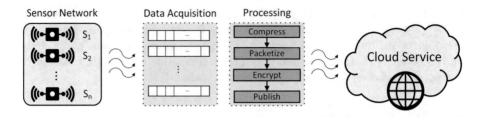

Fig. 2. Flowchart of the proposed BSN platform. The sensors gather a fixed number of samples into individual arrays during data acquisition. Arrays are compressed according to sensor-specific rules, concatenated into packets, encrypted, and finally published to the cloud service.

allowing them to broadcast their output to the rest of the network. Controllers coordinate communication between nodes, sensors attached to these nodes, and clients intending to access data from the BSN platform. Aside from managing the communications of the platform, controllers may also handle any necessary data pre-processing prior to transmitting to other controllers and/or clients. Specifically, controllers on a configured BSN platform instance can take the data returned by its assigned nodes, compress it, encrypt it, and upload it to an AWS server. A flowchart of the process is shown in Fig. 2.

3.2 Compression

An efficient compression routine for BSN data must meet certain criteria:

- **Latency:** computation of the compressed packet should not introduce considerable latency
- **Flexibility:** compression should be suitable for varying packet sizes, as different BSN implementations can have different numbers and types of sensors with varying sampling rates
- **Energy Efficiency:** the total computation energy should not exceed the total energy savings due to encrypting and transmitting a smaller packet
- **Tunability:** if lossy, the compression should be configurable, such that different sensors can be compressed to comply with reconstruction constraints.

Hence, a lightweight, configurable compression routine, which provides a suitable compression ratio for BSN signals is desired. In particular, we utilize a lifting wavelet transform based on the Haar wavelet, with a per-sensor configurable detail coefficient threshold and efficient run-length encoding scheme. The final packet is optimized to account for the (in)compressibility of different sensors, including those with on-chip classification, which enables us to leverage edge computation capabilities and further reduce packet size.

Lifting Transform and Configurable Thresholding. We employ a lifting scheme variant of the Haar wavelet transform, which is ideal for conserving relevant data from body sensors that frequently have extended periods of similar or repetitive readings. Initially, we use lifting stages to separate the fine details in the sensor signal [27]. The split step consists of dividing the sensor signal into even and odd elements. The predictive step (1) is performed, where a linear interpolation function assumes that an odd element will exist at the mid-point of a line between the two even values adjacent to it. The odd element is replaced by whatever difference results from subtracting the odd value's predicted value from its actual value. The update step (2) replaces each even element with an average of both the even element itself and its corresponding odd element. The transform is complete once these steps have been performed on all pairs of even/odd elements. The results of the Haar lifting scheme are easily reversible, such that the original sensor signal can be reconstructed by adding the prediction value back to each odd element and interleaving the even and odd values into one sample array.

$$odd_{j+1,i} = odd_{j,i} - even_{j,i} \tag{1}$$

$$even_{j+1,i} = even_{j,i} + \frac{odd_{j+1,i}}{2} \tag{2}$$

Our implementation groups readings from each **compressible** sensor on the BSN into 16 sample batches. We apply a Level 3 lifting Haar transform, resulting in a transformed signal beginning with two approximation coefficients, which represent the average values of the first half and second half of the original 16-element array, followed by 2, 4, and 8 detail coefficients from levels 3, 2, and 1, respectively. This DWT implementation with the Haar wavelet is computationally inexpensive, requiring few operations per sample and making it ideal for use in this context.

Signals acquired from body sensors (accelerometers, gyroscopes, distance sensors, etc.) often exhibit gradual changes over brief timescales rather than abrupt ones. This yields sequential measurements with similar magnitudes. Such signals, in their transformed state, will have detail coefficients of generally smaller magnitude. A thresholding operation may be applied in the wavelet domain to the detail coefficients to effectively filter minor fluctuations, e.g. noise or less relevant data, making the signal more amenable to compression in subsequent processing stages. In particular, when applied to signals from sensors that do not experience high-magnitude changes, thresholding detail coefficients frequently produces results with large, adjacent groups of zeros in the wavelet domain, which can lead to higher compression ratios, though this comes at the cost of greater reconstruction error [16]. Due to differences in each sensor type and the required fidelity during reconstruction of different signals in different BSN applications, a unique threshold value can be defined for each sensor type. For example, the accelerometer may have a detail coefficient threshold of 3, i.e. any detail coefficient ≤ 3 is set to 0, whereas the gyroscope may have a detail coefficient threshold of 5. This can enable designers to easily trade-off between the compression ratio (and subsequent energy savings from reduced packet transmission), and reconstruction accuracy on a per-sensor basis.

Run-Length Encoding and Packet Generation. After thresholding, the packets will generally be sparse, containing multiple segments of consecutive zeros, making it more amenable to compression. Run-length encoding (RLE) is a well-known lossless compression routine in which repeated values in a signal are represented by the number of times that value is repeated (n_i) in array n, and the value of the data itself, (b_i), in array b. As with other compression routines, random data, or highly variant data which are not amenable to compression, may result in packets larger than the original array. This is important to consider when determining the array size constants and sensor thresholds, as these choices have a direct impact on the overall efficiency of the compression. We elaborate on this point in Sect. 3.4.

While much of the data returned by the body sensors is comprised of raw samples in a time series, some sensors have built-in processing capabilities which return categorical data. For example, an accelerometer may return the X, Y, and Z components of acceleration, but a more sophisticated sensor may directly process this data and attempt to categorize the wearer's current physical activity such as standing, walking, running, jumping, or climbing stairs. Such categorical data are not amenable to transform and thresholding, and there is no guarantee they will naturally repeat, and so compression may not provide any benefit. Hence, while we consider these data incompressible, they may still be encoded in fewer bits with efficient atomic operations, e.g. `shift` and logic `OR`. To account for sensors which may return more than 8 categories, we encode two subsequent readings from these sensors into one 8-bit byte, thus supporting up to $2^4 = 16$ categories for each sample.

Next, the RLE arrays are concatenated in an optimally space-efficient manner. As each packet contains 16 samples from each sensor, there can be at most 16 repetitions n_i for each value b_i. Hence, each element n_i in the n array can also be stored in 4-bit chunks. Moreover, in all but one special case, the total number of non-zero nibbles in the n array provide sufficient information for reconstruction of the b array. This is shown in Fig. 3. For example, the first two bytes, {0x24, 0x19} indicate that the subsequent b array contains just 4 elements, as there are four non-zero nibbles totaling 16 - the maximum size of the b array. The expanded array is shown in Fig. 3(b), as array b_0. Following the 4 bytes of the array b_0, a new n array begins. While this also consists of 2 bytes, the least significant nibble in the 2nd byte is 0; hence, there are 3 non-zero nibbles whose values sum to 16. This indicates that the next three elements comprise the corresponding b array. In n_2, only 1 byte is needed to define the elements of the b array - 0x2E - as the nibbles 0x2 and 0xE sum to 16. Hence, the next two bytes define the corresponding b array. Finally, in the special case of n_3, a 0x0 is encountered in the lower half of the byte, but the preceding nibble is 0xF. This does not sum to 16, but does represent a situation where there are 16 repeated values (in this case, 0x00) with just one element. If the lower nibble were 0x01,

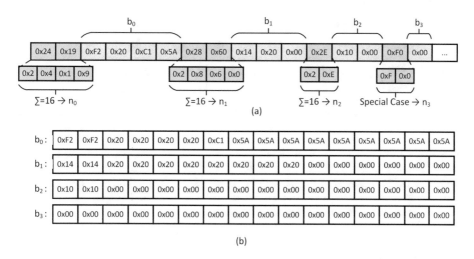

Fig. 3. Example of RLE sensor data: (a) the individual nibbles of the first two bytes (0x2, 0x4, 0x1, and 0x9) sum to 16, which indicates that the n array is complete, and that there are 4 bytes in the b array - 0xF2, 0x20, 0xC1, and 0x5A. These are expanded according to the RLE decoding rules in b_0, shown in subfigure (b). Other n/b array pairs show other possible results from the RLE process, including a special case in b_3. (b) the expanded sensor data packets.

this would have indicated two bytes in the corresponding b array, rather than just one. Thus, there is no need to store the size of the n and b arrays, and it can be efficiently stored and perfectly reconstructed from this encoding. In the worst case, in which no element of b is repeated, the overhead from this encoding is exactly 50%. Due to the previously described wavelet transform and per-sensor thresholding approach, such a situation is extremely rare for the BSN data.

The final packet is therefore comprised of a concatenation of the encoded categorical data with concatenated run-length encoded arrays, as shown in Fig. 4. The maximum size of the packet depends on the number of categorical sensors, the number of raw data sensors, and the compression ratio for that data across the 16 samples. For example, with 3 categorical sensors, 16 samples of 1 byte each (unencoded) would require 48 bytes; with the proposed encoding, this is reduced to 24 bytes. With 10 raw data sensors, assuming 8 bits per sample, and 16 samples per sensor per packet, a total of 160 bytes are required. If there are no repeated values whatsoever, the proposed encoding would require 8 bytes per n array and 16 bytes per b array, for each sensor, or 240 bytes - an increase of 50%. If about half of the values are repeated, the $n + b$ array size for each sensor would be about 12, for an overall size of 120 bytes, a savings of 25%. In practice, at least 33% of the values should be compressible in this manner to effectively reduce the size of the complete data packet comprised of the compressible sensor data. Example compression ratios for various sensors and thresholds are given in Sect. 4, where we also consider the energy savings due to reduced transmission time, as well as overall energy efficiency.

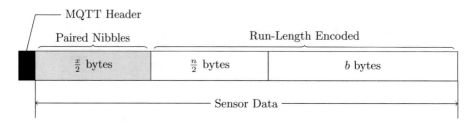

Fig. 4. The final packet is comprised of paired nibbles of categorical sensor data, followed by concatenated run-length encoded arrays for the sensors. These arrays represent thresholded data from the sensors in the wavelet domain. The n array are packed into nibbles, while elements of the b array are then appended. The MQTT header and control bytes are prepended prior to transmission.

3.3   Encryption

The limited computational capability and memory availability of the microcontrollers comprising our BSN platform create a need for algorithms that can perform cryptographic operations reliably on systems with limited resources. There are a number of lightweight cryptography algorithms which have emerged for use in IoT. For this implementation, we have chosen SPARX, a lightweight block cipher readily implemented on constrained platforms [9]. Traditional block ciphers often have elaborate key schedules designed to work on 32-bit or greater architectures. Using these ciphers on sub 32-bit architectures can cause register pressure to increase, forcing round keys to be either computed at runtime or pre-computed and stored in RAM [20]. Even 32-bit systems are hindered by the S-box operations required by many modern encryption standards, further re-enforcing the need for a microcontroller-appropriate alternative.

SPARX is an ideal cipher for this platform because it includes functionality to pre-compute the round keys as well as a variant designed specifically to work well on architectures of 32 bits or less. This is possible because all internal operations are implemented using 16-bit variables. The variant of SPARX used in this work is referred to as SPARX 64–128, denoting that it is configured to encrypt a 64-bit block with a 128-bit key. Because residual bits that exceed the length of the information being processed must still be encrypted, having a smaller blocksize can be advantageous in situations where lower latency and energy are required. In general, this can reduce space wasted due to padding during encryption/decryption. This advantage becomes increasingly apparent when the size of the encrypted message approaches the theoretical minimum packet size of 56 bytes, which is evenly divisible by 64 bits, but not 128 or 256. If a 128-bit or 256-bit block were used, some of the benefits of compression would be undone due to the required padding, and the encryption operation would need to process additional irrelevant data.

3.4   Cloud Uploading and Processing

After compression and encryption of the sensor data has been completed, the data is then uploaded to an AWS server. This was accomplished with an AWS instance with the IoT platform enabled. AWS IoT is a managed cloud platform for secure interactions between connected devices and cloud appliances. In order for microcontrollers on the BSN platform to communicate with the AWS IoT cloud platform, they must be configured with the appropriate connection parameters and credentials. Amazon has created a C++ library to facilitate initializing and maintaining communication between AWS servers and IoT cloud platform devices [2]. We generated the necessary security certificates on the AWS website and exported them to a file included in the programming that was uploaded to each device, giving them provisioned access to AWS IoT cloud resources. For our use, we only needed AWS IoT to listen to incoming data from a configured microcontroller, so although the ability to receive messages from AWS IoT was operational, we did not utilize it for the scope of this research. Nevertheless, we maintained low-latency communication with the server, such that cloud-based computation and feedback to BSN-based actuators would be feasible.

The communication protocol used internally by the AWS library is based on MQTT, a lightweight, publish-subscribe network protocol running over TCP/IP. While MQTT is usually used to send and receive JSON data, it is also capable of passing raw binary data, which was our use case for this platform. We published MQTT data in raw binary form rather than JSON or string data to reduce message size overhead as much as possible. Since each reading was converted into a one-byte representation of its original value, this avoids recasting the data into ASCII and consuming additional space with the structuring of JSON.

3.5   Experimental Setup

Our BSN testbed consisted of a microcontroller flashed with the platform firmware connected to an Inertial Measurement Unit (IMU) and two distance sensors. The IMU itself contains many separate sensing components, such as an accelerometer, gyroscope, and magnetometer, for a total of 21 sensors, which were sampled 2 Hz. To explore the potential trade-offs in preparing data for publishing to the cloud, four separate packet processing schemes were tested in real-time, each consisting of two or more primary functions: 1) **CP:** concatenate and publish; 2) **CCP:** compress, concatenate, and publish; 3) **CEP:** concatenate, encrypt, and publish; and 4) **CCEP:** compress, concatenate, encrypt, and publish.

A National Instruments (NI) Analog Discovery (AD) 2 USB oscilloscope was used to gather all power measurements. A 2.2 Ω shunt resistor was connected in series with the system power. Differential measurements were taken across the resistor at 50 MHz using the two analog inputs. A third, digital channel was used to trigger measurement; a digital GPIO pin on the microcontroller was asserted at startup, deasserted immediately before the function under test, and immediately reasserted once the function had returned. This capture window

was recorded in 100 sequential measurements, which were aligned according to
the recorded digital trigger signal and averaged together to improve signal quality. Execution of the `compress()`, `concatenate()`, and `encrypt()` functions is
very consistent across measurements in different processing schemes; however the
latency of the `publish()` function may depend on a number of external factors.
To ensure as little variance as possible in measurements of the `publish()` function, we ensured only the BSN was connected to the WiFi network, and placed
the BSN in close proximity to the router. In total, two datasets were processed
in real-time on the sensor nodes: one in which the BSN was in motion, and one
while it was still. These are referred to as the `walking` and `standing` datasets.
Together, these demonstrate the capabilities of the system when using different
packet processing schemes under real-world conditions.

4   Results and Discussion

An instance of the BSN platform was implemented as described in Sect. 3. Communication with AWS was confirmed by viewing the packets published on the
MQTT channel. From here, packets can be decrypted, decoded, and further processed or graphed, or simply stored for later viewing. In this section, we provide
detailed results and an analysis of our experiments with respect to the compression routine when applied to diverse sensor data from the example BSN, as well
as overall efficiency of the packet processing schemes.

4.1   Compression

In general, the compression scheme worked well on most of the sensor data.
Table 1 gives an overview of the compression ratios and resulting reconstruction error, computed as RMSE, as a percentage of the total sensing range when
applied to the `walking` dataset. As each sensor type has a unique range of possible values, all of which are mapped to 8-bit values during processing, reporting the error in this manner provides a fair comparison between different sensor types. Furthermore, we define the compression ratio (CR) as the percent
reduction in size; hence, a CR of 25% indicates the compressed packet is 25%
smaller than the original, while a CR of 75% indicates the compressed packet
is 75% smaller than the original. Among the least compressible signal types
in the dataset included the accelerometry signals (Accel. and LinAccel.), which
required relatively high threshold parameter (T_d) ranges to achieve compression,
and then resulted in moderate reconstruction error, e.g. about 5%. Since T_d is
tunable, it is feasible to adjust this parameter for different sensor types, or even
signals from different measurement axes if desired. On average across all sensor
types, this technique achieves a minimum of 28.5% compression with an average reconstruction error of 2.0%, typical compression of 46.4% with an average
reconstruction error of 5.3%, and maximum compression of 53.2% with an average reconstruction error of 6.0%. By comparison, compression achieved on the
`standing` dataset tends to be higher, with lower error. At all threshold levels

Table 1. Compression (% reduction) and reconstruction error for various threshold values on data from the IMU and distance sensors on the `walking` dataset.

Sensor	T_d	CR (%)	Er (%)	T_d	CR (%)	Er (%)	T_d	CR (%)	Er (%)
		X			Y			Z	
Accel.	25	6.3	3.1	–	–	–	25	25.0	4.2
	50	43.8	6.0	50	6.3	10.1	50	50.0	6.4
	75	50.0	7.5	75	43.8	12.1	75	68.8	7.6
		Right			Left				
Dist.	8	12.5	1.3	8	6.3	0.0			
	12	50.0	1.6	12	6.3	0.0			
	15	68.8	1.9	15	6.3	0.0			
		Roll			Pitch			Yaw	
Euler	8	25.0	1.0	2	31.3	0.3	2	12.3	0.3
	15	31.3	1.5	5	68.8	0.4	3	50.0	0.4
	20	68.8	2.2	**	**	**	5	81.3	0.6
		X			Y			Z	
Gyro.	25	6.3	3.6	25	25.0	3.9	25	12.5	3.7
	50	25.0	5.5	50	50.0	5.9	50	50.0	5.7
	**	**	**	**	**	**	**	**	**
		X			Y			Z	
LinAccel.	40	6.3	3.1	–	–	–	20	6.3	2.2
	50	12.3	6.9	–	–	–	40	31.3	5.0
	60	31.3	7.8	–	–	–	50	62.3	7.7
		X			Y			Z	
Magneto.	1	81.3	0.0	1	81.3	0.0	1	81.3	0.0
	**	**	**	**	**	**	**	**	**
	**	**	**	**	**	**	**	**	**
		X			Y			Z	
Quatern.	3	6.3	0.4	3	68.8	0.3	3	68.8	0.3
	5	25.0	0.6	**	**	**	**	**	**
	10	68.8	1.1	**	**	**	**	**	**

–   no suitable threshold could be found for the maximum allowable error
**   optimal compression already achieved at a lower threshold

which provide suitable compression for sensors while active, as in the walking dataset, maximum packet compression (81.3% or 68.8%, depending on the signal) is achieved at an average reconstruction error of under 0.1%. These results confirm the selection of the 3rd level Haar lifting wavelet transform and configurable threshold, which ultimately provided an acceptable balance between minimum sensor packet compression, processing time, and resulting reconstruction error for $T_d > 0$.

4.2   Packet Processing Efficiency

To ensure security of the final system and that the privacy of the end user is protected, the data gathered by the BSN must be encrypted in some way prior to publishing. Because the packet sizes are relatively small, we did not observe an appreciable difference in the latency of the `publish()` function, which was responsible for generating the final MQTT packet and transmitting the data to the remote server via WiFi. It is expected that, for a simpler communication protocol, differences in the actual transmission latency, as measured on the radio itself, would be more apparent, and the latency/energy savings due to reduced packet size would be significantly more pronounced. Therefore, while the CP and CCP variants are included as a reference, the more meaningful comparison is between CEP and CCEP.

Figure 5 shows the total current consumption of the complete system during one full period of packet processing for the `walking` and `standing` datasets. Vertical lines in the graphs indicate the end of a processing stage; for example, in Walking CEP, the three vertical lines indicate the end of the Compression, Encryption, and Publishing stages. In this implementation, there is a high baseline power, but in practice, any number of common power saving strategies may be employed to improve battery life. While actively processing, there is about 100 mA in current over the baseline; this first segment includes all but the `publish()` function, which itself takes around 4 ms. Broadly, our results demonstrate that the net energy efficiency is improved in CCEP when compared to CEP due primarily to the smaller packet size, translating to less data that must undergo encryption; this is most evident when comparing the relative Energy-Delay Product (EDP) difference between CCEP and CEP on the `walking` and `standing` datasets. Note that in these results, lossless compression ($T_d = 0$) was used; in practice, a higher T_d would improve compression, as shown in Table 1.

With this setup, the average time to encrypt a raw data packet in CEP was 737 μS, whereas the time required to encrypt a compressed packet was only 250 μS for the `standing` data and 531 μS on the `walking` data. Meanwhile, compressing the `standing` data required only 58 μS, while compressing the `walking` data required 66 μS. Because the concatenate function execution depends on the type of data (encrypted or raw), there is also variance here: for uncompressed data, concatenation required 3.5 μS, whereas for compressed `walking` and `standing` data, concatenation required 2.8 μS and 1.5 μS, respectively. When considering the latency and energy of just these three functions in preparing packets for publishing, there is a marked improvement in energy efficiency, 34% and 82%, for compressed data relative to uncompressed data, for the `walking` and `standing` datasets, respectively. Overall EDP, which includes publishing, is shown in Fig. 6(a). Here, there is a significant improvement in energy efficiency due to compression in the `standing` dataset, and the primary driver - the improvement in latency - is clearly shown in Fig. 6(b).

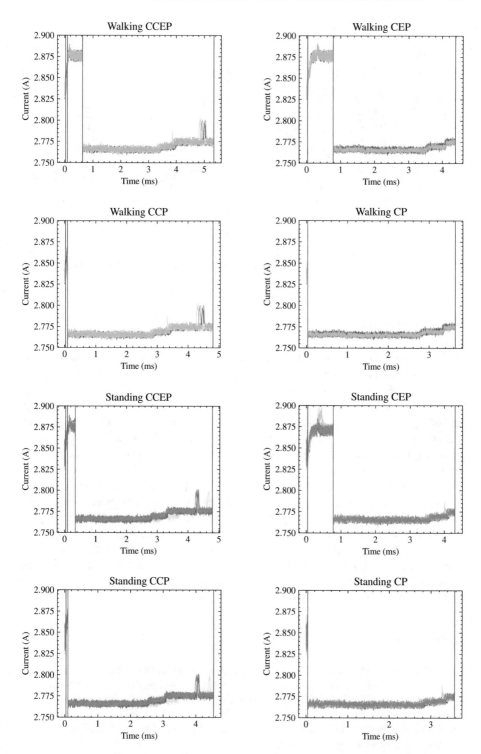

Fig. 5. Power measurements for walking and standing data. Vertical lines in the graphs denote the end of a processing stage.

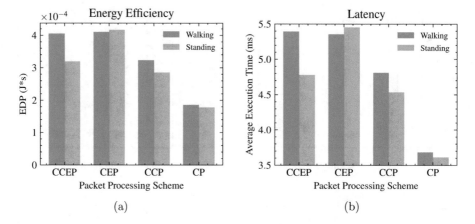

Fig. 6. Average (a) energy efficiency and (b) execution time for different packet processing schemes on the two datasets. Note that for EDP, lower values indicate higher efficiency.

5   Conclusion

In this paper, we have presented a cloud-connected BSN platform that features lightweight cryptography and a configurable compression algorithm suitable for a constrained devices. We have demonstrated through rigorous experimental verification how the compression can be applied to diverse types of sensor data, achieving average compression of 46% with about 5% error in the typical case. We have also presented an efficient packet encoding scheme which supports an arbitrary number of categorical sensors, each of which supports up to 16 categories, as well as an optimal organization for run-length encoded data from the compression routine. Our platform supports connection to Amazon AWS IoT using a lightweight MQTT protocol. In general, the use of a secure lightweight cipher is encouraged to ensure security for the system, and privacy for the individual. We have demonstrated how a sufficiently low-overhead compression algorithm can actually enable energy *savings*, even when used in conjunction with a lightweight block cipher. Future work on this platform includes implementing additional power optimization strategies, investigating alternative compression routines, and overall usability enhancements for BSN developers.

References

1. Alrige, M., Chatterjee, S.: Toward a taxonomy of wearable technologies in healthcare. In: Donnellan, B., Helfert, M., Kenneally, J., VanderMeer, D., Rothenberger, M., Winter, R. (eds.) DESRIST 2015. LNCS, vol. 9073, pp. 496–504. Springer, Cham (2015). https://doi.org/10.1007/978-3-319-18714-3_43
2. Amazon.com Inc.: AWS IoT Device SDK for C++ v2, June 2021. https://github.com/aws/aws-iot-device-sdk-cpp-v2

3. Azar, J., Darazi, R., Habib, C., Makhoul, A., Demerjian, J.: Using DWT lifting scheme for lossless data compression in wireless body sensor networks. In: 2018 14th International Wireless Communications Mobile Computing Conference (IWCMC), pp. 1465–1470 (2018). https://doi.org/10.1109/IWCMC.2018.8450459
4. Beaulieu, R., Shors, D., Smith, J., Treatman-Clark, S., Weeks, B., Wingers, L.: The Simon and speck lightweight block ciphers. In: Proceedings of the 52nd Annual Design Automation Conference, DAC 2015. Association for Computing Machinery, New York (2015). https://doi.org/10.1145/2744769.2747946
5. Bogdanov, A., et al.: PRESENT: an ultra-lightweight block cipher. In: Paillier, P., Verbauwhede, I. (eds.) CHES 2007. LNCS, vol. 4727, pp. 450–466. Springer, Heidelberg (2007). https://doi.org/10.1007/978-3-540-74735-2_31
6. Dey, N., Ashour, A.S., Shi, F., Fong, S.J., Sherratt, R.S.: Developing residential wireless sensor networks for ECG healthcare monitoring. IEEE Trans. Consum. Electron. **63**(4), 442–449 (2017). https://doi.org/10.1109/TCE.2017.015063
7. Diehl, W., Farahmand, F., Yalla, P., Kaps, J.P., Gaj, K.: Comparison of hardware and software implementations of selected lightweight block ciphers. In: 2017 27th International Conference on Field Programmable Logic and Applications (FPL), pp. 1–4 (2017). https://doi.org/10.23919/FPL.2017.8056808
8. Dinu, D., Corre, Y.L., Khovratovich, D., Perrin, L., Großschädl, J., Biryukov, A.: Triathlon of lightweight block ciphers for the internet of things. J. Cryptogr. Eng. **9**(3), 283–302 (2019)
9. Dinu, D., Perrin, L., Udovenko, A., Velichkov, V., Großschädl, J., Biryukov, A.: Design strategies for ARX with provable bounds: SPARX and LAX. In: Cheon, J.H., Takagi, T. (eds.) ASIACRYPT 2016. LNCS, vol. 10031, pp. 484–513. Springer, Heidelberg (2016). https://doi.org/10.1007/978-3-662-53887-6_18
10. Elsayed, M., Badawy, A., Mahmuddin, M., Elfouly, T., Mohamed, A., Abualsaud, K.: FPGA implementation of dwt EEG data compression for wireless body sensor networks. In: 2016 IEEE Conference on Wireless Sensors (ICWiSE), pp. 21–25 (2016). https://doi.org/10.1109/ICWISE.2016.8187756
11. Giorgi, G.: A combined approach for real-time data compression in wireless body sensor networks. IEEE Sens. J. **17**(18), 6129–6135 (2017). https://doi.org/10.1109/JSEN.2017.2736249
12. Gravina, R., Alinia, P., Ghasemzadeh, H., Fortino, G.: Multi-sensor fusion in body sensor networks: state-of-the-art and research challenges. Inf. Fusion **35**, 68–80 (2017)
13. Gravina, R., Fortino, G.: Wearable body sensor networks: state-of-the-art and research directions. IEEE Sens. J. **21**(11), 12511–12522 (2021). https://doi.org/10.1109/JSEN.2020.3044447
14. Habib, C., Makhoul, A., Darazi, R., Couturier, R.: Health risk assessment and decision-making for patient monitoring and decision-support using wireless body sensor networks. Inf. Fusion **47**, 10–22 (2019)
15. Jones, R.W., Katzis, K.: 5G and wireless body area networks. In: 2018 IEEE Wireless Communications and Networking Conference Workshops (WCNCW), pp. 373–378 (2018). https://doi.org/10.1109/WCNCW.2018.8369035
16. Karam, R., Majerus, S.J., Bourbeau, D.J., Damaser, M.S., Bhunia, S.: Tunable and lightweight on-chip event detection for implantable bladder pressure monitoring devices. IEEE Trans. Biomed. Circuits Syst. **11**(6), 1303–1312 (2017). https://doi.org/10.1109/tbcas.2017.2748981
17. Li, Y., et al.: Communication energy modeling and optimization through joint packet size analysis of BSN and WiFi networks. IEEE Trans. Parallel Distrib. Syst. **24**(9), 1741–1751 (2013). https://doi.org/10.1109/TPDS.2012.264

18. Mohd, B.J., Hayajneh, T.: Lightweight block ciphers for IoT: energy optimization and survivability techniques. IEEE Access **6**, 35966–35978 (2018). https://doi.org/10.1109/ACCESS.2018.2848586

19. Mohd, B.J., Hayajneh, T., Ahmad Yousef, K.M., Khalaf, Z.A., Bhuiyan, M.Z.A.: Hardware design and modeling of lightweight block ciphers for secure communications. Future Gener. Comput. Syst. **83**, 510–521 (2018)

20. Mouha, N., Mennink, B., Van Herrewege, A., Watanabe, D., Preneel, B., Verbauwhede, I.: Chaskey: an efficient MAC algorithm for 32-bit microcontrollers. In: Joux, A., Youssef, A. (eds.) SAC 2014. LNCS, vol. 8781, pp. 306–323. Springer, Cham (2014). https://doi.org/10.1007/978-3-319-13051-4_19

21. Muzammal, M., Talat, R., Sodhro, A.H., Pirbhulal, S.: A multi-sensor data fusion enabled ensemble approach for medical data from body sensor networks. Inf. Fusion **53**, 155–164 (2020)

22. Pirbhulal, S., Wu, W., Li, G., Sangaiah, A.K.: Medical information security for wearable body sensor networks in smart healthcare. IEEE Consum. Electron. Mag. **8**(5), 37–41 (2019). https://doi.org/10.1109/MCE.2019.2923925

23. Puthal, D., Wu, X., Surya, N., Ranjan, R., Chen, J.: SEEN: a selective encryption method to ensure confidentiality for big sensing data streams. IEEE Trans. Big Data **5**(3), 379–392 (2019). https://doi.org/10.1109/TBDATA.2017.2702172

24. Qiu, H., Qiu, M., Lu, Z.: Selective encryption on ECG data in body sensor network based on supervised machine learning. Inf. Fusion **55**, 59–67 (2020). https://doi.org/10.1016/j.inffus.2019.07.012

25. Sehrawat, D., Gill, N.: Lightweight block ciphers for IoT based applications: a review. Int. J. Appl. Eng. **13**, 2258–2270 (2019)

26. Solanas, A., et al.: Smart health: a context-aware health paradigm within smart cities. IEEE Commun. Mag. **52**(8), 74–81 (2014). https://doi.org/10.1109/MCOM.2014.6871673

27. Sweldens, W.: The lifting scheme: a construction of second generation wavelets. SIAM J. Math. Anal. **29**(2), 511–546 (1998)

28. Wang, Q., Dai, H.N., Zheng, Z., Imran, M., Vasilakos, A.V.: On connectivity of wireless sensor networks with directional antennas. Sensors **17**(1) (2017). https://doi.org/10.3390/s17010134

29. Wang, S., Ji, L., Li, A., Wu, J.: Body sensor networks for ubiquitous healthcare. J. Control Theory Appl. **9**, 3–9 (2011). https://doi.org/10.1007/s11768-011-0236-7

30. Yang, G., Zhu, B., Suder, V., Aagaard, M.D., Gong, G.: The Simeck family of lightweight block ciphers. In: Güneysu, T., Handschuh, H. (eds.) CHES 2015. LNCS, vol. 9293, pp. 307–329. Springer, Heidelberg (2015). https://doi.org/10.1007/978-3-662-48324-4_16

Methods

EasyDeep: An IoT Friendly Robust Detection Method for GAN Generated Deepfake Images in Social Media

Alakananda Mitra[1] , Saraju P. Mohanty[1(✉)] , Peter Corcoran[2] ,
and Elias Kougianos[3]

[1] Department of Computer Science and Engineering, University of North Texas, Denton, USA
alakanandamitra@my.unt.edu, saraju.mohanty@unt.edu
[2] School of Engineering and Informatics, National University of Ireland, Galway, Ireland
peter.corcoran@nuigalway.ie
[3] Department of Electrical Engineering, University of North Texas, Denton, USA
elias.kougianos@unt.edu

Abstract. Advancements in artificial intelligence, and especially deep learning technology have given birth to a new era of multimedia forgery. Deepfake takes it to a whole new level. This deep learning based technology creates new images with features which have been acquired from a different set of images. The rapid evolution of Generative Adversarial networks (GANs) provides an available route to create deepfakes. They generate highly sophisticated and realistic images through deep learning and implement deepfake using image-to-image translation. We propose a novel, memory-efficient lightweight machine learning based deepfake detection method which is successfully deployed in the IoT platform. A detection API is proposed along with the detection method. To the best of the authors' knowledge, this effort is the first ever for detecting highly sophisticated GAN generated deepfake images at the edge. The novelty of the work is achieving a considerable amount of accuracy with a short training time and inference at the edge device. The total time for sending the image to the edge, detecting and result display through the API is promising. Some discussion is also provided to improve accuracy and to reduce the inference time. A comparative study is also made by performing a three-fold textural analysis - computation of Shannon's entropy, measurement of some of Haralick's texture features (like contrast, dissimilarity, homogeneity, correlation) and study of the histograms of the generated images. Even when generated fake images look similar to the corresponding real images, the results present clear evidence that they differ significantly from the real images in entropy, contrast, dissimilarity, homogeneity, and correlation.

Keywords: Deepfake · IoT · Edge computing · Generative Adversarial Networks (GANs) · Image-to-image translation · Texture analysis · Shannon's entropy · Haralick texture feature · CycleGAN · StarGAN

1 Introduction

Recently, there was a lot of excitement generated by Hollywood actor Tom Cruise's Tik-Tok videos. Those videos went viral. They have more than 10M views in March 2021.

© IFIP International Federation for Information Processing 2022
Published by Springer Nature Switzerland AG 2022
L. M. Camarinha-Matos et al. (Eds.): IFIPIoT 2021, IFIP AICT 641, pp. 217–236, 2022.
https://doi.org/10.1007/978-3-030-96466-5_14

The technology behind these videos is deepfake. The real Mr. Cruise was not present in those videos. They were not shot with a real camera. The videos were synthetically generated from thousands of his video clips or images by deepfake technology. Features of Mr. Cruise were learned by deep neural networks from those photos and videos and deepfake videos were created through image-to-image translation. It is illegal to impersonate someone in social media. But there is a disparity between the way technology is progressing and the way researchers and companies are trying to combat it. As a result, newly advanced deepfake videos are spreading everyday in social media like Facebook, Twitter, Instagram etc. Generative Adversarial Networks (GANs) create such sophisticated images/videos, that it is hard to detect them. The Defense Advanced Research Projects Agency (DARPA) of the U.S. government is collaborating with various institutions to fight image forgery, especially deepfake [4]. The tech giants Facebook, Google, Microsoft, and Amazon are also combating it.

In today's world, social media play a crucial role in everyday life. Frequently checking social media anywhere, anytime has become a habit. People can connect to the world from a small hand held device easily. On the other side, multimedia forgery has spread immensely. These altered images and videos are often being uploaded in social media. They can defame a person, create political tension or spread rumors [29].

This motivates us to propose a machine learning (ML) based deepfake detection system, which can be deployed in an end device of an IoT setting so that people can check the authenticity of any image anytime, anywhere. This will help to stop circulating misinformation or rumors. The overall system overview of the detection method in an IoT environment is shown in Fig. 1.

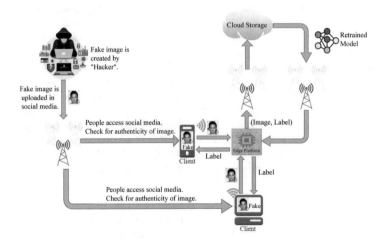

Fig. 1. System overview of the detection method.

In general, GANs [9] have a generator and a discriminator as sub models, but they differ in overall structure and working principles. Hence, fake images generated by different GANs will differ from each other. Initially, we investigate fake images generated by two GANs - CycleGAN [41] and StarGAN [7]. As they have different structures and different working principles, as detailed in Table 1, deepfake image/video produced by CycleGAN will differ from that of a StarGAN. We analyze GAN generated images at pixel level and compute several textural features to obtain more information about the deepfake image textures. This textural analysis helps us to propose a memory effi- cient Machine Learning (ML) based detection method which adapts very well in an IoT environment.

Table 1. Comparison between CycleGAN and StarGAN

	CycleGAN [41]	StarGAN [7]
Network structure	2 generators + 2 discriminators	2 generators + 1 discriminator
Number of domains	2	≥ 2
Loss	Adversarial loss + Forward cycle consistency loss + Backward cycle consistency loss	Adversarial loss + Domain loss + Reconstruction loss
Data for training	Unpaired datasets	Dataset with labeled attributes

The rest of the paper is organized as follows. Section 2 presents challenges and the motivation behind this work. Section 3 focuses on the novel contributions of the paper. Section 4 is a survey of related works in this field. GAN generated images are analyzed in detail in Sect. 5. Our proposed detection method is described in Sect. 6. Experimental verification is discussed in Sect. 7 while Sect. 8 presents the results. Section 9 draws conclusions and suggests directions for future work.

2   Challenges of GAN Generated Deepfake Images

GANs have improved the quality of the generated images [6, 10, 17, 33]. Presently, GAN approaches have achieved monumental success in creating synthetic images [15–17, 36] and in transferring image styles between different domains [41]. Image-to-image trans- lation can be used in changing seasons in a photo, photo enhancement, object trans- figuration, etc. [41]. But, these applications can also be used in negative ways. It is difficult for people to distinguish between a GAN generated deepfake image and a real image with bare eyes. These fake images spread misinformation through social media or news channels. Faking someone's identity ("deepfake") in social media could have a socio-political impact along with financial and security hazards.

For more than a century, audio-visual media have presented the truth, recording the time and history. But fake images, videos and audios change the perception of truth or reality. Thus it is important to look into the threats posed by GAN-generated deepfake images or videos.

3   Novel Contributions of the Current Paper

This paper proposes a ML based technique of detecting GAN generated deepfake images, implementable at an edge device. The novelties of this work are:

– To the best of our knowledge, this work is the first ever effort to detect GAN generated deepfake images at an edge device.
– As edge devices are of limited resources (memory, architecture, storage etc.), high accuracy, heavy computing models can not be deployed. We propose a novel ML based technique which detects deepfake images at an edge device using texture analysis. This is done with lighter computational load. Training time is much shorter and we achieve a considerate amount of accuracy.
– A detection API is proposed to make the overall process automated. Figure 2 shows the overall Detection API diagram.
– We also suggest different ways of achieving higher accuracy.
– Some discussion is provided on strategies to improve inference time.
– Various textural features like Shannon's entropy, and Haralick's texture features of GAN generated deepfake images have been explored to understand the textural difference between generated and real images. It helps us to propose a memory efficient detection method.
– A comparative study on histograms between StarGAN generated images and corresponding real images has been performed to understand the effect of manipulation on color.

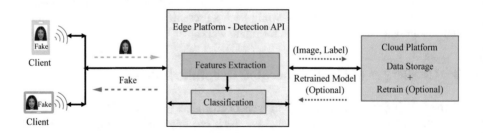

Fig. 2. Detection method API diagram.

4   Related Prior Works

In the last decade, due to the availability of GPUs, the research on GAN generated images has received a huge boost. Various areas of image manipulation such as high quality GAN generated images [5,10,17,20,27,31,33,38], image-to-image translation [7,14,39,42], face completion [13,21], various facial expression and attributes [8,23], domain transfer [19,34], and style transfer [15,16] have received the attention of the computer vision community.

Researchers in image forensics and computer vision have been working to develop methods in detecting those GAN generated fake images. In our previous work [28,29] we detected mostly auto-encoder generated social media deepfake videos. An ensemble deep learning technique via a Random Forest classifier has been proposed in [12]. Three shallow CNN structures have been used to extract features from the images in YCbCr, HSV, and Lab color spaces. Two fully connected (FC) networks with 2048 and 1024 nodes increase the total number of trainable parameters. Parallel processing of the same image in three different color spaces makes the process resource intensive. No IoT implementation effort has been made here. Fake faces have been detected in [37] using a shallow neural network as a classifier and neuron activation has been monitored using deep neural network. The model has been evaluated for four perturbation attacks. This model is also resource intensive. It is not implemented in IoT settings. Gram blocks have been added in ResNet structure in detecting fake faces in [22]. This is not an IoT friendly network either, due to its heavyweight structure. Gray level co-occurrence matrices (GLCM) have been calculated separately on RGB channels and used as the inputs of a DNN structure [30]. GLCM calculation over three channels for an image makes it memory intensive. No effort has been made to deploy it at edge either. Both GAN generated and man made fake images have been detected in a DNN based ensemble network [35].

How a GAN generated image is different from a camera shot image from a color cue perspective, has been investigated in [26]. GAN fingerprints on image attribution have been noted in [40]. Some of the textural properties of fake images generated by StyleGAN and PGGAN have been explored in [24] along with their detection network. All these works claim to have high accuracy, but no effort has been made to deploy them in IoT environments.

5 Analysis of GAN Generated Deepfake Images

In this section, we explore several first and second order statistical texture features of GAN generated fake images, before detecting them in Sect. 6. A comparative study has also been performed between the generated deepfake images and corresponding real images.

When a photo is shot in a digital camera, light from the object gets passed through the lens and falls on the CMOS sensors which breaks the image into pixels after measuring the light intensity and brightness. When a real image is passed through a GAN generator, it transforms the image into a latent space vector. After a zero sum game with the discriminator it generates a fake image. Hence, the way a digital camera takes a photo differs from the process of generation of fake images by GANs. This motivates us to explore the textural features of GAN generated images. We tested CycleGAN and StarGAN generated images.

5.1 Entropy Computation

In information theory, Shannon's Entropy measures the uncertainty of a random variable's possible outcomes. For an image, it is more related to the texture or image information. The difference in entropy between a generated image and its corresponding real image gives some information on texture difference between them. Calculating the entropy of each pixel in an image and summing over all possible gray scale pixels gives a scalar value E of the entropy of that image according to Eq. 1, and makes it easily comparable:

$$E = -\sum_{i=0}^{n-1} p_i \log_b p_i, \tag{1}$$

where n denotes the number of gray levels, p_i is the pixel probability for gray level i, and base b is the base.

To calculate the entropy of an gray scale image E_{gray}, the space of any *RGB* image is first changed to *Gray* scale. With same radiance of *red (R)*, *green (G)*, and *blue (B)* colors, green always looks brightest among those three because the luminous efficiency tops at the green zone of the visible light spectrum, red looks less bright and blue is the darkest. So when the luminance (Y) of an *RGB* image is expressed as a function of R, G, and B, different weights are applied in them to represent the color perception of real life as in Eq. 2 [3]. During conversion of *RGB* image to *Gray* scale image, Eq. 2 is considered as the luminance of the image.

$$Y = 0.2125R + 0.7154G + 0.0721B \tag{2}$$

To compare the entropies of generated and real images, the process described in Algorithm 1 has been used.

5.2   Haralick's Texture Features Analysis

Texture is a spatial property of an image. Computing the Gray-Level Co-Occurrence Matrix (GLCM) of an image is a well known method to capture the spatial dependence of gray level values. It calculates the likelihood of a pixel value and its relationship with other pixels [2].

To explore the fake images more closely, we calculate several Haralick's Texture Features [11] from the GLCM. The features we calculate are contrast, correlation, homogeneity, and dissimilarity.

The GLCM is defined as a square matrix with elements as the frequency of occurrence of pixels with gray levels at a certain distance and angle. Contrast, homogeneity, dissimilarity, and correlation are defined in Eq. 3, 4, 5, and 6 respectively.

Algorithm 1. Process of Comparing Entropy of Generated and Real Images for Section 5.

1: **Input:** Fake Image $I1$ and Real Image $I2$
2: **Output:** min, max, $mean$, and $standard\ deviation$ of entropy difference
3: SAVE the real images with name ending real and fake images with ending word fake
4: SET input image directory $input\_dir$
5: DECLARE two Dictionaries ent_fake_dict and ent_real_dict with keys $filename$ and $entropy$ for fake and real images respectively
6: DECLARE a variable $comp\_entropy$ and initialize it to 0
7: DECLARE a list $comp\_entropy\_list$ for storing the entropy difference and initialize it to $comp\_entropy\_list \leftarrow NIL$
8: ASSIGN a particular fake image to $index\_f$ and a real image to $index\_r$
9: **for** $file \in input\_dir$ **do**
10:     Entropy is calculated.
11:     **if** $file$ contains the word real **then**
12:         STORE the entropy in ent_real_dict along with $filename$
13:     **else**
14:         STORE the entropy in ent_fake_dict along with $filename$
15:     **end if**
16: **end for**
17: **for** $index\_r \in ent\_real\_dict$ **do**
18:     **for** $index\_f \in ent\_fake\_dict$ **do**
19:         GET the fake image ent_fake_dict[$filename$] corresponding to the real image ent_real_dict[$filename$].
20:         COMPUTE $comp\_entropy$ by taking the difference between entropies of the
21:         corresponding fake and real images
22:         STORE $comp\_entropy$ in $comp\_entropy\_list$
23:     **end for**
24: **end for**
25: COMPUTE min, max, $mean$, and $standard\ deviation$ of $comp\_entropy\_list$

$$CON = \sum_{i,j=0}^{n-1} p(i,j)(i-j)^2 \tag{3}$$

$$HOM = \sum_{i,j=0}^{n-1} \frac{p(i,j)}{(1+(i-j)^2)} \tag{4}$$

$$DIS = \sum_{i,j=0}^{n-1} p(i,j)|i-j| \tag{5}$$

$$COR = \sum_{i,j=0}^{n-1} p(i,j) \left[\frac{(i-\mu_i)(j-\mu_j)}{\sqrt{(\sigma_i^2)(\sigma_j^2)}} \right] \tag{6}$$

In the above expressions, n denotes number of gray levels, $p(i,j)$ is the element of GLCM for the distance between gray level values i and j, and μ and σ are the mean and variance of the intensities of all gray values present, respectively.

We have followed the process in Algorithm 2 for comparing contrast, dissimilarity, homogeneity and correlation among real and generated images.

Algorithm 2. Process of Comparing Contrast, Dissimilarity, Homogeneity, and Correlation of Generated and Real Images for Section 5.

1: **Input:** Fake Image $I1$ and Real Image $I2$
2: **Output:**min, max, $mean$, and $standard\ deviation$ of GLCM properties difference
3: SAVE real images with name ending real and fake images with fake.
4: SET input image directory $input\_dir$
5: DECLARE two Dictionaries $glcm\_prop\_fake\_dict$ and $glcm\_prop\_real\_dict$ with keys $filename$, $contrast$, $dissimilarity$, $homogeneity$, and $correlation$ for fake and real images, respectively.
6: DECLARE a list $comp\_glcm\_prop$ for storing the GLCM properties and initialize it to $comp\_glcm\_prop \leftarrow NIL$.
7: DECLARE another list $comp\_glcm\_prop\_list$ for storing the GLCM properties differences and initialize it to $comp\_glcm\_prop\_list \leftarrow NIL$.
8: ASSIGN a particular fake image to $index\_f$ and a real image to $index\_r$.
9: **for** $file \in input\_dir$ **do**
10:　　GLCM is calculated.
11:　　$contrast$, $dissimilarity$, $homogeneity$, and $correlation$ are calculated.
12:　　**if** $file$ contains the word real **then**
13:　　　　STORE $contrast$, $dissimilarity$, $homogeneity$, and $correlation$ in $glcm\_prop\_real\_dict$ along with $filename$.
14:　　**else**
15:　　　　STORE $contrast$, $dissimilarity$, $homogeneity$, and $correlation$ in $glcm\_prop\_fake\_dict$ along with $filename$.
16:　　**end if**
17: **end for**
18: **for** $index\_r \in glcm\_prop\_real\_dict$ **do**
19:　　**for** $index\_f \in glcm\_prop\_fake\_dict$ **do**
20:　　　　GET $glcm\_prop\_fake\_dict[filename]$ corresponding to $glcm\_prop\_real\_dict[filename]$.
21:　　　　COMPUTE $comp\_glcm\_prop$ by taking the difference between contrast, dissimilarity, homogeneity, and correlation of the corresponding fake and real images.
22:　　　　STORE $comp\_glcm\_prop$ in $comp\_glcm\_prop\_list$
23:　　**end for**
24: **end for**
25: COMPUTE min, max, $mean$, and $standard\ deviation$ of $comp\_glcm\_prop\_list$.

5.3　Histogram Analysis

We explore the histograms of the generated images and compare them with those of real images. Histograms for the R, G, and B channels are plotted separately. They show a comparative graphical representation of the distribution of intensity of a generated image and corresponding real image for each channel.

6   The Proposed Novel Deepfake Detection Method at Edge Computing Platform

In this section, we propose a novel machine learning based model for detecting GAN generated images at an edge device using textural features of images. The process is performed automatically through our proposed detection API. The reasons behind this approach are multi-fold:

- The computation cost is very low, therefore it is a good fit for less resource IoT settings.
- As the the approach is based on gray level co-occurrence at pixel locations, it is generic. It can be applied to any type of GAN.

6.1   System Level Representation

The system level overview of the detection method is shown in Fig. 1. In this IoT environment, end users or clients are connected to the edge device. The edge device is connected to the cloud for data storage. Retraining of the model can be done at the cloud with the stored images and corresponding predictions at a later stage, if needed. The detection process is initiated when an image from social media (uploaded by any person of bad intent [1]), to be detected, is sent to the edge platform through our proposed 'Detection API'. Once the image is detected by the model, the detection score goes back to its source. The detection score is also stored in the cloud along with the image to be used for future retraining of the model. Figure 2 shows a detailed representation of the concept when a client sends the image to the edge device.

6.2   Detection Methodology at the Edge Platform

Figure 3 shows the overall diagram of the detection model at edge. It is an automatic workflow. When an user wants to check any picture from social media accounts for authenticity, he calls the Detection API and sends the image to the edge device. Once the image reaches the edge device it is saved in a folder and the GLCM followed by Haralick's texture features are calculated from the corresponding gray level image of the colored image.

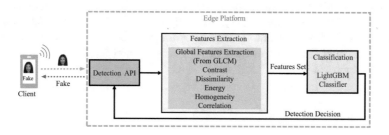

Fig. 3. Overall workflow diagram at edge platform.

A features set is created from those features. We compute five Haralick's texture features. The texture features calculated at this stage are contrast, dissimilarity, homogeneity, energy, and correlation. We calculate those features from the GLCM for four distances at $d = 1, 2, 3, 5$ and three angles $\theta = 0, \pi/4, \pi/2$ to generate the feature vector. After the feature extraction, a machine learning algorithm is used to classify the image. As in IoT environment, the resources are limited, we carefully choose our classifier as LightGBM with boosting type 'Gradient Boosting Decision Tree (gbdt)'. It is a tree based algorithm. The advantage of using this classifier over others are:

- The algorithm [18] uses histograms to learn. It is cost effective because for a histogram based algorithm the time complexity is proportional to the number of bins, not to the data volume once histograms are made.
- Use of discrete bins reduces the memory usage which is a limiting factor at an edge device.
- Training is very fast as it is distributed.

6.3   Phases of Detection Method

The overall detection process has two phases: Training and Testing or Inferring.

- *Training Phase:* In the training phase, the classifier learns how to detect the fake images. Initial training has been done on a PC. The details are mentioned in Sect. 7. At a later stage, if retraining is needed, it can be done in the cloud.
- *Testing Phase:* Testing phase is where the unknown samples are tested. This is implemented at the edge device. The testing phase is performed through our proposed API.

6.4   Detection API

We propose a Detection API hosted at the edge device. The workflow of the API is shown in Fig. 4. The goal is to make the API lighter and faster to work at an edge device.

6.5   Detection Metrics

To visualize the classification performance of our detection model, we define the *Confusion Matrix (CM)* as in Table 2 [29]. Detecting real or GAN generated fake images is a binary classification problem, the corresponding *CM* is a 2×2 matrix. To evaluate the detection model, various metrics have been computed from *CM* according to the following expressions:

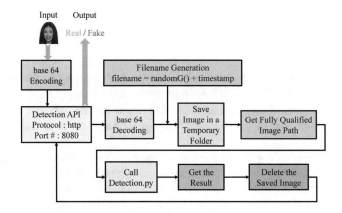

Fig. 4. Detection API workflow.

$$Accuracy = \left(\frac{TP + TN}{TP + TN + FP + FN} \right) \times 100\% \qquad (7)$$

$$Precision = \left(\frac{TP}{TP + FP} \right) \times 100\% \qquad (8)$$

$$Recall = \left(\frac{TP}{TP + FN} \right) \times 100\% \qquad (9)$$

$$F1 - score = \left(\frac{2}{\dfrac{1}{Precision} + \dfrac{1}{Recall}} \right) \times 100\% \qquad (10)$$

Table 2. Confusion matrix

	Predicted label	
True label	True Positive (**TP**): Reality: **Fake** Model predicted: **Fake**	False Negative (**FN**): Reality: **Fake** Model predicted: **Real**
	False Positive (**FP**): Reality: **Real** Model predicted: **Fake**	True Negative (**TN**): Reality: **Real** Model predicted: **Real**

7   Experiments

7.1   Datasets

StarGAN and CycleGAN datasets have been chosen to compare the fake images generated by different GANs. The CycleGAN dataset consists of images which are generated by translating from one image domain to another image domain, whereas StarGAN generates multi-domain images on the fly by changing physical attributes and with different expressions.

StarGAN Dataset: To generate this dataset we follow the process as in [7]. Five different physical attributes, such as different hair color (black, blond, brown), gender, and age have been chosen. No expression or mood change has been done. To generate the images by StarGAN, the first 6,000 images from CelebA [25] dataset have been chosen. Each real image generates five images, so a total of 30,000 images are generated. 500 fake images along with corresponding 100 real images have been tested to compare textural properties of fake images with those of real images. For the detection model a total of 60,000 images (30,000 fake and 30,000 real) have been used for training and validation. Up-sampling of the minority class has been done to provide a balanced dataset. Figure 5 shows some sample StarGAN generated images.

CycleGAN Dataset: To make this dataset, the GitHub page of the original paper has been followed [14,41]. Real images for CycleGAN have been collected from ImageNet, Wikiart, and CMP Facades dataset [32], as suggested by the original paper. A total of 9,809 images have been generated from 9,812 real images. Table 3 presents the detailed list of the dataset generated. Some of the generated CycleGAN images are shown in Fig. 6.

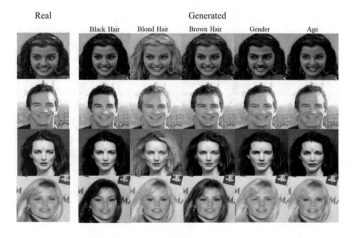

Fig. 5. Sample StarGAN generated images.

Table 3. Generated CycleGAN dataset

	apple2orange	horse2zebra	monet2photo	vangogh	ukiyoe	cezanne	facades
Real	2237	2349	671	1738	194	295	343
Generated	2239	2348	672	1736	193	294	342

Real

Generated

Fig. 6. Sample CycleGAN generated images.

7.2 GAN Generated Image Analysis

Once the datasets are generated, we evaluate various texture statistics for those GAN generated fake images and their corresponding real images. We perform three different experiments with the images.

In the first part, we compute the entropy of the fake images generated by both GANs and compare the result with corresponding real images. Minimum, maximum, mean and standard deviation of the entropy difference between the fake images and real images are also calculated. We evaluate 2,239 "apple2orange", 2,348 "horse2zebra", 672 "monet2photo", 1,736 "vangogh", 193 "ukiyoe", 294 "cezzane", 342 "facades", and 500 StarGAN images. This provides a comparative idea of fakeness of the two sets of fake images.

For the same set of images, GLCM is calculated. Then four Haralick's texture features - contrast, homogeneity, dissimilarity and correlation - are computed and compared with those of corresponding real images. To provide an inter-GAN comparison, the same statistical parameters of the dataset are calculated for both GANs.

Histograms for the R, G, and B channels are observed separately for generated and real images. Histograms of generated image (which has same feature as the real image) are compared with the corresponding histograms of real image e.g., if the sample input image is a black haired young male, comparison is made only when the generated image has the same features ('black haired young male'). For CycleGAN this part is skipped, as the generated image is different than the real image. This has been implemented in Python.

7.3   Implementation of Proposed Detection Method of GAN Generated Images at an Edge Computing Platform

Single Board Computer Platform: The detection model has been implemented on a 4 GB Raspberry pi 4, a single board computer. The input image has been provided through the proposed Detection API and the detection result has been given back through the API.

Initially, the training has been done on a PC with 16 GB total memory and Intel Core i7-9750 processor. No GPU was used. 48, 000 images (24, 000 deepfake images generated by Star GAN and 24, 000 real images) have been utilized for training and 12, 000 images have been used for validation of the model. Total time for training and validation of the model was 27 min. Before constructing the features set, the image is converted to gray level and then resized to 256×256. The features set is constructed from Haralick's texture features. The feature set is of size $48, 000 \times 30$ for the training data. The learning rate of the classifier is kept at 0.05, the maximum depth of 600 trees is 13, and the number of leaves of each tree is kept at 8,500. The boosting algorithm is chosen to be 'Gradient Boosting Decision Tree'. The detection part has been implemented in Python and the API part in Java.

8   Results

8.1   Analysis of GAN Generated Images

In this section, the observations after analyzing and comparing two GAN generated images with real images are reported in detail.

Entropy: The entropy difference of the generated image and its corresponding real image for both GANs is shown in Table 5. The abbreviated terms of Table 5 are explained in Table 4.

Table 4. Definition of abbreviated terms of Table 5

Term	Meaning
ΔE	Entropy difference of real image and generated image $E_R - E_F$
ΔE_1	ΔE when $E_F < E_R$
ΔE_2	ΔE when $E_F > E_R$
ΔE_{mean}	Mean entropy difference of test data distribution
ΔE_{std}	Standard deviation of entropy difference of test data distribution

The entropy difference has been computed by taking the difference of generated images from its corresponding real images. Some results give positive entropy difference and some results negative.

- Negative entropy difference means that the entropy of the generated image is greater than its corresponding real image and is denoted by ΔE_2 in Table 5.
- Positive entropy difference means that the entropy of the generated image is lower than its corresponding real image and is denoted by ΔE_1 in Table 5.

Table 5. Entropy differences between real images and GAN generated fake images

GAN	Data	ΔE_1	ΔE_2	ΔE_{mean}	ΔE_{std}
Cycle GAN	apple2orange	1.8177	−4.6379	0.3965	0.7221
	horse2zebra	0.7999	−2.3821	0.0514	0.2862
	monet	0.5779	−0.83646	0.01031	0.2428
	vangogh	0.5779	−2.3413	0.1046	0.3519
	ukiyoe	0.4335	−0.8343	0.0217	0.2016
	facades	1.448	−3.4454	0.4901	1.3729
	cezanne	0.6253	−1.6657	−0.0171	0.3158
StarGAN		0.4579	−1.3998	−0.1062	0.2310

We tested entropy difference over a certain number of images. Table 5 shows the trend of entropy distribution of a particular GAN generated fake dataset, but changing the images will definitely change the values of maximum, minimum, mean, and standard deviation of entropy difference. StarGAN generates images with lower $|\Delta E|$ on average. The standard deviation of entropy difference in Table 5 also follows the same trend. Other than the ukiyoe dataset, all cases of CycleGAN have larger standard deviation of entropy difference than StarGAN. It means that CycleGAN generates a wide variety of fake images with greater ΔE than StarGAN.

Entropy of an image is the randomness around the pixels of an image. It gives certain information on image texture. Lower $|\Delta E|$ of StarGAN generated images prove that the texture of fake images varies lesser in StarGAN generated images than CycleGAN generated images. StarGAN generates more robust (less varied entropy than real images) fake images than CycleGAN.

Haralick's Texture Features: Table 6 and Table 7 show the differences of texture features between generated image and the corresponding real image. The average difference of contrast, dissimilarity, correlation, and homogeneity are much larger in CycleGAN than StarGAN because CycleGAN generated images are very different from the original images. But StarGAN generated images have varied texture features than real images too. Therefore, we choose these textural features along with energy (inversely proportional to entropy) in forming the features set for detecting fake images.

Histogram: Third, we observe histograms for the StarGAN generated images. They are shown in Figs. 7(a), 7(b), and 7(c). In each case, histograms for red, green, and blue

Table 6. Difference of texture properties of GAN generated images and real images - I

GAN	Data	Contrast		Dissimilarity		Homogeneity		Correlation	
		Δ_{min}	Δ_{max}	Δ_{min}	Δ_{max}	Δ_{min}	Δ_{max}	Δ_{min}	Δ_{max}
Cycle GAN	apple2orange	0.1759	4067.51	0.0025	19.2035	0.6417	4.0771	0.6303	3.3104
	horse2zebra	0.0089	16649.09	0.0002	65.8922	0.00001	0.3731	0.8593	6.9169
	monet	0.9867	2559.67	0.0026	18.8634	0.00001	0.4919	0.0004	0.3023
	vangogh	0.6193	2532.19	0.0025	27.3638	0.0002	0.6615	0.0004	0.6378
	ukiyoe	1.2918	2343.93	0.03824	23.4140	0.00005	0.4478	0.0003	0.4959
	facades	1.2550	1982.35	0.0061	21.2044	0.0014	0.6379	0.00005	0.3006
	cezanne	1.0449	1964.87	0.0071	19.0935	0.00003	0.4021	0.0016	0.4070
	Average	**0.7689**	**4585.66**	**0.0085**	**27.8621**	**0.0919**	**1.0131**	**0.2132**	**1.7673**
StarGAN		0.0003	3175.85	0.0026	24.2543	0.0001	0.4029	0.0001	0.3212

$\Delta \rightarrow$(Difference of a texture property)

Table 7. Difference of texture properties of GAN generated images and real images-II

GAN	Data	Contrast		Dissimilarity		Homogeneity		Correlation	
		Δ_{mean}	Δ_{std}	Δ_{mean}	Δ_{std}	Δ_{mean}	Δ_{std}	Δ_{mean}	Δ_{std}
Cycle GAN	apple2orange	353.3008	339.2468	3.6820	3.0643	0.0964	0.0108	0.0547	0.0522
	horse2zebra	1241.3559	1579.4719	8.7607	8.4865	0.0364	0.0482	0.0001	0.1554
	monet	259.5098	297.9325	2.9529	2.4031	0.0553	0.0605	0.0455	0.0401
	vangogh	663.8957	433.3669	10.1373	5.8673	0.1118	0.0958	0.1661	0.1022
	ukiyoe	935.4261	510.1807	9.7288	4.7253	0.0787	0.0849	0.1719	0.0871
	facades	479.9753	447.9612	6.2992	4.1170	0.2592	0.1790	0.0609	0.0524
	cezanne	542.8389	340.8045	7.1889	4.1682	0.0918	0.0806	0.1110	0.0781
	Average	**639.4718**	**513.8523**	**6.9642**	**4.6902**	**0.1042**	**0.0800**	**0.0872**	**0.0811**
StarGAN		813.0842	679.7914	6.8765	4.9921	0.0729	0.0663	0.0787	0.0579

$\Delta \rightarrow$(Difference of a texture property)

channels of the generated images differ from those of the real images with the same attributes. It means that even if the generated image looks the same as the real image with bare eyes, the color distributions are not the same for those two images.

So, GAN generated images vary in textures and colors from the real images. This observation has been utilized in detecting GAN generated images.

8.2   Evaluation of Edge Detection Model

The performance of the model has been evaluated over $2,000$ total test images. 50% of the images are fake and the rest are real. The *Confusion Matrix* is generated from these images, as shown in Fig. 8(a). We calculate *Precision*, *Recall*, and *F1-score* from *CM* using Eqs. 8, 9, and 10. Table 8 shows the classification report of the model.

To evaluate the model more accurately, we draw the *Receiver Operating Characteristic (ROC)* curve, as shown in Fig. 8(b). *AUC score* for the model is 96%.

Table 9 shows the relation between the accuracy, tree structure, boosting type algorithm and size of the model. We vary the parameters to have a model which can be

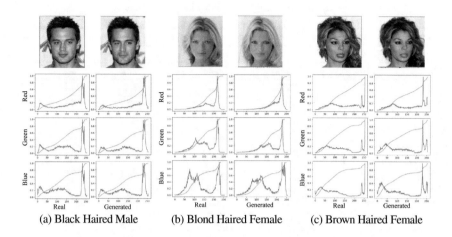

(a) Black Haired Male   (b) Blond Haired Female   (c) Brown Haired Female

Fig. 7. Histogram comparison of StarGAN generated images and real images.

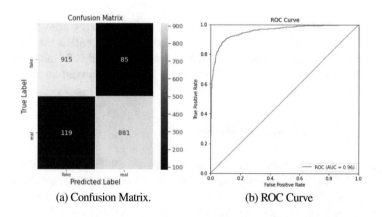

(a) Confusion Matrix.   (b) ROC Curve

Fig. 8. Histogram comparison of StarGAN generated images and real image.

Table 8. Classification report of test images.

Test images	Precision %	Recall %	F1-score %
1000 fake	88.0	92.0	90.0
1000 real	91.0	88.0	90.0
Macro average	90.0	90.0	90.0
Weighted average	90.0	90.0	90.0
Total 2000	Accuracy %	90.0	
Total 2000	**AUC score** %	96.0	

Table 9. Accuracy variation with tree structure

Number of trees	Max tree depth	Number of leaves	Algorithm boosting	Accuracy %	Model size (MB)
100	8	255	dart*	79.4	3.2
100	10	1000	dart	80.4	6.7
100	11	2500	dart	81.8	12.4
100	12	4200	dart	82.1	15.8
100	13	8500	dart	82.9	19.0
100	14	17000	dart	82.7	22.2
100	13	8500	gbdt*	85.5	14.3
100	14	17000	gbdt	85.9	16.4
200	13	8500	gbdt	87.4	21.5
300	13	8500	gbdt	88.2	27.3
400	13	8500	gbdt	89.0	32.8
600	13	8500	gbdt	90.0	43.7

dart* (Dropouts meet Multiple Additive Regression Trees)
gbdt* (Gradient Boosting Decision Tree)

deployed at the Raspberry pi and would also have high accuracy. The final structure is chosen with an accuracy of 90%, 600 trees, and each tree with a maximum depth of 13 and number of leaves 8,500. Training time for our model is 27 min. Accuracy is improved by increasing the number of trees in the algorithm. Maximum tree depth and number of leaves also influence the accuracy.

9   Conclusion and Future Work

It is challenging to implement a computation-intensive computer vision problem like deepfake detection in an IoT environment. We tried to keep the computation as light as possible. We chose only 30 features for each image so that we could infer at a limited resource IoT device with considerable accuracy. Accuracy can be improved by increasing the number of trees and also by changing the feature set. With more features, the accuracy will be higher and the generalization of the model will be achieved. To improve the inference time instead of sending the image in base64 format, binary image can be sent. As a future work, generalization of the model and higher accuracy can be achieved along with improved inference time.

References

1. Image "hacker". image: freepik.com. Accessed 07 June 2021
2. Mathworks. https://www.mathworks.com/help/images/texture-analysis-using-the-gray-level-co-occurrence-matrix-glcm.html. Accessed 28 Jan 2021
3. scikit-image. http://poynton.ca/PDFs/ColorFAQ.pdf. Accessed 02 Feb 2021
4. DARPA News, March 2021. https://www.darpa.mil/news-events/2021-03-02. Accessed 07 May 2021

5. Arjovsky, M., Chintala, S., Bottou, L.: Wasserstein GAN. arXiv: 1701.07875 (2017)
6. Brock, A., Donahue, J., Simonyan, K.: Large scale GAN training for high fidelity natural image synthesis. arXiv: abs/1809.11096 (2018)
7. Choi, Y., Choi, M., Kim, M., Ha, J., Kim, S., Choo, J.: StarGAN: unified generative adversarial networks for multi-domain image-to-image translation. In: Proceedings of the IEEE Conference on Computer Vision and Pattern Recognition, pp. 8789–8797 (2018)
8. Dogan, Y., Keles, H.Y.: Semi-supervised image attribute editing using generative adversarial networks. Neurocomputing **401**, 338–352 (2020)
9. Goodfellow, I., et al.: Generative adversarial nets. In: Ghahramani, Z., Welling, M., Cortes, C., Lawrence, N., Weinberger, K.Q. (eds.) Proceedings of Advances in Neural Information Processing Systems, vol. 27, pp. 2672–2680. Curran Associates, Inc. (2014)
10. Gulrajani, I., Ahmed, F., Arjovsky, M., Dumoulin, V., Courville, A.C.: Improved training of Wasserstein GANs. In: Proceedings of Advances in Neural Information Processing Systems, pp. 5767–5777 (2017)
11. Haralick, R.M., Shanmugam, K., Dinstein, I.: Textural features for image classification. IEEE Trans. Syst. Man Cybernet. SMC-**3**(6), 610–621 (1973)
12. He, P., Li, H., Wang, H.: Detection of fake images via the ensemble of deep representations from multi color spaces. In: Proceedings of IEEE International Conference on Image Processing, pp. 2299–2303 (2019)
13. Iizuka, S., Simo-Serra, E., Ishikawa, H.: Globally and locally consistent image completion. ACM Trans. Graph. **36**(4), 1–14 (2017)
14. Isola, P., Zhu, J., Zhou, T., Efros, A.A.: Image-to-image translation with conditional adversarial networks. In: Proceedings of IEEE Conference on Computer Vision and Pattern Recognition, pp. 1125–1134 (2017)
15. Karras, T., Laine, S., Aila, T.: A style-based generator architecture for generative adversarial networks. In: Proceedings of IEEE Conference on Computer Vision and Pattern Recognition, pp. 4396–4405 (2019)
16. Karras, T., Laine, S., Aittala, M., Hellsten, J., Lehtinen, J., Aila, T.: Analyzing and improving the image quality of stylegan. In: Proceedings of IEEE Conference on Computer Vision and Pattern Recognition, pp. 8107–8116 (2020)
17. Karras, T., Aila, T., Laine, S., Lehtinen, J.: Progressive growing of GANs for improved quality, stability, and variation. arXiv: abs/1710.10196 (2017)
18. Ke, G., et al.: LightGBM: a highly efficient gradient boosting decision tree. In: Proceedings of Advances in Neural Information Processing Systems (2017)
19. Kim, T., Cha, M., Kim, H., Lee, J.K., Kim, J.: Learning to discover cross-domain relations with generative adversarial networks. arXiv: abs/1703.05192 (2017)
20. Ledig, C., et al.: Photo-realistic single image super-resolution using a generative adversarial network. arXiv: abs/1609.04802 (2016)
21. Li, Y., Liu, S., Yang, J., Yang, M.: Generative face completion. arXiv: abs/1704.05838 (2017)
22. Liu, M., Breuel, T., Kautz, J.: Unsupervised image-to-image translation networks. arXiv:abs/1703.00848 (2017)
23. Liu, M., Tuzel, O.: Coupled generative adversarial networks. arXiv: abs/1606.07536 (2016)
24. Liu, Z., Qi, X., Torr, P.H.S.: Global texture enhancement for fake face detection in the wild. In: Proceedings of IEEE Conference on Computer Vision and Pattern Recognition, pp. 8057–8066 (2020)
25. Liu, Z., Luo, P., Wang, X., Tang, X.: Deep learning face attributes in the wild. In: Proceedings of International Conference on Computer Vision, December 2015
26. McCloskey, S., Albright, M.: Detecting GAN-generated imagery using color cues. arXiv:abs/1812.08247 (2018)
27. Mirza, M., Osindero, S.: Conditional generative adversarial nets. arXiv: 1411.1784 (2014)

28. Mitra, A., Mohanty, S.P., Corcoran, P., Kougianos, E.: A novel machine learning based method for deepfake video detection in social media. In: Proceedings of IEEE International Symposium on Smart Electronic Systems (iSES) (Formerly iNiS), pp. 91–96 (2020)
29. Mitra, A., Mohanty, S.P., Corcoran, P., Kougianos, E.: A machine learning based approach for deepfake detection in social media through key video frame extraction. SN Comput. Sci. **2**(2), 1–18 (2021)
30. Nataraj, L., et al.: Detecting GAN generated fake images using co-occurrence matrices. arxiv:abs/1903.06836 (2019)
31. Radford, A., Metz, L., Chintala, S.: Unsupervised representation learning with deep convolutional generative adversarial networks. arXiv: 1511.06434 (2016)
32. Radim Tyleček, R.Š.: Spatial pattern templates for recognition of objects with regular structure. In: Proceedings of German Conference on Pattern Recognition, Saarbrucken, Germany (2013)
33. Salimans, T., Goodfellow, I., Zaremba, W., Cheung, V., Radford, A., Chen, X.: Improved techniques for training GANs. In: Proceedings of the 30th International Conference on Neural Information Processing Systems, pp. 2234–2242 (2016)
34. Taigman, Y., Polyak, A., Wolf, L.: Unsupervised cross-domain image generation. arXiv: abs/1611.02200 (2016)
35. Tariq, S., Lee, S., Kim, H., Shin, Y., Woo, S.S.: Detecting both machine and human created fake face images in the wild. In: Proceedings of the 2nd International Workshop on Multimedia Privacy and Security, pp. 81–87 (2018)
36. Varkarakis, V., Bazrafkan, S., Costache, G., Corcoran, P.: Validating seed data samples for synthetic identities - methodology and uniqueness metrics. IEEE Access **8**, 152532–152550 (2020)
37. Wang, R., et al.: FakeSpotter: a simple yet robust baseline for spotting AI-synthesized fake faces. In: Bessiere, C. (ed.) Proceedings of the Twenty-Ninth International Joint Conference on Artificial Intelligence, pp. 3444–3451, July 2020
38. Wang, T., Liu, M., Zhu, J., Tao, A., Kautz, J., Catanzaro, B.: High-resolution image synthesis and semantic manipulation with conditional GANs. In: Proceedings of IEEE Conference on Computer Vision and Pattern Recognition, pp. 8798–8807 (2018)
39. Yi, Z., Zhang, H., Tan, P., Gong, M.: DualGAN: Unsupervised dual learning for image-to-image translation. arXiv: abs/1704.02510 (2017)
40. Yu, N., Davis, L., Fritz, M.: Attributing fake images to GANs: learning and analyzing GAN fingerprints. In: Proceedings of IEEE International Conference on Computer Vision, pp. 7555–7565 (2019)
41. Zhu, J., Park, T., Isola, P., Efros, A.A.: Unpaired image-to-image translation using cycle-consistent adversarial networks. In: Proceedings of IEEE International Conference on Computer Vision, pp. 2242–2251 (2017)
42. Zhu, J.Y., et al.: Toward multimodal image-to-image translation. In: Guyon, I., et al. (eds.) Advances in Neural Information Processing Systems, vol. 30, pp. 465–476. Curran Associates, Inc. (2017)

A Fuzzy Logic Approach for Self-managing Energy Efficiency in IoT Nodes

Victória Melo$^{(\boxtimes)}$ ⓘ, Gustavo Funchal ⓘ, Jonas Queiroz ⓘ, and Paulo Leitão ⓘ

Research Centre in Digitalization and Intelligent Robotics (CeDRI), Instituto Politécnico de Bragança, Campus de Santa Apolónia, 5300-253 Bragança, Portugal
{victoria,gustavofunchal,jpqueiroz,pleitao}@ipb.pt

Abstract. The collection and analysis of data assume a crucial importance in the digital transformation era. Internet of Things (IoT) technologies allow to gather data from heterogeneous sources and make them available for data-driven systems aiming, e.g., monitoring, diagnosis, prediction and optimization. Several applications require that these IoT nodes be located remotely without connection to the electrical grid and being powered by batteries or renewable sources, thus requiring a more efficient management of the energy consumption in their operation. This paper aims to study and develop intelligent IoT nodes that embed Artificial Intelligence techniques to optimize their operation in terms of energy consumption when operating in constrained environments and powered by energy harvesting systems. For this purpose, a Fuzzy Logic system is proposed to determine the optimal operation strategy, considering the node's current resource demands, the current battery condition and the power charge expectation. The proposed approach was implemented in IoT nodes measuring environmental parameters and placed in a university campus with Wi-Fi coverage. The achieved results show the advantage of adjusting the operation mode taking into consideration the battery level and the weather forecasts to increase the energy efficiency without compromising the IoT nodes' functionalities and QoS.

Keywords: Internet of Things · Energy efficiency · Fuzzy logic

1 Introduction

In the digital era, also known as Industry 4.0 [6], the collection and analysis of data assume crucial importance to support the increase of efficiency and optimization of business processes, strongly contributing for the implementation of the digital transformation. The data acquisition is carried out by smart sensors that have been leveraged by Internet of Things (IoT) technologies. Lately they have been widely applied to collect and send the huge volume and variety of data from heterogeneous sources to remote Cloud applications, where the data is stored and processed to extract information and knowledge aiming, amongst others, monitoring, diagnosis, prediction and optimization. Following the fast advances in IoT technologies, there is a continuous growth in the number of smart devices connected to the Internet, that, according to McKinsey reports,

© IFIP International Federation for Information Processing 2022
Published by Springer Nature Switzerland AG 2022
L. M. Camarinha-Matos et al. (Eds.): IFIPIoT 2021, IFIP AICT 641, pp. 237–251, 2022.
https://doi.org/10.1007/978-3-030-96466-5_15

is expected to exceed 50 billion by 2025 [1]. Additionally, it is estimated that by 2025, IoT can generate up to \$11.1 trillion of economic value each year [8].

The development of IoT devices (or nodes) imposes some important challenges in terms of security, privacy and interoperability. In some specific cases, the energy consumption and supply represents another concern. In fact, several applications require the IoT nodes to be located remotely and without the possibility to be connected to the electrical grid, thus requiring to be supplied by batteries and/or renewable energy sources. In this way, the design of IoT nodes should consider technologies and operating strategies that make the nodes energy efficient while ensuring their correct operation.

The energy efficiency can be achieved in the design phase by using low-consumption technologies, e.g., controllers and communication protocols, or implementing efficient processing algorithms. As example, the use of low-energy communication networks, e.g., LoRa and BLE (Bluetooth Low Energy), often contributes to solve the energy efficiency problems in such situations [2]. However, in some situations this is not enough and requires the implementation of actions that manage the energy consumption during the operational phase, e.g., reducing the sampling, transmission or processing capabilities to save energy and increase the node lifespan and still ensuring the QoS. For instance, Machine Learning (ML) techniques can be used to analyze the available operational data and create models to be used by the node as a self-awareness mechanism that can define the best conditions to perform some tasks that may require more power resources, e.g., adapting the frequency to sample and transmit data.

Having this in mind, the objective of this work is to analyze the energy efficiency in IoT nodes located in restricted areas, isolated from the electrical grid and powered by batteries that are charged by solar panels. In particular, this work considers the development of intelligent algorithms that can be used as a self-awareness mechanism to optimize the energy consumption in IoT nodes, specially those that rely on Wi-Fi or other energy-hungry protocol. For this purpose, a Fuzzy Logic system is proposed to dynamically adjust the operating conditions of an IoT node, based on the current power resource demands, the battery condition and the power charge expectation, aiming to increase its energy efficiency. The proposed approach was implemented in a university campus with Wi-Fi coverage, where an IoT node with no access to the electrical grid, needs to collect and transmit environmental data to the Internet. The experiments focused on studying the influence of running these intelligent algorithms locally or as a service in Cloud platforms, with results showing that performing the fuzzy system locally, on the IoT node, presents less impact, in terms of the response time and energy consumption, than performing remotely on the Cloud.

The rest of the paper is organized as follows: Sect. 2 overviews the related work in terms of energy efficiency in IoT nodes, while Sect. 3 discusses the main aspects that mostly affect such efficiency. Section 4 describes the proposed Fuzzy Logic system to dynamically adapt the operating conditions to improve the energy efficiency in IoT nodes, and Sect. 5 presents the experimental implementation of the fuzzy decision-making system for the case study. Finally, Sect. 6 rounds up the paper with the conclusions and points out some future work.

2   Related Work

The energy consumption represents a crucial problem in the operation of IoT nodes that can affect their functionalities along the time, particularly regarding the data collection, processing and transmission. This assumes an even critical importance in remote applications, where the connection to the electrical grid is not possible and the IoT nodes are powered by batteries. In such situations, the energy management assumes a crucial role to ensure the QoS and reduce the need for battery replacement, which in some cases is an extremely critical issue, e.g., when IoT nodes are placed in locations of difficult access (e.g., forests or remote areas), or operating in adverse conditions (e.g., underwater or underground) where the nodes can be discarded after the completely use of the battery [4].

For this purpose, it is important to select the most appropriate and low-energy consumption technologies and protocols to be used by IoT nodes. In terms of communication technologies, they are required to support the connectivity of each node aiming the data transmission through Internet. The selection of a low-energy consumption communication protocol, that ensures the data transmission requirements, contributes for the energy efficiency of the IoT node, but it depends of the application requirements. For instance, LoRa and BLE are suitable solutions to this purpose due to their low-energy consumption, the first is suitable for applications with long transmission range and lower transmission rate and the second for short transmission range but higher transmission rate. The use of Wi-Fi is not a low-energy consumption option, which means that it is not regularly used for IoT nodes powered by batteries, but it is widely available, provides a direct communication with the Internet, allows an easy connection and disconnection of devices, and has good features in terms of data transmission rate and security [5].

The same applies to the selection of the hardware platforms, e.g., micro-controllers and System-on-a-Chip, that should be chosen to fit the project requirements, since, as much functionalities they provide, e.g., in terms of connectivity and processing capabilities, as higher will be the power consumption.

However, in some situations, the use of proper technologies, and particularly low-energy consumption communication protocols, could be not enough and it is necessary to go one step beyond. In this case, it is important to consider Edge computing approaches to develop intelligent energy management mechanisms that can run continuously in the IoT nodes, adapting its operating conditions in a dynamic and efficient manner, for optimizing the battery usage and consequently extending its lifetime.

In this context, some research works use Artificial Intelligence (AI) techniques to manage the node's behavior. As example, a fuzzy-based optimization model is used for energy management in wireless sensor networks (WSN), aiming to maximize the lifetime of the network and minimize the traffic load [11]. In this case, the sleep and wake-up procedure of the nodes are adapted based on the classification of the nodes as good, normal or bad, defined according to parameters like, the degree of the node, link quality, residual energy and traffic rate. A Fuzzy Logic based mechanism is also used to determine the sleep time of IoT devices in a home automation environment based on BLE [3]. The hibernation time of IoT devices is determined according to the battery level values and the ratio of Throughput to Workload, allowing to reach a 30% increase in the device's lifetime.

An algorithm using the Long Short Term-Memory (LSTM) technique, running in Edge devices, is used to improve the energy efficiency of wearable sensors, aiming to reduce the volume of communication between devices [9]. This implementation recognizes event data and transfers them when necessary, being the majority of the computational and storage load handled away from the data source. A Fog-based system is used to minimize the energy consumption of IoT nodes in Industry 4.0 applications, using the MQTT protocol and ML algorithms, e.g., Multiple Linear Regression, Bagged Decision Tree and Artificial Neural Network, to predict future data measurements, which consequently reduces the transfer rate from the devices to the control unit [10]. This model takes into consideration the energy consumption per bit, the total number of bytes needed for communication between the broker and the IoT devices, and the predictive algorithm's degree of accuracy.

Another approach describes a power management model for a battery operated IoT-based weather station, comprising a micro-controller unit (MCU), solar panel, battery, power management circuit and sensors [12]. Algorithms are used to estimate the energy stored in the battery based on the information from the solar panel, converter, charger circuit and solar irradiance. The MCU uses this information to optimize the system's overall energy consumption, maximizing its lifespan.

The existing approaches to minimize the energy consumption on IoT nodes typically use the intrinsic parameters to the local IoT node, e.g., the battery status and the transmission rate. In order to achieve more adaptable solutions, these intelligent algorithms should also consider other parameters, e.g., weather forecasts when considering renewable power sources, to obtain the best mode of operation of an IoT node, e.g., sleep and wake-up times, sampling frequency and data transmission, according to the power supply conditions that keep the node running for longer while maintaining the QoS.

3   Energy Consumption in IoT Nodes

The energy management is an essential task in battery-operated systems, e.g., IoT nodes that operates without connection to the main grid. In this context, the energy management in an IoT node depends on several factors related to the characteristics of hardware and software elements, as illustrated in Fig. 1.

In this sense, the development of such IoT nodes requires that both hardware and software are optimized for the application scenario. However, this is not a simple task in dynamic environments, where the demands of the node resources can vary along the time.

In such environments, the power source is one of the main aspects that should be considered. It is related to two factors: the battery capacity and the power energy harvesting system. The first determines the life span of the node if the battery is not rechargeable, otherwise the time the node can last disconnected from the power source. The second is mostly based on renewable energy sources, usually solar, that are known by instabilities caused by weather conditions.

Other important parameters are the consumption of the hardware platform, particularly the processor, and the communication platform (technology and protocol). In this case, powerful processors allow to run advanced processing algorithms but implies a

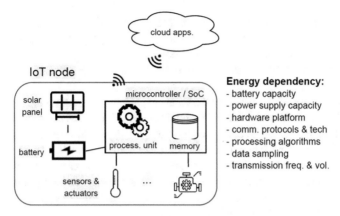

Fig. 1. Factors that influence the operation of an IoT node.

higher energy consumption. Similarly, communication technologies that allow higher bandwidth have a higher energy consumption, and the same for robust protocols. The energy consumption also increases with the number and characteristics of connected sensors, the sampling rate, and the data transmission (frequency and volume).

Many of these factors cannot be dynamically adapted, instead should be chosen at the design time. On the other hand, some of them can be dynamically tuned by software procedures, aiming to control the energy consumption, e.g., reducing the data transmission frequency or volume. In this context, being aware of the battery level and the prediction of the weather conditions can help to save energy to overcome long periods of lack of renewable power supply (e.g., rainy days). Note that, the knowledge of the battery voltage requires a dedicated sensor embedded in the IoT node, while the weather conditions can be provided by external services. Although this will cost extra energy consumption with the extra communication, these values do not need to be updated constantly, given their low variability over time.

In this way, IoT nodes should be able to manage their operating conditions over time aiming to save energy to extend its lifespan without degrading the QoS. Note that in these cases, the QoS refers to the capability of the node to fulfil its goals, specially in critical situations in which the variables monitored by the sensors of the IoT nodes indicate alarming situations, requiring greater performance by the monitoring system. For instance, a node designed to monitor a given environmental condition needs to work with its full resources when the monitored condition reaches critical levels. In this sense, the node can operate using less resources during the periods that the monitored conditions are stable, e.g., work with lower sample or transmission rate.

AI-based algorithms can be considered to develop such intelligent and self-awareness mechanisms to perform efficient energy management. Such algorithms should run continuously or periodically, analyzing the operating and power conditions in order to optimize QoS and lifespan. The output of the algorithm should consider the parameters that strongly influence the energy consumption, and adjust them properly during its operation, mainly the:

- Data acquisition: determined by the sampling rate (volume, e.g., different frame rate of a camera) and measurement granularity (quality, e.g., picture size of camera). For both parameters, higher values implies more energy consumption. Besides the energy required by the sensing interfaces, it indirectly affects the energy required by the processing unit.
- Data transmission: determined by the volume (package size, e.g., multiple samples can be transmitted in the same message) and frequency (messages per second) that data is sent to other systems. The energy consumption is determined by the communication interfaces. Although for both parameters, higher values generally implies more energy consumption, in the cases that the data size is lower than the package metadata, sending more data per package can contribute to reduce the energy consumption. These cases must also consider the energy required to setup the transmission (e.g., connect to the network and then to the server/application).
- Operating mode: determined by the hardware management capabilities of the device (e.g., some devices can have different operating modes/states, like active, stand-by, or sleep) that define the energy consumption of the hardware units, components and interfaces (like the I/Os, CPU and communication). The operating modes can be set according to internal conditions of the device (e.g., a device can be active during the daytime and be in stand-by/sleep mode during the night).

These algorithms can be embedded directly in the IoT nodes, using Edge computing, or made available as services in the Cloud. This design option is dependent on the local processing capacity, the type of intelligent mechanism to be executed, and desirable response time. The execution of such algorithms is another concern, since they require extra energy from the IoT node. This trade-off should be analyzed during the design of the IoT node and algorithms.

4   Fuzzy Logic System for Energy Efficiency

A Fuzzy Logic approach is proposed to introduce intelligence in IoT nodes, regarding mechanisms to self-regulate its operation and to manage the energy efficiency overtime, keeping the QoS requirements. The Fuzzy Logic technique was selected, mainly because it is a rule-based system that does not require complex mathematical models and can map imprecision and subjective aspects through linguistic terms. Furthermore, when compared with some ML techniques, it has a deterministic behavior, and does not need training data sets and powerful computational hardware platforms.

This approach considers IoT nodes powered by a photovoltaic system, comprising a battery and a photovoltaic panel. Figure 2 illustrates the proposed Fuzzy Logic approach, which considers 5 input variables, combined in two Fuzzy inference systems. The first variable, called resource demand, indicates the node demand of power resource. It is computed based on the operating conditions and the QoS requirements. This variable can be defined by a single or multiple parameters, e.g., based on the value of a temperature sensor, or the combination with the humidity value. In the second case, another fuzzy system can be used to define the resource operating condition.

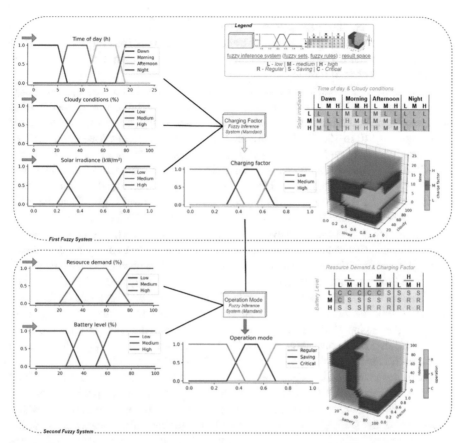

Fig. 2. Fuzzy logic approach, including the fuzzy sets, their membership functions and the fuzzy rules.

The second input variable, called battery level, also represents an internal measurement of the node, and defines the current status of the battery charge and together with the previous variable, plays an important role in the definition of the power saving modes.

The other 3 input variables represent the conditions that affect the power supply, being responsible to define the battery charging factor. This value is obtained by a fuzzy inference system that combines the input of these variables. Different from the other 2 variables, their values should be obtained from external systems and represent short-term predictions, e.g., for the next hour interval. In particular, they represent the time of day that provides a perspective of the power supply (e.g., if it is morning there will be plenty of sun light to charge the battery, and the opposite for the afternoon). The solar irradiance has a similar role for charging the battery, where its value presents a characteristic behavior along the day, slightly varying along the seasons of the year. Different from the previous variables, the cloudy conditions has a more dynamic behavior, affected by the weather conditions, and is also essential to determine the expectation of power supply to charge the battery.

In this approach, the fuzzy sets and membership functions (MFs) for the input and output variables were defined by using trapezoidal functions (see Fig. 2). They were chosen based on the performance observed during the preliminary tests, and their low computational cost requirements.

In this context, the resource demand is defined by its level (0 to 100%), comprising 3 Fuzzy sets (Low, Medium, High). The battery level is based on its battery voltage value, where, according to the type of the battery used, should be mapped to the charge percentage level (0 to 100%). This variable has 3 Fuzzy sets: Low, Medium and High. The time of day has four Fuzzy sets covering a 24 h period: Dawn, Morning, Afternoon and Night. The cloudy conditions was defined based on a scale from 0 to 100%, and three Fuzzy sets: Low, Medium and High. The solar irradiance was defined based on a scale from 0 to 1 kW/m^2 and three Fuzzy sets: Low, Medium and High. While the value of the cloudy conditions is usually provided by the weather services in percentage, the min/max values of the solar irradiance varies according to the earth geolocation and the photovoltaic panel orientation, requiring to be properly mapped to this percentage level.

The output of the Fuzzy system was defined in terms of the power saving levels. In this case, three Fuzzy sets, representing the power saving operating modes for the IoT node were defined, namely Regular, Saving and Critical modes. The Regular mode relates to the condition where the node must operate with its full resources, thus consuming more energy. In the Saving mode, the node can take actions, e.g., disabling or reducing some capabilities, in order to save some energy. On the other hand, the Critical mode is related to the situation when the node must save as much power as possible.

The power saving modes is just a label for specific operating settings, such those listed in Sect. 3, e.g., regarding data transmission frequency/volume or sleep time interval. In this case, a particular assumption to be considered in this mechanism is the context-aware, which reflects the DoFs (Degrees of Freedom) of some operating parameters, e.g., the frequency and volume of data transmission (default and minimum values). These DoFs are used by the Fuzzy Logic system as the boundaries to adjust the operation mode of the IoT node, and the minimal values are considered the minimum values of operation without degrading the QoS.

The Fuzzy inference engine requires the definition of IF-THEN rules that associate the linguistic values of the input variables to the output variables. The decision tables, also illustrated in Fig. 2, presents the rules defined for this approach, where the two Fuzzy inference systems, the Charging Factor and Operation mode, have 36 and 27 rules, respectively. Each cell of the tables represents the output of the AND combination of the input variables (rows and columns). Considering the two Fuzzy inference systems, the fuzzy rules can be interpreted as in the following example: IF the next period will be "Dawn" (e.g., 3 AM), AND with "High" cloudy conditions (e.g., 90%), AND "Low" solar irradiance (e.g., 0.1), THEN the charging factor (output of the first inference system), is "Low", indicating that the conditions are not good to recharge the battery. In this condition and applying the second Fuzzy inference system, it is possible to determine the operation mode for this scenario example, illustrated in Fig. 3.

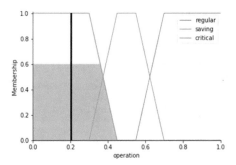

Fig. 3. Result of the operation mode Fuzzy inference for the given example.

In this case, IF a "Low" charging factor is present AND the battery level is "Low" (e.g., 25%), AND the resource demand is "Low" (e.g., 28%), THEN the power saving operation mode is "Critical", meaning that the IoT node must adopt the procedures defined to save as much energy as possible.

5   Fuzzy Logic System for Energy Efficiency

The proposed Fuzzy Logic approach was implemented and tested in a real case study, comprising an IoT node, based on an ESP8266 micro-controller, that collects environmental measurements in a university campus by using sensors that measure the temperature and humidity (SI7021), the light intensity (BH1750), the UV index (VEML6070) and the soil moisture (resistive sensor). These data are measured every 10 s in the intermediary operating condition (i.e. power saving mode) and transmitted at the same rate in a package of 118 bytes.

The node is powered by a Li-ion battery (3.7 V) that is charged by an external energy harvesting system based on a small PV panel (110 × 60 × 2.5 mm-6 V/1 W). The IoT node uses Wi-Fi to connect to the Internet and the publish-subscribe MQTT (Message Queuing Telemetry Transport) protocol to send the measured data to a Cloud application implemented using the Node-RED platform. The data can be visualized in real-time in a dashboard, it is stored in an InfluxDB database and analyzed to detect anomalies or trends.

In this paper, the objective of the experiment was to test the performance and trade-offs when the Fuzzy Logic was deployed on the node (Edge) as a mechanism for self-regulation of energy consumption, or performed on the Cloud, as a service. In the first configuration the node request the information required to perform the Fuzzy system to a Cloud service, while in the second configuration, the IoT node sends its information to a Cloud service, that executes the Fuzzy Logic system and sends back the indication about the operating mode that should be adopted. The implemented algorithms to execute the Fuzzy Logic system at the Edge or at the Cloud are illustrated in Fig. 4 and 5, respectively.

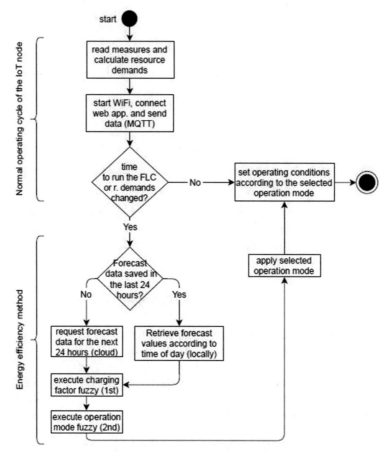

Fig. 4. Algorithm to run the energy efficiency method locally at the edge.

5.1 Application of the Fuzzy Logic System

The Fuzzy system was implemented in the Edge and Cloud computing layers, in order to verify the required response time and energy consumption. The Edge computational platform is the ESP8266 that is a low-cost computing platform that has constrained computational resources. For this reason, the lightweight eFLL library [7] was used, while for the Cloud the python skfuzzy library was used. In spite of the different implementation of the Fuzzy Logic algorithm by the two libraries, they were tested with the same configuration (Mamdani Fuzzy type and centroid defuzzyfication method), and for the same set of values, presenting extremely small differences in the outputs. The output space of the Fuzzy system for the proposed approach is illustrated in the charts of the Fig. 2.

The value of the resource demand is based on the measured data and can be obtained by several means (e.g., from simple rules to Fuzzy systems or ML-based algorithms). For the case study, the values of temperature and humidity were considered, in which

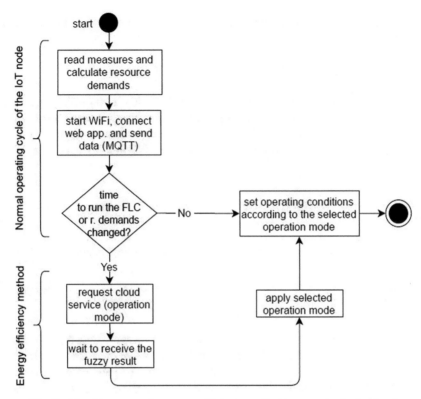

Fig. 5. Algorithm to run the energy efficiency method as a service in the cloud.

the temperature was mapped from 20 °C to 40 °C (corresponding to the range of 0 to 100%). The values are combined to determine critical conditions, e.g. temperature above 30 °C and humidity below 30%, indicating a high risk of fire and consequently greater demand for resources. The cloudy conditions is already provided by the weather services in percentage and the solar irradiance parameter can vary from 0 (night) to 1 kW/m^2 (summer day, solar noon, no cloud). For the battery parameter, the actual behavior was considered to implement a linear model for the voltage level drop. The voltage range considered for the operation of the system was 3.3 V (minimum voltage required for the operation of the system) and 4.1 V (maximum voltage obtained from the battery), mapped from 0 to 100% in the fuzzy variable.

The optimization of the IoT node's energy efficiency comprises the regulation of the frequency in which the node measures and publishes data, that in this case is based on the sleep time between the measurements. The operating modes are defined according to the battery level, resource demand and charging conditions of the solar panel.

When in "Regular" mode, the IoT node must operate continuously (i.e. no sleep), measuring and sending data at highest frequency (every second). In the "Saving" mode, it must adapt to reduce the power consumption, entering in the deep sleep mode for 10 s after the measurements. Similarly, when the operation mode is "Critical", the battery savings need to be even greater, thus the IoT node goes into deep sleep mode for 30 s.

This mode is used in situations where the battery level and the demand for resources is not high, since this approach prioritizes the QoS over the battery lifespan.

5.2 Analysis of Results

The experiments were conducted in order to analyse the trade-offs, regarding the response time and the energy consumption, when performing the Fuzzy locally on the Edge or as a service on the Cloud. Table 1 presents the response time required for the data acquisition, transmission and processing at the Edge (ESP8266/12E) and Cloud (Virtual Machine-Ubuntu 18 i5-8400).

Table 1. Execution time of fuzzy logic system running locally at the edge and as a service at the cloud (ms).

	Measurement time	Preparing time	Execution time	Total time
Locally at Edge	277,5	5,3	13,4	296,2
Service in Cloud	277,5	5,3	89,9	372,7

The measurement time refers to the time required to acquire data from all sensors in the node, and the preparation time refers to the time taken to serialize the collected data in JSON format to be sent to the Cloud application. The main difference between the two approaches is related to the execution time of the Fuzzy Logic system: 13,4 ms if processed locally in the IoT node and 89,9 ms (i.e. 86,6 ms for the data transmission and 3,3 ms for the processing of the algorithm). This clearly shows that running the Fuzzy Logic system directly in the IoT node allows to get a fast response time. Mapping the achieved results in terms of energy consumption, and considering that the Fuzzy algorithm runs 24 times a day (once an hour), and that the IoT node has an average consumption of 81,13 mAh, the consumption for executing the Fuzzy Logic system at the Edge is 13,2 μA, and for accessing as a service in the cloud is 50,9 μA. The achieved values highlight the advantage of running the Fuzzy Logic system directly in the ESP8266 since less energy is required to execute the intelligent mechanism.

The previous results were related to a scenario where the Fuzzy Logic system is running once a hour and the weather forecast information is retrieved once a day since its variability is low (i.e. forecast values for the next 24 h are saved in ESP's RTC memory). In case, the weather forecast information needs to be retrieved more often from a Cloud application, then the Edge approach starts to loss advantage related to the Cloud since in this case it is necessary to add the time (and consumption) associated to request the forecasting data from the Cloud. As example, in the extreme case that the frequency to retrieve weather forecast data is equal to the frequency to run the Fuzzy Logic system, then the execution time is 234 ms at the edge and the same 89,9 ms at the Cloud. It is noteworthy that in this case, the cloud is connected to the same network and, due to this, it will present low latency (quick response). However, if the cloud is connected to another network, it would present a higher latency and, consequently, a higher response time (increasing the consumption of the IoT node).

Thus, these results allow to conclude that if light intelligent algorithms are used combined with reduced external forecast data requests (due to its inertia), the best option is to run them directly on the IoT nodes; otherwise, it is preferable to run complex algorithms in Cloud platforms.

The IoT node was also tested to analyze the benefits of using the proposed approach, considering a scenario with good solar radiation conditions, but also some cloudy periods. The energy management in the IoT nodes was analyzed considering the normal operation and the use of the proposed Fuzzy Logic system, with the achieved results being illustrated Fig. 6.

As mentioned before, in normal operation, the IoT node has an average consumption of 81,13 mAh, causing the IoT node to operate for approximately 5 h without recharge by the solar panel. Using the Fuzzy Logic system embedded directly in the IoT node, depending on the input variables, the system suggests changing the operating mode when it is identified that according to weather conditions, there would be no way to recharge the battery and it would be more advantageous to save energy and operate with a lower QoS. This allows to save energy since a much smaller number of readings are performed by the IoT node, increasing the lifespan to approximately 12 h. Note that the percentage of improvement is strongly dependent of the values for the sleep modes established for saving and critical operation modes.

It is noteworthy that for this test the solar panel was not used, allowing to observe the lifetime gain of the IoT node only with the fuzzy approach applied. However, when using the solar panel, the system will always have priority in the regular mode as it presents a source of energy for the node whenever the weather conditions are favorable, allowing the node to operate for much longer and without the need for replacement of batteries.

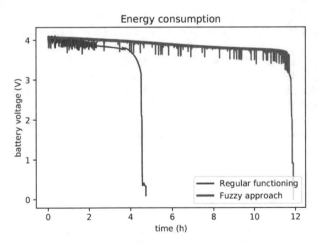

Fig. 6. Analysis of system operation in normal operation and with fuzzy logic management.

6 Conclusions

The operation of IoT nodes in constrained environments, without connection to the electrical grid and being powered by a battery, requires the use of technologies and operating strategies that make the nodes energy efficient while ensuring their correct operation. In some situations, the use of proper hardware and technologies, and particularly low energy consumption communication protocols, could not be enough or attend the application requirements, being necessary to consider intelligent mechanisms to optimize their operation.

This paper presents a Fuzzy Logic system to dynamically self-manage the local energy consumption by self-adjusting some operation parameters, namely the sleep time and frequency of transmission, to increase the energy autonomy of the IoT node without compromising its QoS. The proposed Fuzzy approach considers the node's resource demands, the battery level and the charging factor to determine the most suitable operation mode. This approach was implemented in an ESP8266 that has connected sensors to measure the temperature, humidity, luminosity, UV index and soil moisture, transmitted to the Cloud using Wi-Fi.

The experimental results show that the proposed approach was able to dynamically adjust the operating conditions to maintain the QoS, efficiently extending the battery lifespan for an extremely long time when compared to the standard operation of the IoT node. In addition, the experimental tests allowed to analyze the influence of running the Fuzzy Logic system locally in the IoT node or as a service in cloud platforms. The achieved results show the advantage of running locally in the IoT node in case that the update of the weather forecast is reduced when compared with the frequency to run the Fuzzy Logic algorithm.

Future work is devoted to analyze the effects of running intelligent mechanisms for energy efficiency in the overall energy consumption, as well as to analyze the dependency of the number of sensors, processing workload and ML technique in the energy efficiency.

Acknowledgments. This work has been supported by FCT-Fundação para a Ciência e Tecnologia within the Project Scope: UIDB/05757/2020. This work has been also partially conducted under the project "BIOMA-Bioeconomy integrated solutions for the mobilization of the Agro-food market" (POCI-01-0247-FEDER-046112), by "BIOMA" Consortium, and financed by European Regional Development Fund (ERDF), through the Incentive System to Research and Technological development, within the Portugal2020 Competitiveness and Internationalization Operational Program.

References

1. Behm, S., Deetjen, U., Kaniyar, S., Methner, N., Münstermann, B.: Digital ecosystems for insurers: Opportunities through the internet of things (2019). https://www.mckinsey.com/industries/financial-services/our-insights/digital-ecosystems-for-insurers-opportunities-through-the-internet-of-things
2. Cerchecci, M., Luti, F., Mecocci, A., Parrino, S., Peruzzi, G., Pozzebon, A.: A low power IoT sensor node architecture for waste management within smart cities context. Sensors **18**(4), 1282 (2018). https://doi.org/10.3390/s18041282

3. Collotta, M., Pau, G.: Bluetooth for internet of things: a fuzzy approach to improve power management in smart homes. Comput. Electr. Eng. **44**, 137–152 (2015). https://doi.org/10.1016/j.compeleceng.2015.01.005

4. Abbasian Dehkordi, S., Farajzadeh, K., Rezazadeh, J., Farahbakhsh, R., Sandrasegaran, K., Abbasian Dehkordi, M.: A survey on data aggregation techniques in IoT sensor networks. Wirel. Netw. **26**(2), 1243–1263 (2019). https://doi.org/10.1007/s11276-019-02142-z

5. Feng, X., Yan, F., Liu, X.: Study of wireless communication technologies on Internet of Things for precision agriculture. Wirel. Pers. Commun. **108**(3), 1785–1802 (2019). https://doi.org/10.1007/s11277-019-06496-7

6. Kagermann, H., Wahlster, W., Helbig, J.: Securing the Future of German Manufacturing Industry: Recommendations for Implementing the Strategic Initiative INDUSTRIE 4.0. Technical Report, ACATECH (2013)

7. Kridi, D., Alves, A., Lemos, M., Rabelo, R.: Desenvolvimento de uma biblioteca fuzzy para o controle autônomo de um robô móvel em ambiente desconhecido (2011)

8. Manyika, J., et al.: Unlocking the potential of the internet of things (2015). https://www.mckinsey.com/business-functions/mckinsey-digital/our-insights/the-internet-of-things-the-value-of-digitizing-the-physical-world

9. Mengistu, D., Frisk, F.: Edge machine learning for energy efficiency of resource constrained IoT devices. In: SPWID 2019: The Fifth International Conference on Smart Portable, Wearable, Implantable and Disability-Oriented Devices and Systems (2019)

10. Peralta, G., Iglesias-Urkia, M., Barcelo, M., Gomez, R., Moran, A., Bilbao, J.: Fog computing based efficient IoT scheme for the industry 4.0. In: 2017 IEEE International Workshop of Electronics, Control, Measurement, Signals and their Application to Mechatronics (ECMSM). IEEE, May 2017. https://doi.org/10.1109/ecmsm.2017.7945879

11. Rani, K.S., Devarajan, N.: Fuzzy based optimization for power management in wireless sensor networks. Int. J. Comput. Appl. **48**(4), 10–16 (2012)

12. Turos, L., Csernáth, G., Csenteri, B.: Power management in IoT weather station. In: 2018 International Conference and Exposition on Electrical and Power Engineering (EPE), pp. 0133–0138 (2018). https://doi.org/10.1109/ICEPE.2018.8559865

Hydric Resources and Meteorological Monitoring IoT System
The Software Architecture

Raúl Sousa Carvalho(✉), João Miguel Santos(✉), João C. Martins(✉),
João Filipe Santos(✉), Patrícia Palma(✉), and José Jasnau Caeiro(✉)

Instituto Politécnico de Beja, Beja, Portugal
756@stu.ipbeja.pt,
{joao.santos,joao.martins,joaof.santos,ppalma,j.caeiro}@ipbeja.pt

Abstract. An Internet of Things system designed for the collection and processing of surface water quality and meteorological data is presented. The open source software architecture is an important aspect of the design of this system, based on common commercial of the shelf components. It integrates: low power microcontrollers and single board computers to acquire and process the data from the most common parameters measured by water quality monitoring systems; long range communications using the LoRaWAN protocol allowing the system to be deployed over large and remote areas; asynchronous and reliable communications; a container based software design for easy, scalable and controllable deployment, thus reducing the complexity of the reproduction of the experimental setup in systems research. This paper also describes the design and implementation of a geospatial database using free and open source software. The system allows the user to visualize and plot the acquired data from the measurement of water quality parameters and meteorological data of various water-bodies at different time periods. Real-time measurements of parameters such as: air and water temperature; electrical conductivity; pH and evaporation, among others, can be correlated with other important properties. Remote sensing data providing real-time information to predict, prevent and act on water quality is also incorporated in the system.

1 Introduction

Water quality is one of the main challenges related to the sustainability and development of human life as part of the urgent effort to combat climate change (United Nations, 2018) [21]. Water management systems belong to the set of critical infrastructures. The development and rapid growth of the world population contribute to the deterioration of the environment, with a strong impact on the quality of available water.

Making its evaluation, constant monitoring and management crucial tasks. Water scarcity has been one of the main constraints in the development of the Alentejo region, limiting the modernization of agriculture and the sustainability

© IFIP International Federation for Information Processing 2022
Published by Springer Nature Switzerland AG 2022
L. M. Camarinha-Matos et al. (Eds.): IFIPIoT 2021, IFIP AICT 641, pp. 252–267, 2022.
https://doi.org/10.1007/978-3-030-96466-5_16

of the public water supply. The Alentejo region is characterized by a semi-arid climate with the precipitation going from about 450 mm per year until near or more than 800 mm on the highest altitudes, with the precipitation being below potential evapotranspiration for most of the year, which emphasizes the importance of irrigated agriculture. To accomplish this availability-demand task, the role of high storage capacity reservoir, in order to regulate the supply between dry and wet periods, is an essential aspect, built mainly with the purpose of water storage and for the smoothing of interannual precipitation variability [14], especially when the region is affected by 3–4 year cycle droughts, when using the Standardized Precipitation Index (SPI) for the south of Portugal [18].

Currently, the methodologies used to monitor water quality are based on laboratory analysis, not allowing real-time monitoring and limiting the results to a small geographical area. The Internet of Things (IoT) is based on the possibility that uniquely identifiable things, with sensing and/or actuation and/or processing capabilities, can be connected via the Internet into a huge network of collaborating agents. Among the current environmental problems that can benefit from this ecosystem of technologies is the monitoring and management of water quality. Two of the 17 sustainable development goals (SDGs), adopted by all United Nations member states in 2015 [22] are: goal 6, *Achieve access to water and sanitation for all* and goal 13, *Take urgent action to combat climate change and its impacts.*

Recent advances in sensors, microcontrollers (MCU), single board computers (SBC), and communication technologies, with a significant drop in power consumption and cost, made possible to meet the growing need for water quality monitoring using systems with IoT based architectures, an approach that has been the subject of study over the past few years [1,17,19].

Automatic *in-situ* monitoring substantially reduces the labor costs involved in sampling, which requires to travel to the sites under study, in addition to maintenance services at those sites. IoT-based systems, in particular those made with open source hardware and software, have lower costs making them better suited to replication and scalability. This allows a significant increase in the amount of available real-time data from *in-situ* monitoring that can be combined with data from other sources, such as remote sensing and laboratory analysis. On the other hand, the continuous monitoring of water allows a real understanding of the limnological and physicochemical dynamics of the water bodies.

The system carries out a comparative analysis of the results obtained with the limits defined in the standards. The variation of the water quality provides an indication of possible abnormalities in the water system. It will help in the decision-making of water utilities to reduce the contamination risk.

This paper presents the software architecture aspects of a prototype of an IoT-based system for monitoring the surface water quality of rivers and lakes in regions far from monitoring centers, or with difficult access. Starting from a hardware architecture that collects a set of physical and chemical parameters of the water and atmosphere, the software architecture suitable for reading, processing and visualizing the data is presented. Sensor data is acquired by a set of local modules and transmitted using the LoraWAN protocol to a gateway that can be kilometers away. The gateway transmits the data to a central server running a database management system (DBMS), allowing real-time management and display. In addition to information on water quality and atmospheric parameters, georeferenced information is added with the stations locations (geographic information system (GIS)). Communications are based on the LoRa technology and are supported by the ChirpStack software stack. All software infrastructure components are launched using container technology, reducing the complexity of software management, deployment and portability. The possibility of replicating and adapting the developed hardware and software architecture to other sensors and the possibility to add more local modules highlights the diversity of possibilities that this prototype offers.

Section 2 presents a survey of published work using this kind of IoT systems, demonstrating and contextualizing the environment in which the project is inserted. Projects with identical bases or similar aims are also indicated, highlighting specific characteristics. The system architecture is presented in Sect. 3, including the framework of the IoT platform with an emphasis on the software architecture. In Sect. 4, experimental analysis, a field testing activity for gaining a preliminary understanding of the water quality monitoring project is provided. The components that make up the software framework of the IoT platform carried out are presented, identified, specified and evaluated. Section 5, concludes the paper by summarizing the main contributions and suggesting possible future work.

2   A Review of IoT Based Surface Water Quality Monitoring Systems

Surface water quality monitoring implies the acquisition of data at a set of different locations along the water surface, at different depths and at regular time intervals [3,6]. IoT is playing a major role in monitoring the water quality and quantity, in real and in continuous time. An IoT system comprises both the monitoring of a single *thing* up to the interconnection of millions of *things*, with the ability to deliver complex services and applications [10]. Research has been done in recent times to develop intelligent systems for the identification and monitoring of water parameters. From published reviews on the subject [5,13,19] three main subsystems stand out: the data collection subsystem; the data transmission subsystem and the data management subsystem [9]. Some the operational challenges include the power consumption, security and interoperability. In general, the three subsystems are interconnected as described below. Sensors are responsible for gathering information either about themselves or about their environment. The collection of data from sensors is carried out through MCUs and/or SBCs, connected through different protocols like UART, I^{2}C or SPI. Once collected, the data is transmitted using communication technologies, for example: WiFi, Bluetooth, ZigBee, LoRa, NBIoT, 3G/4G/5G, *etc.* The data collected is processed, cleaned, modeled, analyzed and stored, usually in a DBMS. The data collected from various IoT devices is combined to provide valuable information to the end user. The goal is to provide information as simply and transparently as possible across multiple platforms: tablets, smartphones and desktops.

A survey over published work presenting this kind of systems was carried out to collect the most common options and their evolution within these three subsystems.

A low-cost aquaculture water quality monitoring system with communication based on LoRaWAN is presented in [8]. The system has remote collection and data storage of multi-sensor processor information. A Raspberry Pi controlled LoRa gateway receives data from field devices and transfers water quality parameters into a database. The data is presented on a Website, with a responsive web design, and with the remote monitoring screen, users can track changes of water quality and make timely adjustments with no need to be at the aquaculture site. The database is implemented with MySQL, using XAMPP, in a Window OS.

An agro-intelligence IoT system, with communications also based on LoRa technology, was proposed in [23]. Some nodes were developed to measure a set of environmental parameters, including air and soil temperature, solar radiation, precipitation and barometric pressure, which are sent to a server through a LoRa gateway. The data is decoded and sent over Ethernet to an Internet-of-Things analytic platform where it is aggregated, viewed and analyzed. The nodes are based on Heltec MCUs with LoRa radios and sensors connected to the MCUs over SDI-12 and I^2C interfaces.

ARM microcontrollers from the SMT32 family are used in two systems presented by [25] and by [24]. In the first system a water quality monitoring system collects and stores values of quality parameters of water used in aquaculture. Pre-processed data is stored on a local server that can be accessed remotely. Time-series data is displayed with the Grafana software package. In the second system, water quality monitoring sensor data is acquired and pre-processed by the ARM MCU and transmitted over WiFi to a cloud server for analysis and storage in a SQL Server database. The web client (mobile app) reads information from the interactive through the HTTP protocol.

An IoT system the monitoring water quality using a publisher/subscriber architecture with Message Queuing Telemetry Transport (MQTT) protocol with HiveMQ broker was proposed in [16]. The system is composed of a network of relay nodes (publishers), the sensors are controlled by an Arduino and communicate using the Zigbee protocol with a gateway node (subscriber). Data is also sent to a server via the Zigbee protocol.

Also making use of the MQTT protocol, the design and implementation of a IoT water quality monitoring system for crab farming to help the farmer to maintain acceptable levels of water quality is described by [11]. The MQTT system consists of sensor nodes acting as publishers, an SBC acting as broker and mobile client devices as subscribers. Sensor nodes are built with MCUs, LoRa radios and water quality sensors. The monitoring system allows remote access to water quality levels through Node-RED. In [2] an environmental and water management monitoring system, using standard water quality monitoring sensors is presented. The probe is connected to a Raspberry Pi via RS232 and the SBC is connected via WiFi to a router/modem which connects the system to the Internet. Data transmission to a SQLite database is done over the MQTT protocol, as in the two previous systems. For data storage, the authors use a DBMS app and a database system built over MariaDB. To monitor sensor devices, the data visualization app uses a Web UI system using PHP and HighChart Javascript to display graphics.

A solution in the field of aquaculture that aims to help fish farmers with intelligent control and water quality management is proposed in [7]. The data collected from sensors using a MCU is transmitted using LoRa technology. The resulting information is transmitted through a GPRS module to a remote server and stored in a database, making it available for visualization. App software development was based on the Browser/Server mode framework and used the LAMP framework development system. For front-end construction, the mature HTML5+CSS+JSP+JQUERY mobile technology stack was used. For the back end, the Java programming language and MYSQL database technology was adopted.

3   System Architecture

The subject of this section is the presentation and description of the IoT based system architecture for water quality monitoring with emphasis on the software structure.

A widely adopted IoT reference layered architecture is the one defined by the International Telecommunication Union (ITU), consisting of four layers: devices; network; service support and application support [9]. The layer-based diagram is presented in Fig. 1. It shows how the data starts to be collected at the lowest levels and flows through the system up to the point where it is presented to the users. At the lowest level there is the data sources: surface water and atmosphere parameters. It comprises sensors, MCUs and SBCs. Sensors are responsible for providing a measure of the physical and chemical parameters from the surface water and from the surrounding atmosphere. Using data acquisition computing modules, communications hardware, and software protocols, MCUs and SBCs receive and transmit the collected data to the network layer responsible to send data at a long distance to other network devices and servers. The network layer comprises the communication technologies and data transmission protocols. The choice of communication technologies is determined by the existing conditions at the data collection site, in particular the physical conditions, the availability of communications, and the type of power sources.

The top level includes the visualization of the collected and processed data, interacts with users through screens, forms, menus, reports, etc. It is the most visible layer of the application. It defines how the application looks. Comprises the data storage, analysis apps, and visualization layers. This level entails the treatment, analysis and storage of the collected data. The data must be stored and used for smart monitoring and actuation.

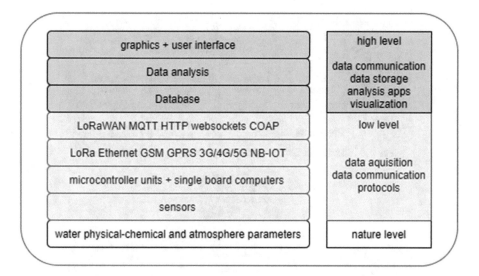

Fig. 1. A layer diagram of a general IoT water data collection system: each layer consists of modules that offer a cohesive set of services.

The proposed architecture of a water quality and weather data collection and analysis system is represented in Figs. 2, 3 and 4. The system may be roughly divided into the following types of data processing subsystems: data collection, data transmission and data management, which includes storage and high-level processing. The data collection subsystems are represented in Fig. 2. These include the Water Quality Module and the Weather Station Module. Both modules deliver data to the gateway via LoRa technology. The Water Quality Module provides the acquisition of the most common physical and chemical water quality parameters, namely: *pH*; *ORP*; *DO* and *EC*. The Weather Station is a device which provides meteorological data from the surrounding environment, namely: air temperature, air humidity, air pressure, precipitation, wind velocity and wind direction, luminosity and UV radiation.

The data transmission system adopts ChirpStack, an open source LoRaWAN Network Server stack with five major components: a LoRa Gateway Bridge; a LoRa Network server; a LoRa Application Server and a MQTT Broker [4], Fig. 3. The LoRa Gateway receives the information from the data collection modules, that can be placed at distances ranging from some tens of meters to some kilometers. A single LoRaWAN Gateway can accommodate thousands of devices or nodes. It transforms the format produced by the Packet Forwarder, and the LoRa gateway forwards the data using an MQTT broker to publish the sensor data and exchange control data with the LoRaWAN network/application server. The LoRa Gateway Bridge converts the packet forwarded UDP protocol data into JSON and sends/publishes it to the LoRa Network Server, using a subscription on a MQTT server. The LoRa Network Server eliminates duplicated or redundant information and handles the received uplink frames from

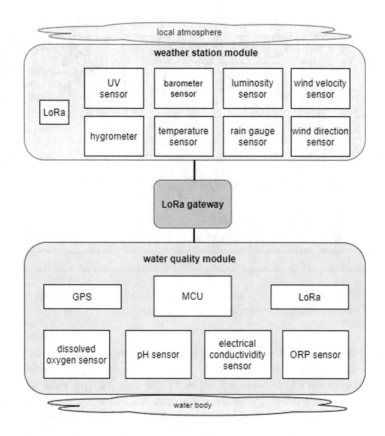

Fig. 2. Data collection and device communication architecture.

gateway(s), handles the LoraWAN MAC layer and schedules the downlink data transmissions. The LoRa Application Server handles the join-requests, encryption of application payloads and offers external services.

LoRaWAN defines a protocol to implement security from the end device to the application server, encrypting the messages exchanged between the two. This protocol uses the AES-128 algorithm to encrypt the message with two different keys. The first key (NwkSKey) is used to encrypt all the messages between the end-device and the network server. The second key (AppSKey) is used to encrypt only the data between the end-device and the application server. In the architecture, the network server and the gateway have no access to the data encrypted with AppSKey. The MQTT Broker requires authentication to implement security during connection establishment. It supports both username/password based authentication and TLS certificate based authentication.

The LoRaWAN protocol is designed to allow long-range communications at a low bit rate for things (connected objects), operating on battery with low power requirements. Provides low bandwidth communication, this being almost

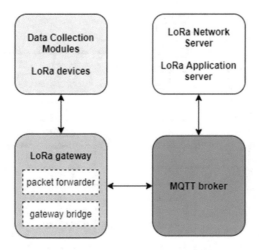

Fig. 3. LoRaWAN communication architecture.

the ideal solution for practical IoT deployments that require less data. The data produced by data collection modules, water quality monitoring or environment control, are applications with a reduced number of periodic messages and relaxed delay constraints. One or two readings per hour is acceptable, with a small amount of data, which does not bring any constraints to the LoRa network. The LoRaWAN characteristics can be summarized as:

- covers long distances, making it well suited for rural and inland solutions;
- consumes less power, which makes the technology convenient for battery powered devices;
- provides low bandwidth communication, this provides a solution for practical IoT deployments that require less data;
- it has relatively low deployment costs, compared to mobile or WiFi due to the lower number of Gateway devices required;
- supports bi-directional communication.

A single LoRaWAN gateway can accommodate 1,000s of devices or nodes, and multiple gateways can provide resilience to smart solutions.

The data management subsystem, Fig. 4, comprises DBMS data storage, web server, GIS system, data storing and visualization app, and Node-RED. The MQTT Broker that interfaces between the LoRa Gateway Bridge and the LoRa Network Server, publishes the data from the data collection modules. The *Data Storing App* subscribes the *MQTT broker* for all the topics from the sensors and stores the information at the *DBMS data storage*. In the field of database technology, there are two primary types of databases to store data: relational databases and non-relational databases. There are numerous commercial and open-source options for each type of DBMS. It was chosen the relational PostgreSQL database management system, with the geographical PostGIS extensions, and the geographical information system QGIS because they are provided

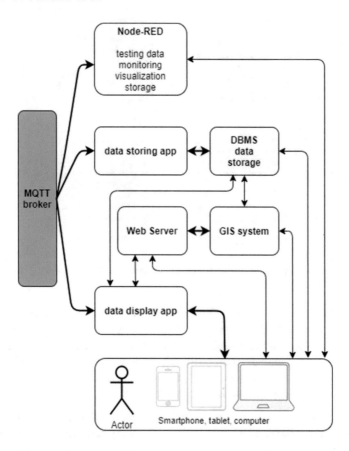

Fig. 4. The general data management software architecture.

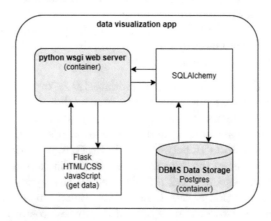

Fig. 5. Flask web application (Python ecosystem microframework). It processes the data in real-time and makes it available with a web environment using JavaScript, CSS, and HTML.

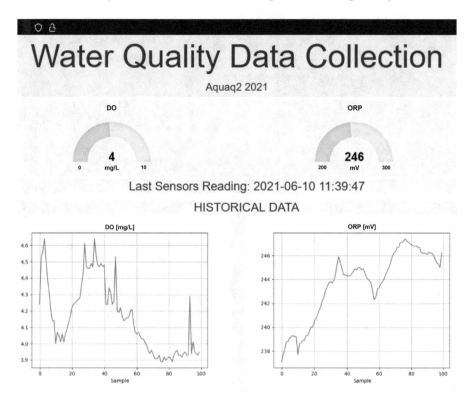

Fig. 6. Result of the execution of the data visualization application. Displays real-time readings from each sensor in the water quality monitoring module and graphically displays the readings history.

as open source software and have an simple integration procedure. The *Node.js* based *Node-RED* server provides a browser-based low code flow editor for fast and flexible prototyping. Flows can be easily created [12] thus making this software a popular tool for the rapid deployment of IoT systems.

The *data visualization app* filters the information in the database and provides information to users through a web server based on the NGINX proxy server and the Gunicorn UWSGI web server. This application is written in Python and adopts the Flask web framework, Fig. 5. The Flask web framework uses a standard Model-View-Controller approach and SQLAlchemy is used as the Model component. The View and Controller are already part of Flask. A sample of the visualization output is presented in Fig. 6. The Javascript *JustGage* library and the Python *matplotlib* packages are used for this visualization.

The deployment of the software services is based on several major choices: reliable deployment using modern container technologies; the choice of the Python programming language for most of the development, and open source

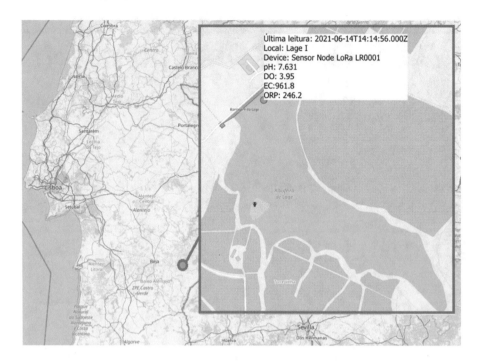

Fig. 7. GIS system image. Provides real-time data from the water quality monitoring station located in the Laje Dam (Alentejo, Portugal), including the date of the last reading, device name, and the parameters read from the sensors.

code. The servers are based on the Linux Ubuntu Server 20.04 LTS (Long Term Service) distribution. The servers are deployed and managed with Docker, with Dockerfiles and docker-compose configuration files. The data storage and processing applications are written in Python and use the available APIs for PostgreSQL (psycopg2) and QGIS.

4   Software Setup

It was conducted preliminary field testing for water quality monitoring at the Lage Dam, located in Alentejo near Pias, at the south of Portugal (Fig. 7), at approximately 160 m altitude. The implemented IoT solution utilizes a LoRaWAN network. The data is provided as represented in Fig. 8. The top layer is represented by the applications that store, process and visualize the data received from the ChirpStack LoRaWan stack. This data is received, using MQTT, from the lower level end devices. The water quality and Weather Station modules are each considered and registered as devices in the LoRaWAN network/application server. An MQTT broker interfaces between the LoRa Gateway Bridge and the LoRa Network Server. The data is published by the data collection modules (end devices). The LoRa Network Server subscribes and receives

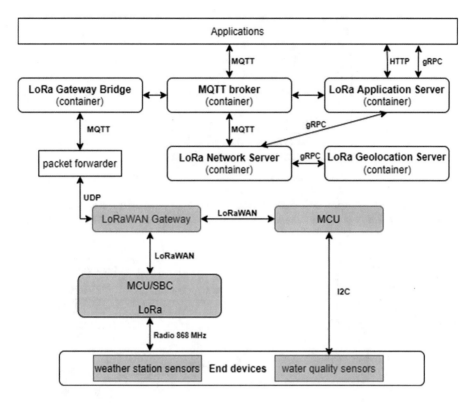

Fig. 8. Communications structure using container technology. The data collected by the devices are sent to the MQTT broker, through LoRa gateway. The data published by the MQTT broker is subscribed by the applications for analysis, processing and storage.

data from the LoRa Gateway Bridge over MQTT and sends the data to the LoRa Application Server. The *Data Storing App*, shown in Fig. 9, subscribes the MQTT broker for all the topics from the sensors and stores the information using the data storage management system, presented in greater detail in Fig. 10. The database's growth was monitored and recorded an increase of less than 50KB per day, with 2 readings per hour from each data acquisition station. It is estimated to be less than 20 MB per year.

The *Data Visualization App* module filters the information in the database and provides information to users through a web server. To make geographic information available on the internet a QGIS Server is used to deploy maps as a service. The service is deployed using the proxy web server NGINX with a FastCGI (Common Fast Gateway Interface). The geographical information system consists of the PostGIS extensions and the QGIS Server. PostGIS is a spatial database extender for PostgreSQL object-relational database. It adds support for geographic objects allowing location queries to be run in SQL [15].

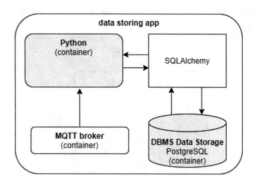

Fig. 9. Data storage application architecture. The data subscribed and received from the MQTT broker is stored in the DBMS with an application written in Python using the SQLAlchemy package.

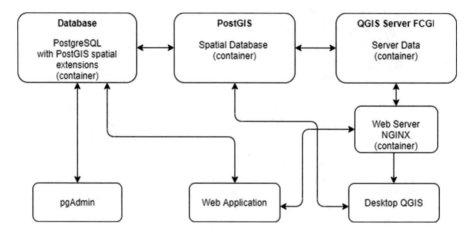

Fig. 10. Database management and geographical information systems. The data is stored in a database with geographical extensions. It is accessed for different purposes and forms through different software platforms and applications.

5   Conclusions

A design and implementation of a real-time water quality monitoring system with an IoT hardware and software structure that collects a wide set of physical and chemical parameters of the water and atmosphere is presented. The system stores data in a database management system, allowing real-time management and display, generating knowledge and facilitating real-time environmental decisions.

Essential attributes are: low cost, namely by adopting open source software; easy to deploy, maintain and scale services, by choosing a container based technology approach, and a consistent programming environment with the Python programming language. The data is collected with the support of a LoraWan stack, stored within a relational database with geographical extensions and visualized with the help of a web framework. Additional visualization using Node-RED is also provided. It is important to stress the integration level that is achieved by the geographical information system, connecting the water and weather data collected by the hardware, to the data introduced from other geo-referenced sources.

The presented proposal distinguishes itself from others, mainly in the implementation of a robust and easy to deploy and maintain software architecture. It's easy adapt to any other type of IoT project, with scopes different from water quality monitoring.

In the future the system software will provide data on the power consumption of all devices. It is foreseen the integration of this monitoring system with a smart lysimeter module and the entry of non-periodic manual chemical data, resulting from water samples analyzed in laboratory. Due to the critical nature of water data, an external blockchain technology system for data storage and sharing, is thought to offer the benefit of providing a safe, easy-to-manage, and accessible mechanism to share data. The evolution of this system will encompass building a data model of modern pattern recognition systems, machine learning, and artificial intelligence software that allows relating all data collected to be able to predict events and allows monitoring long-term threats to water quality, anticipating of environmental issues. To predict the long-term impacts of water management measures and input of agricultural chemicals (loss of nutrients), the application of The Soil and Water Assessment Tool (SWAT) model, will be considered [20].

This system is envisaged to become a first class instrument for water resources sensing and analysis with wide scientific possibilities.

References

1. Benedict, S., Gowtham, N., Giri, D., Sreelakshmi, N.: Real time water quality analysis framework using monitoring and prediction mechanisms. In: 2018 Conference on Information and Communication Technology. CICT 2018 (2018). https://doi.org/10.1109/INFOCOMTECH.2018.8722381
2. Budiarti, R.P.N., Tjahjono, A., Hariadi, M., Purnomo, M.H.: Development of IoT for automated water quality monitoring system. In: 2019 International Conference on Computer Science, Information Technology, and Electrical Engineering (ICOMITEE), pp. 211–216 (2019). https://doi.org/10.1109/ICOMITEE.2019.8920900
3. Chapman, D.V., World Health Organization., UNE UNESCO Programme: Water Quality Assessments : A Guide to the Use of Biota, Sediments and Water in Environmental Monitoring, 2nd edn. E & FN Spon, London (1996)
4. ChirpStack open-source LoRaWAN Network Server. https://www.chirpstack.io/
5. Dong, J., Wang, G., Yan, H., Xu, J., Zhang, X.: A survey of smart water quality monitoring system. Environ. Sci. Pollut. Res. **22**(7), 4893–4906 (2015). https://doi.org/10.1007/s11356-014-4026-x

6. EPA (ed.): Parameters of Water Quality: Interpretation and Standards. Environmental Protection Agency, Ireland (2001)
7. Gao, G., Xiao, K., Chen, M.: An intelligent IoT-based control and traceability system to forecast and maintain water quality in freshwater fish farms. Comput. Electron. Agric. **166**, 105013 (2019). https://doi.org/10.1016/j.compag.2019.105013
8. Hsieh, C.W., Tsai, Y.J., Stefanie, C., Wang, C.C., Chang, W.T.S.: The preliminary design of water quality monitor system for the ecological pond based on LoRaWAN. In: 2020 International Symposium on Computer, Consumer and Control (IS3C), pp. 365–367 (2020). https://doi.org/10.1109/IS3C50286.2020.00100
9. Telecommunication Standardization Sector of ITU: ITU-T Recommendation Y.4000/Y.2060 : Global Information Infrastructure, Internet Protocol Aspects and Next-Generation Networks, Next Generation Networks-Frameworks and Functional Architecture Models, Overview of the Internet of Things. ITU (2012). https://www.itu.int/rec/T-REC-Y.2060-201206-I
10. Chebudie A.B., Minerva, R., Rotondi, D.: Towards a Definition of the Internet of Things (IoT) (2014)
11. Niswar, M., et al.: IoT-based water quality monitoring system for soft-shell crab farming. In: 2018 IEEE International Conference on Internet of Things and Intelligence System (IOTAIS), pp. 6–9. IEEE (2018). https://doi.org/10.1109/IOTAIS.2018.8600828
12. Node-RED. https://nodered.org/
13. Olatinwo, S.O., Joubert, T.H.: Enabling communication networks for water quality monitoring applications: a survey. IEEE Access **7**, 100332–100362 (2019). https://doi.org/10.1109/ACCESS.2019.2904945
14. Palma, P., Ledo, L., Soares, S., Barbosa, I., Alvarenga, P.: Spatial and temporal variability of the water and sediments quality in the Alqueva reservoir (Guadiana basin; southern Portugal). Sci. Total Environ. **470–471**, 780–790 (2014)
15. PostGIS - Spatial and Geographic Objects for PostgreSQL. https://postgis.net/
16. Pranata, AA., Lee, J.M., Kim, D.S.: Towards an IoT-based water quality monitoring system with brokerless pub/sub architecture. In: 2017 IEEE International Symposium on Local and Metropolitan Area Networks (LANMAN), pp. 1–6. IEEE (2017). https://doi.org/10.1109/LANMAN.2017.7972166
17. Sadgir, P., Sarda, P.: Assessment of multi parameters of water quality in surface water bodies-a review. Int. J. Res. Appl. Sci. Eng. Technol. **3**, 331–336. ISSN 2321–9653 (2015). https://www.researchgate.net/publication/282356694
18. Santos, J.F., Pulido-Calvo, I., Portela, M.M.: Spatial and temporal variability of droughts in portugal. Water Resour. Res. **46**, W03503 (2010). https://doi.org/10.1029/2009WR008071
19. Santos, J.M., Caeiro, J.J., Martins, J.C., Santos, F., Palma, P.: Physical and chemical water quality parameters sensing IoT systems for improving water productivity. Water Prod. J. **1**(2), 33–46 (2020)
20. SWAT — Soil and Water Assessment Tool. https://swat.tamu.edu/
21. UN: Sustainable Development Goal 6 Synthesis Report 2018 on Water and Sanitation. United Nations (2018)
22. UN-2018: Sustainable Development Goal 6: Synthesis Report 2018 on Water and Sanitation. UN-Water. United Nations (2018)
23. Valente, A., Silva, S., Duarte, D., Pinto, F.C., Soares, S.: Low-cost LoRaWAN node for agro-intelligence IoT. Electronics (Switzerland) **9**(6), 987 (2020)

24. Zhang, C., Wu, J., Liu, J.: Water quality monitoring system based on Internet of Things. In: 2020 3rd International Conference on Electron Device and Mechanical Engineering (ICEDME), pp. 727–730 (2020). https://doi.org/10.1109/ICEDME50972.2020.00171
25. Zhang, Z., et al.: Development of remote monitoring system for aquaculture water quality based on Internet of Things. IOP Conf. Ser. Mater. Sci. Eng. **768**, 052033 (2020). https://doi.org/10.1088/1757-899X/768/5/052033

Author Index

Printed in the United States
by Baker & Taylor Publisher Services